'Steering clear of well-funded newsrooms and glitzy TV studios in metropoles, this book provides a deeply researched and beautifully written account of journalism in mofussil India. Through carefully observed and richly detailed accounts of stringers, Nimmagadda Bhargav charts a new path for regionally grounded studies of news production'.

– **Aswin Punathambekar,** *Professor of Communication, University of Pennsylvania's Annenberg School for Communication, and Director, Center for Advanced Research in Global Communication*

'Increasingly precarious forms of employment for cultural workers such as journalists and its implications not only for the lives of these workers but more broadly for society is becoming an important issue for scholars writing about the Global North. Precarity for journalists in the Global South has been a fact of life for longer and this ethnographic study illuminating the lives of stringers working in small towns in southern India should be essential reading for those interested in understanding the nature and consequences of precarity whether at a local, national or global level. Based on careful and empathetic research of much maligned journalists and grounded in an impressive grasp of sociological and communication theory, this is a major contribution to the field of journalism studies in its quest to become global in orientation'.

– **John Downey,** *Professor of Comparative Media Analysis, Centre for Research in Communication and Culture, School of Social Sciences and Humanities, Loughborough University and President, European Communication Research and Education Association*

'In this excellent exploration of newspaper stringers in small towns of Telangana and Andhra Pradesh regions in India, Bhargav employs a grounded analytic framework by drawing theoretical and conceptual insights from Pierre Bourdieu's field theory and "Ambedkarite social philosophy" to examine "marginality, social organization, division of labour, precarity, and informality" in Indian language journalism culture in India. The topic of stringers in local Indian language newspapers remains unexplored in India, and Bhargav should be commended for undertaking this study that offers fresh new theoretical insights into the local journalistic field and the world of the stringers'.

– **Sanjay Asthana,** *Professor, School of Journalism and Strategic Media, Middle Tennessee State University*

STRINGERS AND THE JOURNALISTIC FIELD

This book is one of the first ethnographic works on small-town stringers or informal news workers in Indian journalism. It explores existing practices and cultures in the field of local journalism and the roles and spaces stringers occupy.

The book outlines the caste, gender, class and region-based biases in the production of Indian-language journalism with a specific focus on stringers working in Telugu dailies in small towns or 'mofussil' areas of Andhra Pradesh and Telangana, states in south India. Further, it captures their daily work and processes of news production, and the precarious lives they often lead while working in small towns or *mofussils*. The author, by using Bourdieu's field theory, introduces the journalistic practices of stringers working on the margins and how they negotiate the complex hierarchies that exist within the journalistic field and outside it.

This book will be of great interest to scholars and researchers of ethnography, media sociology, journalism and media studies, labour studies and Area studies, especially South Asian studies.

Nimmagadda Bhargav earned his Ph.D. degree from the Department of Communication, University of Hyderabad. Currently, he is Assistant Professor at the Manipal Institute of Communication, Manipal Academy of Higher Education, Manipal, Karnataka, India.

ETHNOGRAPHIC INNOVATIONS, SOUTH ASIAN PERSPECTIVES

Series Editor: Niharika Banerjea
Associate Professor, Ambedkar University Delhi
Paul Boyce
Senior Lecturer, University of Sussex and
Rohit K. Dasgupta
Senior Lecturer, Loughborough University

The book series Ethnographic Innovations, South Asian Perspectives (EISAP) will offer a new writing space that will draw together work from across the social sciences and the humanities. The series will focus on ethnographic engagements within and across disciplines and creative styles. Our intention is to engender a publishing environment for interdisciplinary conversations that query various uses of ethnography as a methodological and representational form – in the context of South Asia and beyond.

This will include a focus on ethnographic theorization and method at intersections of public policy and private lives. Our aim is to open new perspectives on how the intimate contextualization of ethnographic knowledge might translate into engagements with civil society and modes of governance. The series will also offer a space for questioning factual modes of ethnographic narration and evidencing in respect of work that proffers fictional forms and 'counter-truth' claims. Connections and divergences between new media, digital intimacies and analogic life-worlds will comprise another key focus along with new scholarship that extends the legacies of South Asian scholarship on caste, class and race into new conversations with queer, race and sexualities theories. In doing so the series aims to bring about new ethnographic engagements with life making projects in their relation to social theory and regional epistemologies and geographies.

STRINGERS AND THE JOURNALISTIC FIELD
Marginalities and Precarious News Labour in Small-Town India
Nimmagadda Bhargav

For more information about this series, please visit: www.routledge.com/Ethnographic-Innovations-South-Asian-Perspective/book-series/EISAP

STRINGERS AND THE JOURNALISTIC FIELD

Marginalities and Precarious News Labour in Small-Town India

Nimmagadda Bhargav

Routledge
Taylor & Francis Group
LONDON AND NEW YORK

First published 2023
by Routledge
4 Park Square, Milton Park, Abingdon, Oxon OX14 4RN

and by Routledge
605 Third Avenue, New York, NY 10158

Routledge is an imprint of the Taylor & Francis Group, an informa business

British Library Cataloguing-in-Publication Data
A catalogue record for this book is available from the British Library

ISBN: 978-1-032-32642-9 (hbk)
ISBN: 978-1-032-43895-5 (pbk)
ISBN: 978-1-003-36926-4 (ebk)

DOI: 10.4324/b23313

Typeset in Sabon
by Apex CoVantage, LLC

To stringers carrying out newswork precariously remaining in the margins of society and the journalistic field . . .

CONTENTS

Acknowledgements x
A note on translation, transliteration, language and style xii

1 Introduction: studying small-town stringers 1

2 Locating the stringer: caste as space, capital, politics 18

3 At the bottom of the ladder: the stringer in the journalistic field 46

4 'Lift irrigation, torture and kismet': the wayward fortunes of stringer's newswork 72

5 Never the *sūtradhār*?: the logic of local journalistic practice 102

6 Damaged and damaging: the insecure masculinity of the small-town stringer 126

7 Informal labour and invisibilised precarity: working lives of stringers before and after the global pandemic 144

8 Conclusion 179

Appendix 184
Index 194

ACKNOWLEDGEMENTS

This book is based on my field and archival research conducted from the early 2010s to the present. I'm grateful to all the stringers, journalists, editors and journalists' union leaders for their time and support offered throughout this period. I thank the people in my sites of research Gannavaram (Andhra Pradesh) and Sangareddy (Telangana) for their generous time and letting me carry out ethnographic research.

I'm indebted to my guide Prof. Vinod Pavarala, who encouraged me to pursue this research from the inception and stood by me through the turbulent phases I had gone through. I thank him profusely for guiding this research and helping me grasp the dense theoretical framework this study demanded. None of this would have been possible without his support.

I would like to extend my sincere thanks to my doctoral committee members Prof. Kanchan Malik and Dr. Arvind Susarla for pointing me towards some missing elements in my research, which became solid sections in my chapters. I thank my teachers in the Department of Communication (University of Hyderabad) Prof. P. Thirumal, Prof. Usha Raman, Prof. B.P. Sanjay, Prof. Vasuki Belavadi and Prof. Sathyaprakash. My debt also goes to Prof. Sheela Prasad for training me in social geography and regional studies.

My gratitude to three persons who left indelible intellectual impressions on me: Prof. G. Aloysius, Chittibabu Padavala and late Dr. K. Balagopal. I would like to thank Jude Mario for offering professional help with my academic writing. I benefitted immensely from all the mentors and participants in the British Academy writing workshop.

Sincere thanks to Prof. John Downey (Loughborough University) who encouraged me with his kind words over emails and during online interactions. I owe him more than saying a mere thanks and look forward to working with him in near future. Thank you to Dr. Madhavi Ravikumar and Debasreeta Deb, my Hyderabad team members of the UKRI project for their support.

I affectionately acknowledge the support received from Dr. K. C. Bindu, AUD, Delhi, Mr. K.V. Nagesh, TISS, Mumbai, Prof Sowmya Deccamma,

University of Hyderabad, Dr Gundimeda Sambaiah, Dr. Babu Remesh, AUD, Delhi, Dr. Alok Pandey and Prof. N. Sudhakar Rao from the Department of Anthropology.

I'm grateful to ICSSR for providing me with a doctoral fellowship, IAMCR for the travel grant, and the University of Hyderabad for the BBL fellowship. I also thank the IGML staff and Ǣ for enabling my research even during the lockdown.

I'm ever grateful to Prof. Pradip Ninan Thomas (University of Queensland) for his encouragement, Prof. Ravi Vemula, EFLU, Shillong for introducing me to IAMCR and Dr. Jagadish Thaker, University of Auckland New Zealand for never saying no to my 'book demands' and scholarly needs. I thank Dr. Jilukara Srinivas and Dr. Pasunoori Ravinder for providing some insights into Telugu culture and society.

My heartfelt gratitude goes to my doctoral batchmates Dr. Sumana Kasturi, Dr. Nookaraju and Husain Abbas. I sincerely appreciate Dr. Sumana, Dr. Bridget Backhaus and Dr. Aditya Deshbandhu for helping me in the process of publishing my research.

I'm grateful to Ethnographic Innovations, South Asian Perspectives series editors Dr. Niharika Banerjea, Dr. Paul Boyce, Dr. Rohit K. Dasgupta and anonymous reviewers, whose suggestions proved to be invaluable while writing this book. My gratitude goes to Shloka Chauhan, Aakash Chakrabarty and their team for making this publishing process enjoyable.

I can never sufficiently thank P. Dinakar, V. Krishna, V. Asheesh, Anubhuti Dayal, R. Roy, G.B. Wilson, L. Rahul, B. Anish, Dr. V. Prasad, and Dr. R. Smith for their constant support.

I find it silly to say mere thanks to Amma, Nanna, Akka and Bava *gāru* for being sources of strength in my academic pursuits. Thank you to Appa, Amma, Aṇṇi and my co-brother for being very cooperative throughout the fieldwork and writing period.

I'm indebted to my wife and soul mate Dheeksha Charan, who stood by me through thick and thin. She was always there for me whenever I felt weak and helped me survive my academic and personal life. If not for her unflinching support, despite my irritating and intolerable idiosyncrasies, this work would not have seen light.

A NOTE ON TRANSLATION, TRANSLITERATION, LANGUAGE AND STYLE

I retained transliterated Telugu to highlight the context and culture specificities. Sometimes, based on how intonation happens, a single transliterated Telugu word becomes a full sentence when translated into English. Throughout the book, transliterated text is in italic immediately followed by its translation in English.

Transliteration is done from the voice records of the interviews and may not follow the literary or standardised Telugu. The variant of Telugu, which respondents and people in Gannavaram, Krishna district (coastal Andhra) usually talk has elongated vowels; in case of Medak (Telangana), people use short or 'normal' vowels. In standardised Telugu and the variant of the language spoken in Krishna district, most words end with vowels or the consonant 'm' (in Telugu). It need not be the case with the Medak variant. English words in Telugu prose quotes, proper names along with accepted non-English words are in Roman script to avoid confusion. I did not use diacritics for Hindi, Dakhni and Urdu language words or sentences. I followed the convention of using diacritics for the Telugu language prescribed by Krishnamurti (2003). Macrons are used for elongated vowels (ā = aa; ē = ee; ī = ii; ō = oo; ū = uu).

A NOTE

Pronunciation:

Vowels	*Consonants*
a = u in nut	k = k in king
ā = farm but for longer duration	g = g in good
e = e in pet	c = ch in chair
ē = above e for twice the duration	j = j in judge
i = i in pit	t = th in width
ī = ee in feel	ṭ = t in tonne
o = o in oak	d = Article 'the' before a consonant
ō = above o for longer duration	ḍ = d in den
u = u in put	ṇ = retroflex the tip of tongue while saying na
ū = oo in food	ñ = pronounced as 'nya' (nasal), when used as a combination (e.g., Hindi word Gyan becomes Gnyana in Telugu, similarly pragya becomes pragnya in Telugu).
	r = r is always strong like r in tree.
	ṛ = rolling r; when used as combination it is pronounced as ru with rolling r.
	ḷ = retroflex the tip of tongue while saying la
	s = s in sea
	ṣ = sh in shine
	ś = pronounced with flat tongue with a hiss

1

INTRODUCTION

Studying small-town stringers

When this ethnographic study was still in an embryonic stage in 2009–2010, I was working as a reporter with an English language national daily. On the one hand, the demand for a separate Telangana state was at its peak, which resulted in a divide among journalists on regional lines, especially in the Telugu language media. On the other hand, the Great Recession, or the global financial meltdown, resulted in job cuts and insecurity across all sectors, including the media industry.

While on the hunt for news stories, 'spot' reporting and press meets at the 'usual places' [Desoddharaka Bhavan in Hyderabad and Hyderabad Press Club, Somajiguda], Telugu stringers always made their presence felt. When I enquired with fellow journalists about them and their role, I often heard two extreme responses: (a) unethical and immoral guys 'who tarnish the reputation of the press' and (b) a near down-and-out figure on the margins of the Indian-language press, who struggles to make ends meet (stringers are invariably men, a point discussed later).

The more I tried to learn about the figure of the 'stringer', the more elusive and enigmatic he became. How much are they paid? Do they have accreditation? Are they tied up with local politics? These were my initial questions. However, Communication Studies' book racks in university libraries stacked with literature on journalism did not have much to offer on the working lives of stringers. Whereas researchers in Social Science departments were working on the professional lives of lawyers, medical professionals, farmers, and IT workers (sociology of professions and related aspects of professionalisation), Media Studies focused on new phenomena and new forms of media. I realised that this topic fell in the no-persons land between established departments and disciplines such as Economics, Sociology, Social Anthropology and Communication Studies.

In this study, I attempt to understand existing practices in the field of local journalism and the role of newsworkers in the Telugu-speaking states with respect to markers of domination and resistance such as caste, gender, class, ability and region/space. In doing so, I present an ethnographic exploration of less-explored aspects in the labour of news production and the precarious

DOI: 10.4324/b23313-1

lives of small-town or 'mofussil' stringers in Indian-language newspapers, using the specific case of Telugu.[1]

Stringers are local news contributors, not on the payroll of the organisation for which they work. Most of them function as part-time journalists and are paid on the basis of the number of lines or the word length of their published contributions. They are recruited in an informal manner with little or no job security. The term 'stringer' can be traced back to a time when part-time news reporters were paid by the column-inch or column-centimetre. Instead of receiving a set compensation for each story written, a stringer would use a piece of string to measure the amount of newspaper space occupied by his/her writing. The stringer would then provide the newspaper with her/his string, cut to the appropriate length.

The newspaper would make a payment to the stringer based on the length of the string published in the district editions (A3 size supplements) of Telugu dailies. At the time of research and writing, the payment was INR 2 per column-inch or column-centimetre (lineage) and for a published photograph; they were paid around INR 10–15. Newspaper establishments maintain an unofficial account for paying stringers known as the 'line account'.

Every *mandal* (administrative division comprising a block of villages) in every district has stringers. While there are stringers in urban areas too, the focus of my study is primarily on newsworkers in mofussil areas. Apart from contributing news to the organisations for which they work, most stringers are also responsible for generating revenue by procuring local advertisements and boosting circulation, along with taking on informal work assigned to them by the heads of reporting/editorial bureaus and managements. Importantly, apart from not having regular salaries, stringers do not have any specific work timings, medical and life/accident insurance, holidays, weekly offs, among other perks to which formal workers usually are entitled. They are referred to as mofussil correspondents (MC), rural contributors (RC) and part-time correspondents. They introduce themselves as stringers or MCs or RCs, mentioning the name of the news establishment for which they work.

The stringer in India was noticeably mentioned within the field of Journalism Studies in India by Robin Jeffrey (2010) in his pan-Indian study, journalist Sevanti Ninan (2007) in her informative work on local news gatherers in *Headlines from the Heartland* and Srirupa Roy (2011, pp. 761–777) in what is a sparse field in India. While Jeffrey (2010, pp. 143–148) briefly discusses the role of stringer while describing the nature of reporting and editing in the Indian-language press, Ninan (2007, pp. 113–141) presents stringers as local news gatherers who play an important part in 'localisation strategy' of Hindi newspapers. While Srirupa Roy (2011, pp. 761–777) discusses how the expansion of television news in Hindi language had a 'provincialising effect of enabling the social, political, and economic empowerment of non-metro actors' with a specific focus on freelance stringers working in TV channels in the Eastern state of Bihar in India, Rajagopal's (2001, 2009, 2016) works provided the base for understanding the relationships between journalism with that of polity, social and economy in the Indian context.

Focusing on the economic conditions of reporters and stringers in the National Capital Region, Remesh (2018, p. 151) suggested that the 'fast-increasing trend of contractualisation of media labour is essentially the root cause of most of the insecurities and vulnerabilities in the sector'. He (2021, pp. 36–41) also pointed out the informal nature of wok assigned to part-time correspondents by news organisations in his study conducted in Aligarh and Hisar districts of Uttar Pradesh and Haryana, respectively.

Journalism Studies and research work emerging from the advanced Western countries or the Global North in the twenty-first century has scholarship on issues concerning the work of foreign news correspondents in which stringers or 'fixers' are mentioned (Hannerz, 2004; Aufderheide, 2004). Studies, since the 2010s, on the role of stringers and fixers, highlight cultural differences in international reporting (Palmer, 2016) and engage with informal arrangements and the labour issues associated with them (Palmer, 2018), the role of 'local-national' stringers in covering a particular international crisis (Bunce, 2011), and how stringers and fixers are increasingly becoming organised in international reporting (Murrell, 2019). Notably, most of these studies emerged in the wake of the 9/11 attacks in New York.

There is a difference between the roles of fixers, freelancers and stringers. In the Indian context, a fixer is expected to be a translator (*dubashi*), to organise and schedule meetings with local officials or industry players or other stakeholders and become 'subjects' for the journalist visiting from outside the state/region/country.[2]

In contrast, a freelancer in a news organisation offers her/his work at will; either she/he has to 'deliver' the requirement or should be in a position to 'sell' the write-up or work. But, for a freelancer, especially in the print media, having a name or established credentials in the industry is considered essential. This aspect will become more obvious when we consider the historical meaning of the term 'freelance':

> A term used by writers denoting one of those military adventurers, often of *knightly rank*, who in the Middle Ages offered their services as mercenaries, or with a view to plunder, to belligerent states; a 'condottiere', a 'free companion' [Italics mine]. . . . In recent usage, a person working for himself [herself] and not for an employer.
>
> (Simpson and Weiner, 1989)

Freelancers are offered payment based on industry standards and also keeping in mind the credentials. This, however, is not the case with stringers.

The emergence of the stringer as a figure in Communication Studies and in journalism in both Global North and Global South (especially South Asia) is interesting, as it reflects not only the imperial politics and technological 'advances/hindrances' but also the historical, cultural and social features of the respective locations. Writing about the relation between technology and public opinion in the United States, one of the founding figures of Canadian Communication Studies, Harold Innis, observed a shift in the nature of work and roles in newswork in the newspaper 'industry' with the coming of the telephone and telegraph. He (1968, p. 173) noted:

> The linotype with at least five times the typesetting speed of the compositor was introduced about 1886 and was followed by a marked increase in the use of typewriters. It made possible the modern newspaper. The régime of the tramp printer came gradually to an end. The telephone supplemented the telegraph for local news and *the reporter saw his work divided between the leg man who visited the sources of news and the rewrite man to whom he telephoned his information* and who prepared it for the paper [Emphasis mine].

By mentioning the role of a 'leg man', Innis anticipated not only the emergence of the stringer in the US context but also the changing nature of news labour with the advent of the then-new technologies, the telegraph and the telephone. This observation was to become more apparent in the writings of US Communication Studies scholar, James Carey in his writing about technology and culture/ideology. In a chapter dedicated to the topic of telegraph and its implications for the communication and journalism field, Carey (2009, pp. 162–163) writes:

> [T]he telegraph eliminated the correspondent who provided letters that announced an event, described it in detail, and analysed its substance, and replaced him with the stringer who supplied the bare facts. As words were expensive on the telegraph, it separated the observer from the writer. Not only did writing for the telegraph have to be condensed to save money – telegraphic, in other words – but also from the marginal notes and anecdotes of the stringer the story had to be reconstituted at the end of the telegraphic line, a process that reaches high art with the news magazines, the story divorced from the story teller.

For Carey, the coming of the telegraph service not only separated the observer from the writer but also resulted in distinguishing the words, 'communication' and 'transportation'. Raymond Williams presents a more nuanced understanding of the difference between communication and transportation. He suggests that a mere one-way transmission technology (telegraph) did not eliminate the synonymous relation; but the two-way transmission (telephone) brought about the distinction (Williams, 1988, pp. 72–73).

But what was the case in the Indian subcontinent or for most of South Asia, where the telegraph service and network did not penetrate as much as it did in the case of the advanced western countries? Even though the trans-atlantic oceanic cable and British India cable from the United Kingdom were laid out roughly with a time gap of a little more than a decade (1858 and 1870, respectively), the penetration of the telegraph into the South Asian subcontinent was not as wide as it was in the case of the North American for various historical, linguistic and cultural reasons.[3]

In retrospect, it appears that these were the reasons for Innis to author key works, such as *Empire and Communications* (1986) and *The Bias of Communication* (1968) with a particular focus on the role of technology, capital and statecraft, and later for McLuhan (1997) to come up with ideas like the 'global village' and 'the medium is the message' in the North American context.

However, in the South Asian context, it can be argued that the telegraph technology did not directly result in the emergence of the stringer or local news reporter or information gatherer, as social communication was contingent on social, economic and historical factors. C. A. Bayly's *Empire and Information* provides a historical account of the social communication and statecraft in India during colonial rule and attests to previous work that highlights socioeconomic factors as opposed to mere technological advancements coming from the West (1999, pp. 315–337). One obvious cultural and technological difference between the West and the dominant culture in the subcontinent is the literacy/orality factor. Moreover, South Asia in general and the Indian subcontinent, in particular, are marked by social, cultural, religious and linguistic plurality and disparity.

The inseparable relationship between the cultural and social factors of caste and the concept of communication in Indian society must also be taken into account. Understandably, the social and cultural aspects in understanding 'communications' were as important as the advancement and introduction of communication technologies in this part of the globe.

Terms and concepts such as labour, social organisation, forces and relations of production and cultural production are crucial for this study which seeks to understand the conditions of news production and the social backgrounds and formations of stringers in Indian-language journalism.

Why study marginal newsworkers and culture of news production?

This research attempts to address the relatively less-explored issue of 'labour' in news and cultural production within Communication(s) Studies in general and the sub-discipline of Journalism Studies in particular.

Instead of addressing media or forms of communication as abstracted from processes of labour, this study attempts to highlight issues within the field of journalism such as division of labour, culture of news production, marginality, social organisation, informal labour and precarity.

I arrived at this research problem based on my own experience in the journalism industry (print) as well as through the academic literature that has been insisting that there is a gap in the research on media producers and their working lives in Communication Studies.

The shaping of the idea, the ethnographic fieldwork and writing were carried out between two great global recessions in the twenty-first century, which had a significant impact on media workers, just as with all kinds of workers of the world. The first one was the Great Recession or global financial meltdown (2008–2009) and the second one is the ongoing global pandemic due to the novel Coronavirus disease (COVID-19).

One of the salient features of this research is that it captures the transformation of the newswork of stringers who earlier sent their news articles and reports through state-run bus services and now have migrated to the latest technologies such as the Internet and mobile phones to file stories and send photographs. Yet, as we shall see, nothing substantial has changed for the stringer. Moreover, this might be one of the last field-based studies on Indian-language journalism focusing on the working lives of stringers and journalists when the Working Journalists and other Newspaper Employees (conditions of service) and Miscellaneous Provisions Act, 1955, was still in operation in mainland India. This Act was scrapped and included in the Wage Code Act, 2020, giving further scope for media organisation to casualise, contractualise and informalise the workforce.

'Locating' the research

> Our cities are not India. India lives in her seven and a half lakhs of villages.
>
> – Mohandas Karamchand Gandhi (1921), cited in Jodhka, 2012, p. 48.

> [Let this city be] 'symbolic of the freedom of India, unfettered by the traditions of the past . . . an expression of the nation's faith in the future'.
>
> – Jawaharlal Nehru on the planned city of Chandigarh (1950), cited in Kalia, 2006, p. 143.

> The mofussil correspondents, still the Scheduled Caste of Indian journalism, are slowly coming into their own, but too slowly.
>
> – Manikonda Chalapathi Rau, 1968, p. 23.

The radically different visions propagated by Mohandas Gandhi and Jawaharlal Nehru – the village as an 'existing ideal space to be rediscovered' and the city as a 'space of becoming or aspiration' – continue to dominate the political enunciations and populist rhetoric of Indian political leaders even in the twenty-first century. But lived realities are more complicated. The permeation of such narratives through government schemes and media narratives has a clear demarcation of the 'urban' and the 'rural' that have certain associations indelibly linked to both poles. The Jawaharlal Nehru National Urban Renewal Mission (JNNURM), 2005, and Mahatma Gandhi National Rural Employment Guarantee Act (MNREGA), 2005, introduced under the erstwhile United Progressive Alliance government and the 100 Smart Cities Mission and Deen Dayal Upadhyaya Gram Jyoti Yojana (rural electrification scheme) by the National Democratic Alliance since 2014 are cases in point. But these narratives do not capture the mobile and dynamic socio-scapes of the mofussil.

Even as the Constitution of India (Part-I) stated the name of the republic as 'India, that is Bharat', the immediate and popular ideated spaces that get associated with India are only the urban (urban India) and rural (*grameen* Bharat). The 'intermediate space' – the small town – has not garnered much attention both in Communications and Journalism Studies scholarship and in the popular media until the 2010s in mainland India that it deserves.[4] Sevanti Ninan (2007), who takes readers to *kasbahs*, *ganjs* and *purs* (suffixes of small towns in Uttar Pradesh) in her writing on local journalism, is perhaps the only exception but there is almost no work in the field by academics.

In reality, the number of small towns is growing at an unprecedented rate in India and have a particular character. The 2011 Census of India documented 2,774 new geographical entities listed as either statutory (242) or census towns (2,530), whereas the 2001 Census noted an increase of 500 towns in the country. This increase was 'unprecedented in the history of the Indian Census' (Kundu, 2017, p. vi).[5] Economists, urban planners, geographers, population studies scholars, anthropologists and policy scientists have realised the importance of understanding the rise of the small-town phenomenon (both existing/thriving and new/emergent ones) since the late 2010s (Denis and Zerah, 2017; De Bercegol, 2017). In their introductory article – 'Reclaiming small towns' – Denis and Zerah (2017, p. 2) stress the need to capture the dynamics of 'ordinary' towns in India and pointed out: 'Small towns need to be studied for themselves, as sites of urbanity, economic activities and social transformations and for their place in urbanisation, rural-urban linkages and the global economy'.

On similar lines, this study began as an attempt to understand Indian-language journalism culture with a specific focus on stringers in small towns. The choice of space was a conscious one inspired by the work of geographers such as David Harvey (2001, 2007), Doreen Massey (2005) and Edward Soja (2011). They helped me understand the notions of space intrinsically present in the works of communication thinkers with varied ideologies and approaches, from Williams (1969, 1975, 1995) to Carey (2009) and from Innis (1968) to McLuhan (1997).

The primary reason for choosing small towns to carry out ethnographic work was not to present a 'fresh' exotic narrative about stringers. It was partly based on the fact that most of the atrocities committed against mofussil journalists and stringers take place in small-town India (Seshu and Sarkar, 2019, p. 4). This has been the case with small-town correspondents since the 1990s and India ranks 142 (out of 180) in 2021 in the Press Freedom Index compiled by 'Reporters Without Borders' (*Reporters sans frontières*).[6] The remark made by one of the luminaries of Indian journalism, Chalapathi Rau in the late 1960s about mofussil correspondents being the 'Scheduled Castes' of journalism was the more important reason to undertake this exploration. The implications of this striking analogy demanded explanation. The structural violence Scheduled Castes (SCs) face both persists and is transformed in complicated ways in the present.

Attacks and atrocities on journalists and issues concerning their safety were not then the primary focus of this study. I was more interested in tracking the lives of stringers in a transforming and dynamic social space. I narrowed down on the mofussil areas with Massey's caveat in mind, that while studying social relations, materiality of practices, and culture in/of 'space', one needs to be wary of nostalgic emotions and utopian ideals (Massey, 2005, pp. 123–125). Those marred both Gandhi's and Nehru's visions and awareness of them would be imperative to avoid a totalising reading of Rau's analogy as well.

The small towns in which the research was carried out were Gannavaram in Krishna district of Andhra Pradesh (AP) and Sangareddy in Sangareddy district of Telangana State (TS) between April 2012 and October 2014. The rationale was their proximity to big cities (capital regions) of Amaravati (AP) and Hyderabad (TS), respectively. More importantly, the two sites of research are *mandals*, towns and legislative Assembly constituencies at the same time. Both sites have a mix of urban and rural characters which offered an opportunity to obtain a sense of relatively unexplored small-town journalistic formation. I revisited both the sites in September 2021 and January 2022, respectively, and spent a week at each place to update the research on stringers during the COVID-19 crisis.

Before plunging into the field to capture the workings of stringer in 'his' work sites and settings, an Appendix attached at the end of the book presents some of the features of Telugu newspapers, which are crucial in understanding the nature of work and the relation the Telugu journalistic field has with the economic and social fields. This understanding is important for the present study as the Telugu language press was one of the first to have cannibalised the specialised magazines for women, cinema, family, business and children content by including them in pull-outs within the main and district editions. Brief profiles of Sangareddy and Gannavaram are also included in the Appendix as separate sections to provide an overview of the sites of research.

Entering the field

On a humid and hot summer morning YSS[7] received a call on a rather routine day for him at work to visit *Grama Sachivalayam* (Village Assembly) of Veerapanenigudem, where scores of people were present to discuss their problems with the Village Revenue Officer (VRO). In a minute he concluded the chat we were having till then at the Gannavaram Police Station and Court complex and offered to take me to the 'spot'[8] on my motorcycle, which I readily agreed.

As soon as we reached the 'spot,' YSS approached the person who called him to find out about the situation as I strolled towards the Village Assembly office. The officials were carrying on with their work taking down the complaints from the farmers of the village in a casual manner.[9] While the officials were working in the *verandah* of the office building the VRO was present inside the building notwithstanding the presence of a crowd in the office premises.

In some minutes, YSS entered the office and went into the room in which the VRO was present. The crowd which was seemingly agitated but cool-headed so far suddenly became insistent and vociferous with support from an ex-sarpanch, who was shouting at the top of his voice against the laxity of the officials. As soon as YSS ended his discussion with the VRO and reached the *verandah* outside the office taking pictures of the event, then the farmers stood-up on their feet blaming the officials who stalled their work. The local correspondent managed to calm down the crowd and started negotiating with the officials, who explained to him that nothing was in their hands. Then he told the ex-sarpanch to write a representation as per his earlier consultation with the VRO, which was duly done. The officials too shared their problems with the stringer explaining their limitations. Once this was done, they asked the villagers if there were any other problems which they faced apart from the sand quarrying issue. Meanwhile, some villagers (from an influential community of the village: Reddy) urged YSS to take note of leaking water pipeline in the third ward of their village (mostly inhabited by people from Reddy community). I followed him, as he noted down the details of the problems, took quotes along with the respondents and finally took photographs of some of them. He quickly turned

> to me and suggested that we need to return to Gannavaram. After having lunch with a local politician (I was also included), he filed both the reports and sent a fax to the edition centre by 5:30 pm and informed the edition in-charge.
>
> (Field notes, Gannavaram, 16 April 2012)

In this instance, this particular news gatherer did not confine himself to the role of a reporter. He performed many roles as a negotiator, pacifier and solution provider. The stringer interacted with officials who were representatives of the state and its subjects – citizens – before filing a report, which was an invitation to a variety of agents into the journalistic field. Given the social background of this journalist, who happens to be from an Other Backward Classes (OBC) community, calling the shots in a traditionally upper-caste village prompted me to understand and theorise 'journalistic capital'.

The aforementioned detailed event substantiated my claim that it was possible to map the role of journalistic activity in a different way by identifying and understanding different agents extant in the bureaucratic, political and social fields hinging on the work of Pierre Bourdieu. However, the fact that both reports did not get published in the next day's paper further demanded an understanding of the interactions/relations/hierarchy, daily routine of the news desk (editorial and managerial department) within the 'journalistic field'.

There were instances where one PCB, who used to handle rural beat for another leading newspaper, helped a staffer from Vijayawada (edition centre), when the latter wanted to get a piece of land registered in his name in Gannavaram Mandal Revenue Office (MRO). This is the same organisation, which had sacked ARP accusing him of too much indulgence in 'brokerage' and 'blackmailing' (personal communication, 7 May 2012). There were stringers who used to write speeches for local politicians at the time of research. These political connections along with relationships with local businessmen and elite were important for stringers to meet the advertisement target set by newspaper organisations.

Taking Pierre Bourdieu to small-town India

The aforementioned experiences in the field convinced me to carry out ethnographic research to understand the autonomous and heteronomous character of small-town journalism. As I progressed in the fieldwork, I was able to make cultural interpretations of newswork from the perspective of stringers. The ethnographic method helped me to a great extent in understanding and then writing about news production at the local level from an emic (phonemic) perspective with an emphasis on the everyday language of stringers. I was also forced to be reflexive throughout the research, interaction and interviewing process of respondents, classification of the primary data and writing.

The habitus of the agents is as important as the professional standing, as practice is the result of the dynamic relationship between the individual habitus and various forms of capital in the field of action (Bourdieu, 2005, p. 101). In the journalistic field, it appeared that the question was not about bureaucratic organisation or social organisation but a combination of both, as they were intertwined.

However, some scholars seemed to be constructing a Bourdieusian universe well within the sub-discipline of Journalism Studies by mechanically augmenting core concepts of his field theory such as 'editorial habitus', 'reporter habitus' or 'intern habitus' and even argue that it is theoretically possible to differentiate the concept of habitus 'based on journalistic genres such as a "foreign correspondent habitus", an "investigative reporter habitus"; forms of habitus according to the media form "magazine habitus", "newspaper habitus", "television habitus"' (Schultz, 2007, p. 194; Willig, 2012, p. 8) and so on using the concepts of capital and doxa. Based on Bourdieu's field theory, this work seems to be practicing field theory, as opposed to coming up with a theory of practice, an error of which the French sociologist persistently warned.

In the present book, Bourdieu's field theory is put into work: (a) to understand the journalistic and non-journalistic practices; (b) to map the relationship between the dispositions of the agents (social space) and the positions (professional space) they occupy in the field; and (c) to understand the simultaneous operation of strategies of domination in organisational structures and channels of resistance by the agents. Methodologically, field theory allowed me to integrate ethnographic evidence on stringers and their journalistic labour in relation to other fields of power. At the same time, I added to the class conditioning aspect embedded in field theory by taking into account factors such as caste, gender and space that were more pronounced at the sites of this research.[10]

The *formal conversions* of capital from one to the other(s) were central to the understanding of the journalistic field. Bourdieu's field theory and its conceptual triad was crucial to this study, as it helped in comprehending the particularities of issues in the sites and individuals (micro-level) and at the same time allowing an analytical understanding of the social, political and economic orders at the macro-level (society, polity, media economy, states). Field theory served as a mezzo-level tool to connect the micro- and macro-levels of analysis (Benson, 2006, pp. 187–202).

The principles of vision and division (*nomos*) inherent in the praxeological framework of Bourdieu's works (1998, pp. 46–47, p. 53, 2021, pp. 70–71) are imperative for this ethnographic study as opposed to replicating his analysis or fitting data into existing theories or concepts, which often leads to deterministic arguments and offers little justice to developing a nuanced understanding of the field in study.

My approach for this research draws largely from Bourdieu's seminal essay – 'Understanding', in which he states:

> A *reflex reflexivity* based on a craft, on a sociological 'feel' or 'eye,' allows one to perceive and monitor *on the spot*, as the interview is actually taking place, the effects of the social structure within which it is taking place.
>
> (1996, p. 18). [Emphasis original]

Throughout the fieldwork, I tried to practice this principle to the best possible extent. Before I set out to jot down my observations during the fieldwork, I used to inform respondents and agents about my project and offer basic personal details. It is not only at the time of writing but also during the interactions in the field, I used 'to make explicit the intentions and the procedural principles' (Bourdieu, 1996, p. 18) which were put into practice at that time. Practicing the 'non-violent form of communication' suggested by Bourdieu, especially while interviewing respondents and interacting with different agents in the field benefitted me during the course of research.[11] I ensured that there was a flow of information from both sides, rather than a 'one-dimensional' interviewer–subject equation.

The voice recordings of the interviews conducted during fieldwork were transcribed immediately keeping the questions of tone, context and ambience in mind. After completing fieldwork at Sangareddy, I was convinced that the ethnographic method, which I was hesitant to adopt initially, is the only systematic process of study by observing the journalistic field on a first-hand basis. At the end of the fieldwork in Sangareddy, my primary data consisted of field notes, transcripts of interviews, profiles of 39 stringers, reporters and editorial staff members and transcripts of selected speeches by senior journalists and politicians in various journalist meetings held at Kanchikacharla in Krishna district, Gajwel in erstwhile Medak district (now in Siddipet district) and Nampally, Hyderabad. I have informally interviewed and interacted with hundreds of stringers, journalists and veteran journalists at journalists' union meetings and workshops for training mofussil stringers and cite them whenever needed throughout the book. Additional interviews were taken to update the study to incorporate changes that took place in the field due to COVID-19 and the Wage Code Act, 2020.

Organisation of the book

Exploring the heteronomous character of the journalistic field, Chapter 2 presents the world in which stringers operate. This chapter unfolds the entanglements of the social, economic and political fields and develops a conceptual understanding of the complexities that stringers navigate while carrying out newswork. This understanding from the ground serves as a foundation to construct arguments related to the journalistic field throughout this book.

I discuss how these structures are refracted into the journalistic field in Chapters 3 and 4. Chapter 3 attempts to address the questions: What is the social background of stringers, reporters and editorial staff members? How do they get recruited or enter the journalistic field? Along with presenting the demographic details of stringers and staffers (both editorial and reporting), the chapter also deals with the patterns of recruitment/entry into the field. I also unravel the aspect of relegation in the recruitment processes, which demonstrates how social reproduction takes place in the field. Chapter 4 discusses the nature of newswork and the prevalence of hierarchies in local journalism. This chapter picks up Bourdieu's concept of relegation and extends it to the issue of delegation of journalistic work. In this part of the book, I encapsulate the roles of stringers, editorial staffers and reporters and detail the multiple hierarchies that dynamically interact with each other in newswork and journalistic practices.

In Chapter 5, I move beyond the ways in which the stringer, seemingly confined by much larger structures, works around and despite them to present the logic of local journalistic practice. Cracking this logic helps in understanding how stringers negotiate the complex multiple hierarchies that exist within the field and outside of it on a daily basis while carrying out newswork. Also, the inseparability of journalistic and non-journalistic work by stringers while negotiating with various fields of power is discussed in this chapter.

One of the unused columns in the demographic details sheet during the fieldwork was gender/sex of stringers and reporters, as almost all of them were male. Chapter 6 moves beyond merely pointing out that there is a meagre representation or 'absence' of women in the local journalistic field and attempts to understand the masculinity of stringers at the intersection of domination and subordination in relation to sex, gender, caste, class and social space. In this chapter, I discuss in detail the exclusionary practices in the gendered journalistic field that cut both ways for these men, producing a damaged and damaging gendered subjectivity.

Chapter 7 points out how the understudied and under-theorised aspects of news labour are crucial to understanding journalism as a profession. I argue that even as the localisation strategy of Telugu newspapers has resulted in a relative democratisation of the field, it has also resulted in heightened informalisation. Based on life-stories of stringers, ethnographic observations, and bringing them to the present crisis of the pandemic, I present the forms of precarity associated with the field. The chapter suggests that the symbolic aspects of precarity are equally important as economic precarity in local journalism in mofussil areas. But show how precarity is not new for the stringer and in many ways the crisis of the pandemic was not a new crisis for them.

I conclude with the implications of this ethnographic research and offer possibilities and departures from it. The promise of the book is to offer an ethnographic understanding of newswork and journalistic practices in the field in relation to the political, social, economic and bureaucratic fields at play. One of the features of carrying out such field-based ethnographic study on news production, as opposed to newsroom ethnography, is the realisation of the relatively less autonomous nature or heteronomous nature of the journalistic field. This is especially the case for players marginalised in that field. The small-town stringer is one such player and in offering a full-bodied account of him, the hope is not just the invisibilising of his labour but the delineating of his importance in the journalistic field as well.

Notes

1 Mofussil is an important term/entity for this study. It loosely means any area that falls outside of the district headquarters or sometimes state capital. If not the same, it is an equivalent to the English word 'province'. Yule and Burnell (2008, p. 275), in their Anglo-Indian glossary noted, 'The provinces – the country stations and districts, as contra-distinguished from "the Presidency"; or, relatively, the rural localities of a district as contra-distinguished from the chief station, which is the residence of the district authorities'. Mofussil and small towns are used interchangeably throughout this research.

2 In the role of a fixer, I accompanied a journalist working with a reputed Dutch newspaper on the issue of suicides associated with the micro-finance sector in the then Telangana region in 2010. In another instance, I worked as a fixer for an English-language magazine reporter from New Delhi who was covering the issue of cotton farmer suicides in 2007 in the United Andhra Pradesh (Warangal and Guntur). I was paid an amount of US$100 for the 2010 assignment and in the second mentioned instance; I received two invaluable books of my choice as payment in kind. But this experience is not universal. See Borpujari (2019), who presents a range of issues associated with the work-life as a 'fixer' in India.

3 Thomas (2019) delineates the complex history of telecommunications in India from the colonial to the present times. He points out how the Indian Telegraph Act 1885 framed during the colonial times ironically continues to remain the root legislation bestowing exclusive powers to the Indian state in maintaining and controlling both wired and wireless communications in the country severely compromising on democratic ideals. Thomas suggests that the Act continues to bolster the expanded nature of surveillance in the IT Act of 2000, which was amended in 2008, giving state agencies unquestionable access to information exchanges between citizens over any device.

4 India and Bharat also carry religious and linguistic connotations. For a perceptive commentary on the Indian Constitution on these aspects, see Austin (2013, pp. 145–179, pp. 330–383).

5 Statutory towns are notified under legislation by state or union territory governments and have civic bodies such as municipal corporations/committees, cantonments, regardless of population, population density or nature of work (agricultural/non-agricultural workers). For a geographical place to be listed as

a census town, it needs to have a minimum population of 5,000 with a population density of at least 400 per sq. km and at least 75 per cent of the male main working population engaged in non-agricultural work. The number of census towns rose from 1,362 to 3,892, while the number of statutory towns increased from 3,799 to 4,041. See https://censusindia.gov.in/2011-prov-results/paper2/data_files/india2/1.%20data%20highlight.pdf

6 See https://rsf.org/en/india In 2002, the country ranked 80 (out of 180), as reported threats and deaths of journalists and media persons continued to rise. See https://rsf.org/en/ranking/2002#.

7 Names of stringers anonymised throughout the book. Diacritical marks are used in transliteration of Telugu quotes and utterances following renowned linguist on Dravidian languages Krishnamurti (2003). However, names of Telugu newspapers are retained as in the original.

8 'Spot' is a term used by journalists to refer to a site which has some potential to gather news. In other words, a place where some unplanned event takes place, unlike the case of press conferences, political gatherings, inaugurals, masjid/temple/church events and planned protests among others. Sub-editors insist the stringers to inform them over mobile, while in the spot. In this instance, the spot was the Village Assembly of Veerapanenigudem, an upland area, which was 7 km from the Court complex. This will be discussed in Chapter 4.

9 The problem which I found out later was about digging their fields for gravel in order to use it for their own building construction purposes. The officials acting upon the orders by the then district collector S.A.M. Rizvi did not permit the villagers from doing so. This was the time when sand quarrying mafia was being dealt seriously by the state government of (United) Andhra Pradesh.

10 Bourdieu (1962, pp. 132–133, pp. 145–155) wrote at length on the caste factor in Algeria in a different context, which is not relevant for the present research.

11 Highlighting that the entire process of interviewing as a spiritual exercise, Bourdieu (1996, p. 22) explained:

> The sociologist may be able to impart to those interviewees who are furthest removed from her socially a feeling that they may legitimately be themselves, if she knows how to show them, both by her tone and, most especially, the content of her questions, that, without pretending to cancel the social distance which separates her from them (unlike the populist vision, which is blind to the reality of its own point of view), she is capable of mentally putting herself in their place.
>
> [Emphasis original]

References

Aufderheide, P. (2004). Big media and little media: The journalistic informal sector during the invasion of Iraq. In Allan, S. and Zelizer, B. (Eds.), *Reporting war: Journalism in wartime*. Abingdon, Oxon: Routledge.

Austin, G. (2013). *The Indian constitution: Cornerstone of a nation*. New Delhi: Oxford University Press.

Bayly, C. A. (1999). *Empire and information: Intelligence gathering and social communication in India, 1780–1870*. New Delhi: Cambridge University Press.

Benson, R. (2006). News media as a "journalistic field": What Bourdieu adds to new institutionalism, and vice versa. *Political Communication*, 23(2), pp. 187–202. DOI:10.1080/10584600600629802.

Borpujari, P. (2019). The problem with 'fixers'. *Columbia Journalism Review*. Retrieved from: www.cjr.org/special_report/fixers.php.
Bourdieu, P. (1962). *The Algerians* (Tr. by Alan C. M. Ross). Boston: Beacon Press.
Bourdieu, P. (1996). Understanding. *Theory, Culture & Society*, 13(2), pp. 17–37. DOI:10.1177/026327696013002002.
Bourdieu, P. (1998). *Practical reason: On the theory of action* (Tr. by Loïc Wacquant and Samar Farage). Stanford, CA: Stanford University Press.
Bourdieu, P. (2005). *Distinction: A social critique of the judgement of taste* (Tr. by Richard Nice). Abingdon, Oxon: Routledge.
Bourdieu, P. (2021). *Forms of capital: Lectures at the collège de France, 1983–1984* (Tr. by Peter Collier), *General Sociology, Vol III*. Cambridge: Polity Press.
Bunce, M. (2011). *The new foreign correspondent at work: Local-national 'stringers' and the global news coverage of Darfur*. Oxford: Reuters Institute for the Study of Journalism.
Carey, J. W. (2009). *Communication as culture: Essays on media and society*. New York: Routledge.
De Bercegol, R. (2017). *Small towns and decentralisation in India: Urban local bodies in the making*. New Delhi: Springer.
Denis, E. and Zerah, M. (Eds.). (2017). *Subaltern urbanisation in India: An introduction to the dynamics of ordinary towns*. New Delhi: Springer.
Hannerz, U. (2004). *Foreign news: Exploring the world of foreign correspondents*. Chicago: University of Chicago.
Harvey, D. (2001). *Spaces of capital: Towards a critical geography*. New York: Routledge.
Harvey, D. (2007). Space as a keyword. In Castree, N. and Gregory, D. (Eds.), *David Harvey: A critical reader*. Oxford: Blackwell.
Innis, H. A. (1968). *The bias of communication*. Toronto: University of Toronto Press.
Innis, H. A. (1986). *Empire and communications*. Toronto: Press Porcépic.
Jeffrey, R. ([2000]2010). *India's newspaper revolution: Capitalism, politics, and the Indian-language press*. New Delhi: Oxford University Press.
Jodhka, S. S. (2012). Nation and village: Images of rural India in Gandhi, Nehru, and Ambedkar. In Jodhka, S. S. (Ed.), *Village society: Essays from economic and political weekly*. Hyderabad: Orient BlackSwan.
Kalia, R. (2006). Modernism, modernization and post-colonial India: A reflective essay. *Planning Perspectives*, 21(2), pp. 133–156. DOI:10.1080/02665430600555289.
Krishnamurti, B. (2003). *The Dravidian languages*. Cambridge: Cambridge University Press.
Kundu, A. (2017). Foreword. In Denis, E. and Zerah, M. (Eds.), *Subaltern urbanisation in India: An introduction to the dynamics of ordinary towns*. New Delhi: Springer.
Massey, D. (2005). *For space*. New Delhi: Sage.
McLuhan, M. (1997). *Understanding media: The extensions of man*. London: Routledge.
Murrell, C. (2019). Fixers as entrepreneurs. *Journalism Studies*, 20(12), pp. 1679–1695. DOI:10.1080/1461670X.2019.1636705.
Ninan, S. (2007). *Headlines from the heartland: Reinventing the Hindi public sphere*. New Delhi: Sage.

Palmer, L. (2016). "Being the bridge": News fixers' perspectives on cultural difference in reporting the "war on terror." *Journalism*, 19(3), pp. 314–332. DOI:10.1177/1464884916657515.

Palmer, L. (2018). Lost in translation: Journalistic discourse on news "fixers". *Journalism Studies*, 19(9), pp. 1331–1348. DOI:10.1080/1461670X.2016.1271284.

Rajagopal, A. (2001). *Politics after television: Religious nationalism and the reshaping of the Indian public.* Cambridge: Cambridge University Press.

Rajagopal, A. (2009). Introduction. In *The Indian public sphere: Readings in media history.* New Delhi: Oxford University Press.

Rajagopal, A. (2016). On media and politics in India: An interview with Paranjoy Guha Thakurta. *South Asia: Journal of South Asian Studies*, 40(1), pp. 175–190. DOI:10.1080/00856401.2017.1250194.

Rau, M. C. (1968). *The press in India.* New Delhi: Allied Publishers.

Remesh, B. P. (2018). Unpaid workers and paid news: Working conditions of journalists in India. In Athique, A., Parthasarathi, V. and Srinivas, S. V. (Eds.), *The Indian media economy, Vol. II: Market dynamics and social transactions* (pp. 134–151). New Delhi: Oxford University Press.

Remesh, B. P. (2021). News hunters or ad gatherers? Precarious work of rural stringers in print media. *Economic and Political Weekly*, 56(15), pp. 36–41.

Roy, S. (2011). Television news and democratic change in India. *Media, Culture & Society*, 33(5), pp. 761–777. DOI:10.1177/0163443711404467.

Schultz, I. (2007). The journalistic gut feeling. *Journalism Practice*, 1(2), pp. 190–207. DOI:10.1080/17512780701275507.

Seshu, G. and Sarkar, U. (2019). *Getting away with murder: A study on the killings and attacks on journalists in India, 2014–2019, and justice delivery in these cases.* Retrieved from: www.thakur-foundation.org/report-on-attacks-on-journalists-in-india-2014-2019.pdf.

Simpson, E. S. C. and Weiner, J. A. (Eds.). (1989). *The Oxford encyclopedic English dictionary.* Oxford: Clarendon Press.

Soja, E. W. (2011). *Postmodern geographies: The reassertion of space in critical social theory.* London: Verso.

Thomas, P. N. (2019). *Empire and post-empire telecommunications in India: A history.* New Delhi: Oxford University Press.

Williams, R. (1969). *Communications.* London: Chatto & Windus.

Williams, R. (1975). *The country and the city.* New York: Oxford University Press.

Williams, R. (1988). *Keywords: A vocabulary of culture and society.* London: Fontana Press.

Williams, R. (1995). *The sociology of culture.* Chicago: University of Chicago Press.

Willig, I. (2012). Newsroom ethnography in a field perspective. *Journalism: Theory, Practice & Criticism*, 14(3), pp. 372–387. DOI:10.1177/1464884912442638.

Yule, H. and Burnell, A. C. (2008). *The concise Hobson-Jobson: An Anglo-Indian dictionary.* London: Wordsworth Editions.

2

LOCATING THE STRINGER

Caste as space, capital, politics

> The Hindu society insists on segregation of the Untouchables. The Hindu will not live in the quarters of the Untouchables and will not allow the Untouchables to live inside Hindu quarters. This is a fundamental feature of Untouchability as it is practised by the Hindus. It is not a case of social separation, a mere stoppage of social intercourse for a temporary period. It is a case of territorial segregation and of a *cordon sanitaire* putting the impure people inside a barbed wire into a sort of a cage. Every Hindu village has a ghetto. The Hindus live in the village and the Untouchables in the ghetto.
>
> – Ambedkar, 1948/2014, p. 266

Introduction

Two unrelated incidents that took place during the course of my fieldwork at different locations and times show the relationship between the social, political and journalistic fields. In the first instance at Gannavaram:

> In a bid to publicise Rajiv Yuva Kiranalu – a state sponsored scheme for the benefit of unemployed youth by the then Congress government – a person (LC Babu) equipped with a microphone and loudspeaker set on a moped went around the villages in Gannavaram playing a pre-recorded announcement about the schedule of the programme.
>
> (Field notes, 8 May 2012)

> With a towel wrapped around his head to protect himself from the scorching summer heat, Babu on his gearless, two-wheeler used to carry out such publicity for most of the public activities taken up by the government such as grievances regarding rural employment scheme (MNREGA), health awareness messages, important announcements regarding agriculture and related activities.
>
> (Field notes, 17 May 2012)

 DOI: 10.4324/b23313-2

> Babu, who was quite popular among stringers and used to inform them (while on the go) about the latest happenings in the nearby village he just visited, belonged to the Madiga community.[1]
>
> (Field notes, 8 May 2012)

During the by-polls in Medak parliamentary constituency, after it was vacated by the Telangana Rashtra Samithi President K. Chandrasekhar Rao (KCR), the contestants (both belong to the influential Reddy caste) for parliament by-polls from the Telangana Rashtra Samithi (TRS) and the Bharatiya Janata Party (BJP) took out separate rallies as part of door-to-door political campaigning at different times of the day. Rallies of both political parties were led by a small group of drum beaters. While one group was playing the *ḍappu* (drum) slung over their shoulders to garner public attention, another group of dancers were dancing to the beats. *Nava Telangana* stringer, PR, pointed out that the persons playing the instrument belonged to the Madiga community and it was a common practice during elections. He also mentioned that they make quick money during occasions like these [elections] (Field notes, 10 September 2014).

It was noteworthy that on both occasions for public and political announcement purposes, persons from the Madiga community played a key role. After pointing that there was an intrinsic and organic relationship between the *ḍappu* and the Madigas since ancient times, Ilaiah (2009, p. 45) notes:

> The *dappu* is used to make public announcements (*dandora*); it was the only mode of announcing the dates of village functions, official announcements by the government, and so on. Thus, it was/is an instrument of music and mass communication. Village folk working in the fields or grazing their cattle in nearby pastures and forests could figure out from the sound of the *dappu* whether it was celebrating a wedding, mourning a death or making a proclamation.
>
> [Emphasis original]

> Even as the person in Gannavaram town did not use the traditional *ḍappu* to carry out publicity activity by replacing it with modern paraphernalia, the very fact that he belonged to the same community that had been involved in such activities (*danḍora*) strongly indicated a very clear and internalised presence of caste in everyday life. It was more obvious in the case of the Sangareddy political rallies.[2]

Responding to my observation that the loudspeaker has replaced the *ḍappu*, but that the 'mass communicator on two-wheeler' was performing the age-old role that their caste-men did, a senior stringer DD pointing towards PCB (a stringer from Madiga caste, who was working with *Eenadu* at the time of research), who was present on the occasion, jovially said, '*ēm māriddi sār? ēmi māradu. ippudu mā PCB gādu kammollaki vāḷḷa paperlo ḍappu kottatlēda? vādiki vērē option ēmannā undā?*' (Nothing will change, Sir. What great job was PCB 'fellow' doing in his paper? He was playing *ḍappu* to the Kammas in his reports. Was there any other option?)[3] With a smile, PCB told DD to shut his mouth (Field notes, 9 May 2012). In Sangareddy town, in a very casual tone, MPR too expressed that it (Madigas playing *ḍappu* in political rallies) was a very common sight in Telangana. These observations and responses from stringers on the nature of their work along with internalisation of hierarchies and dispositions reflected the social and political worlds in which they operate. The following sections of this chapter discuss the conflation of the social and political fields from the ground and its implications on the journalistic field.

Caste appeared as a crucial factor in understanding local journalism at the inception of the fieldwork itself. The ideas surrounding caste, roles and hierarchy were concretised while coding my primary and secondary data along with reading the academic literature.

Caste Studies has engaged with the idea of caste from both textual and field perspectives (text view and field view). Two major conceptions within the text view are 'caste as hierarchy' (Dumont, 1999) and 'caste as colonial construction' (Dirks, 2001).[4] Even as there are differences within this tradition, they engage with the idea of *varnashrama dharma* that suggests a classification of Hindus in the order: (1) Brahmana (priests); (2) Kshatriya (kings and royals); (3) Vysya (traders, traditionally large-scale farmers); and (4) Shudra (*Śūdra,* peasant castes and productive labouring communities). Many studies pointed out that this classification was done on the basis of occupation or purity or ritual status among many other considerations. Susan Bayly notes (1999, p. 9), 'Most Indians who would classify themselves as Hindus are likely to be at least broadly familiar with two distinct concepts of corporate affiliation: the *jati* (birth group) and the *varna* (order, class)'.

More relevant to the present study is the field view, which engages with caste as a lived reality in the society. In the field view of caste, some of the dominant conceptions were: 'caste as power/dominance' (Srinivas, 1959, 1960), 'caste as association' (Rudolph and Rudolph, 1999; Shah, 1975) and 'caste as discrimination/emancipation' (Ambedkar, 1916/2014, 1944/2014; Omvedt, 2010).[5]

Outside of this four-tier classification were people who were labelled earlier as untouchables (SCs or Dalits) along with many people who live in forests or on hills (STs or Adivasis). This classification was based on centuries-old code or text: *Manusmriti*. The usage of the word untouchables and practice of untouchability was outlawed as per the Constitution of India. The fact that the *Census of India* (2011) report compiled that more than 25.2 per cent (SC – 16.6 and ST – 8.6) of the country's population belong to these communities and groups that fall outside of the aforementioned stratification indicated its highly exclusive nature of the *varṇaśramadharma* (Telugu and Sanskrit) or *chaturvarnavyavastha* (four-tier varna system).

There was relatively lesser ambiguity when it came to the understanding of the Savarna category (collectively, Brahmana, Kshatriya and Vysya castes) in the *varna* system. The fourth category Shudra or *Śudra* (Telugu) along with *Panchamas* – the excluded sections of population from the hierarchical Hindu code of classification (fifth category or the category that lies outside of the classification) needed to be understood before proceeding to get an understanding of the social positions of agents within and without the journalistic field.

Gundimeda (2016, pp. 322–323) suggests that there were four types of nomenclatures were associated with the *Panchamas*. They were (1) Depressed classes or Scheduled Castes (imposed by colonial authorities); (2) Ati-Shudras or Harijans (attributed by social reformers, such as Jotirao Phule and Gandhi, respectively, striving for the upliftment of those communities); (3) Dalit (politically aware individuals and leaders identifying themselves as ex-untouchables in contemporary India); and (4) Jati (self-description of Dalits in specific local contexts such as Madiga, Mala, Chamar, Pariah).

During the interactions and while carrying out interviews for the present study, most of the Dalits referred to themselves as *Mādigalu* or *Mālalu* (depending on their caste), *Daḷitulu & SC-lu*.[6] This was how they described themselves during general descriptions and conversations. While talking about the oppression they faced in society and profession, they used terms such as *kindi kulālu* (downtrodden castes), *takkuva jāti* (lower by birth), *aṇagārina kulālu*. On the other hand, forward caste stringers, editorial and reporting staffers, and locals referred to Dalits as SC *vaḷḷu*, SC-STlu, *dēvuni biḍḍalu* (children of God),[7] *mādigōḷḷu or mādigalu*, *mālōḷḷu or mālalu*, *Daḷita kulāla vāḷḷu*, and *Daḷitulu*. While asking questions or interacting, I used the term Dalit or *Daḷitulu* both in Andhra Pradesh and in Telangana.

The fourth category in the *Varna* classification – the Shudras – was highly contextual and region specific. Without presenting a general picture of the variations in this category, beyond the scope of this study, I list the names of Shudra castes (Hindus) that agents from the journalistic field. They are (1) Kamma; (2) Reddy; (3) Velama; (4) Kapu (Delta region of Andhra Pradesh); (5) Goud; (6) Padmasali; (7) Nayi Brahmin; (8) Rajaka; (9) Chakali; and (10) Mudiraj. There was one person from the Madiga caste who converted to Christianity (BC-C) and the remaining were Muslims (3), who belonged to religious minorities. There were no stringers or reporters or editorial staffers from the Vysya and Kshatriya (Telugu Rajus) castes at the time of research in both Sangareddy and Gannavaram.

Persons belonging to communities such as Goud or Gouda (toddy tappers), Padmasali or Padmashali (weavers), Nayi Brahmin (barbers), Rajaka and Chakali (washermen), and Mudiraj (soldiers and fishing community members) in Andhra Pradesh and Telangana are categorised as the Backward Classes and fall under the Shudra category at the same time (Ilaiah, 2009; Swamy, 2019, pp. 90–115).[8]

The remaining castes in the Shudra category were Kammas, Reddys, Velamas and Kapus. All these castes were land-owning and agrarian communities in the Telugu-speaking regions: Telangana, Andhra and Rayalaseema. Harrison (1960, p. 209) noted that Sat-shudra (sat = good) status was accorded to Kammas, Reddis, Velamas and other Telugu peasant castes to distinguish them from less affluent Shudras in the Census of India, Madras Presidency in the year 1901.

Social hierarchies and volatilities

On the way to Gannavaram from Vijayawada on the National Highway-16 (NH-16), there are vast expanses of green farmland at a distance on either side of the highway along with state-of-the-art automobile showrooms and service centres that have mushroomed in swanky commercial complexes situated closer to the highway. There are private engineering and junior colleges, and a Best Price-Walmart wholesale store and occasional '*dhabas*' (eating joints on highways) on the way. After crossing the Medha IT Park and the NTR College of Veterinary Science on the left and the Vijayawada International Airport at Gannavaram on the right, I took a left after reaching Gandhi *Bomma* (statue) Centre to reach Gannavaram centre. If the IT Park, multinational FMCG store, commercial complexes and an airport were signs of globalising India, the story of neoliberal modernity ended at the Gannavaram centre, as a statue of Gandhi with his walking stick welcomed the passers-by to the *mandal*. Notably, in most villages, Ambedkar statues are found in 'SC colonies' or 'labour colonies' or 'Ambedkar colonies', as they were referred to, sidelined from the main and approach roads.

The Gannavaram *mandal* or town, referred to interchangeably, is neither urban nor rural in character. If one were to associate modernity with the principle of egalitarianism, the town was not modern, as the residential localities and housing patterns are divided on caste lines. Each caste occupies a solid block of contiguous houses in a lane or locality. The influential or 'upper' castes named their colonies as Ram Nagar colony, Raya Nagar colony, Srinagar colony and Subba Rao Nagar colony.[9] There was VN Puram colony in Kesarapally village, in which influential caste people resided. The remaining villages were inhabited on the basis of castes classified under Other Backward Classes (OBC) category, with a handful of upper caste houses at the centre of villages near a school (*baḍi*) or temple (*guḍi*), while the Scheduled Caste (SC) colonies and Ambedkar colonies were scattered on the fringes of villages in the *mandal*. Savarigudem in Gannavaram *mandal* is exclusively inhabited by the Sugali (Scheduled Tribe) community.

Not only are housing and residential localities differentiated on the basis of caste and community places of worship are as well. There were *ramalayams* (temples of Lord Rama) for each caste in different villages and localities. The notable ones were Kammavari *ramalayam*, Tagarula, Yadavula, Razakula, Kapula and Gouda *ramalayams* in the villages of Gannavaram *mandal* and town. The Kodanda *ramalayam* was the oldest temple in the *mandal*, which does not have any caste tag attached to it. There is the Kanyaka Parameswari temple, open to everyone, but built by the Vysya community. Similarly, the foundation plaques of all these *ramalayams* revealed that they were built by raising donations with a significant contribution made by an affluent person(s)/family from that particular community. Even the churches were said to be differentiated on the basis of class and caste in Gannavaram. Unlike the temples, there are no visible caste-based markers of the churches in the form of plaques or names. During the time of research, I observed that the majority of the Christians who had converted from forward castes such as Brahmin, Kamma, Kapu and Reddy belonged to the Roman Catholic Missionary (RCM) churches, while Christians from the Dalit (mostly the Malas and the Madigas belonging to SC category) and OBC communities frequented Lutheran, Telugu Baptist and Pentecostal churches (Robinson and Kujur, 2010; Webster, 2012; Kumar, 2015).

Sangareddy in Telangana is similar in terms of segregation of geographical locations on the basis of social differentiation but the castes and communities were different from that of Gannavaram. While multinational pharmaceutical companies along with regional, national and international institutes of research and education indicated the influx of global capital, the social geography of the town mirrored differentiations based on religion. If the main religious minority (not in terms of numbers but stakes in various spheres) community in Gannavaram was Christian, it was the Muslim community in Sangareddy. Even as most residential colonies had people from various communities and castes, the town was divided into two parts: old and new. It was the new bus stand that stood at the centre dividing the town.

Ahmed Nagar was the biggest colony in the 'older' (*pāta*) part of Sangareddy, inhabited by the Muslim community, while Shanti Nagar was the biggest colony in the new Sangareddy town. The Muslims from lower economic strata were located in Nalsabgadda and Meeda Bazaar areas, while the rich and upper-middle-class households were scattered across the town. Most of the masjids (Islamic worship places) were located in the older part with the biggest and oldest being Jama Masjid. On the other hand, temples were located in both parts. There were colonies bearing caste names such as Brahman Wada, Mudiraj Colony, Golla Gudem, and Vaddera basti (colony).[10] Middle-class Hindu households were, predominantly, located in Bhavani Nagar, Ram Nagar, Prashanth Nagar, Sanjeev Nagar, Someshwarwada, Veerabhadra Nagar, and Shivaji Nagar.

Moreover, I observed a strong presence of *śaivam* (Shaivite tradition; worship of Lord Shiva) tradition with statues of Lord Basaweshwar (seen with a sword riding on the back of a white horse) at the entrances of villages in and around Sangareddy *mandal* and town areas.[11] There were many temples of Lord Shiva at different places in the town itself reinforcing the tradition. These temples and statues appeared to be powerful reminders indicating the proximity of the region with Karnataka.[12] There was a considerable population of Lingayats, who act as priests in some temples, in this region (Robinson, 1988, p. 65).

As part of the Shaivite tradition, goddess worship was common in the form of Renuka Yellamma,[13] Nalla Pochamma, Chowdamma Thalli and Katta Maisamma (deities that ward off evil spirits and diseases and secure water bodies). The Edthanur *tāṇḍa* (hamlet), located on the outskirts of Sangareddy, had two temples of Chowdamma (a descendent of Lord Shiva) one each for the Mala and the Madiga castes. The Kanyaka Parameswari temple in Sadashivpet was built by Vysyas, as the goddess residing in the temple is their *kula daivam* (caste deity). On the other hand, the relatively new religious structure, the Sri Vaikuntapuramu temple, along with *goshalas* (Hindu cow shelters) located outside Sangareddy town are related to the *vaiṣṇavam* (Vaishnavite tradition; worship of Lord Vishnu).[14]

This aspect of location on the basis of social stratification (caste and religion) in Indian villages, in the Deccan village to be precise, dealt with in detail by social anthropologist S.C. Dube in his classic work: *Indian Village* (1967, pp. 161–166) focused on the hierarchical (social and economic) differentiations in the village of Shamirpet in Ranga Reddy district (now Medchal-Malkajgiri district) of Telangana. Parallels could be drawn with the small towns (Gannavaram and Sangareddy) considered in which this study is located.

At both locations of research, I found that the names of the villages that end with the suffix – *uru/oor, -palle/-pally* (small village), and *puram/pur* have significant influential or upper-caste populations or the land is owned by them, while *-peta/-pet* (residential locality on the fringe of a major town),[15] *-gudem/-guda or khed* (hamlet), *-kal/-gal/-kallu* (rock/hillock) are inhabited by agricultural labourers from the Dalit (SC) and OBC communities.

It was not only in villages but also in the town areas that caste mattered the most in the space, everyday life and language of people.[16] On most of the occasions, when I tried asking for the address of a person in Sangareddy, the locals required the *mārpēru*[17] of the person for identification purposes. The *marpēru* ('nickname') would bear the caste of the person or geographical location (like groundwater well, temple, school) or age or physical attributes (fat/lean, tall/short, fair/dark), including physical ability. Even in Gannavaram, the locals would ask for caste or religion marker or occupation or surname (the last two could supplement the caste and religion in some cases) to identify a person.

Restaurants, eateries and food-joints (referred to as hotels in Telugu) reflect the cultures present at the research location. For instance, on the Sangareddy town main road itself, there is a Kalyani Biryani[18] point and another one at Pothireddipalli village, adjacent to the town. There are the usual tiffin centres (places offering breakfast or snacks) mushrooming in the town. Reportedly one of the largest meat-exporters in the country, the Al Kabeer group's mechanised slaughterhouse (abattoir) was located at Rudraram village near Sangareddy. It was always in the news for dumping animal waste in the nearby localities.

While there is an increasing presence of tiffin centres in Sangareddy, there are many Hyderabadi biryani food joints in Gannavaram along with a couple of places offering 'Irani chai'. Unlike in Sangareddy, sale of uncooked and cooked beef was not a public or commercial affair in Gannavaram. Those who consumed it did so surreptitiously. However, the absence of beef and pork, affordable sources of protein, in commercial spaces indicated the hegemonic forces in the context.[19] Gannavaram had a government-run bacon factory, which was converted into a veterinary sciences college in 1998. The college premises located on NH-5 had a centre exclusively for fattening and breeding of pigs, at the time of fieldwork.

There were two courts in Gannavaram with the principal junior civil court complex located near the gram panchayat office and an additional junior civil court complex adjacent to the sub-registrar's office. The Gannavaram sub-jail and the Gannavaram police station were located in and around the MRO office area. Constables walking the accused from the police station to produce them in the courts was a common sight. The district and sessions court at Sangareddy was commonly referred to as the court complex. Even the Sangareddy jail was huge. Being the headquarters of the district, the court complex was always abuzz with activity with people from all corners of the district visiting. This was a good resource point for stringers to file stories of human interest.

Sangareddy was considered a communally volatile area with the latest such major incident occurring in March 2012.[20] Police were seen on an alert mode every Friday during the *Jumma* (early afternoon congregational *namaz* [prayer] practiced by Muslims) and it was the only occasion when they were lenient on triple riding on bikes, as Muslim youths rushed to the Jama Masjid – the oldest worship place in the area.

In Sangareddy, apart from the regular duties to maintain law and order along with allied responsibilities, police were faced with three major concerns: (a) communal tensions; (b) close observation on Maoist activities; and (c) *ganja* (marijuana) cultivation.[21] In the case of Gannavaram, the police had to deal mainly with (a) illegal sand business; (b) land dealings and settlements; and (c) caste conflicts in villages among other issues of concern. Most issues in both towns boiled down to communal/caste-based conflicts.

Caste capital: solidarities, assertions and discriminations

Even as caste remained a crucial factor in everyday life in both Krishna and Medak districts, the way it was articulated in public places was starkly different. Caste articulation in Vijayawada and Gannavaram by the influential communities was supremacist in nature, while in Sangareddy and Medak districts, it was more of expressing solidarity or communal camaraderie among caste groups.

The offices of caste associations (*sanghams*) such as the Mudiraj *Sangham*, the Telangana Goud *Sangham* and the Yadava *Sangham* are everywhere in and around Sangareddy town. These caste-based welfare associations have marriage function halls that also serve as convention centres (during off-season for marriages) for income generation purposes. They are rented at discount rates, – priority is given for marriages between members of the same caste – as a way of expressing caste-based solidarity.

In the case of Vijayawada and Krishna district, the thin line between caste-based solidarity and assertion is blurred, as caste forced itself into every sphere of life. Vijayawada is an arena for a show of might between the Kammas and the Kapus. The dynamics and assertive strategies of these castes are visible at movie theatres,[22] political publicity material (giant flexi-posters, wall posters, pamphlets, and so on), and even on their vehicles. Unlike in Sangareddy, the manifestation of caste in the public arena is not restricted to a mere expression of solidarity among caste and community persons in Krishna district.

The Kammas take pride in labelling themselves as 'Royal Chowdarys' in general and 'Nandamuri fans' at theatres, while the Kapus proudly asserted 'Royal Kapus' taglines in public and 'Mega fans' when it came to cinemas. While 'Nandamuri fans' denoted an umbrella of fan associations of 'Tollywood heroes' from the NTR family[23] (sharing the surname Nandamuri), the 'Mega fans' tag was about heroes from the family of 'Megastar' Chiranjeevi (Srinivas, 2009; Gundimeda, 2009a).

'Caste feeling', as most locals articulated the assertion of their caste, was relatively higher in Vijayawada in Krishna district compared to Sangareddy in Medak district. This caste feeling was prevalent even in job fairs in some of the caste *sanghams* (associations) in and around Vijayawada city. Most *sangham* offices have a hostel attached to them, served as marriage function halls and offered vocational training for unemployed youths and homemakers. Advertisements for these programmes were published in district editions of newspapers, along with posters stuck on the walls at public places. These training centres and hostel facilities along with marriage halls appeared to be spaces of social capital for persons belonging to that particular caste.

To understand the nature of caste-based solidarities, assertions, articulations and discrimination in the social order, Bourdieu's (1986, pp. 241–258) conception of various forms of capital was is interpretatively helpful. His notion of capital forms the triad of field theory along with field and habitus. The French sociologist's conceptualisation offered a fresh lease of life to an otherwise reified Marxist and economic deterministic conception of capital, augmenting it as he did with the academic works of Weber (cultural roots of capitalism) and Durkheim (social order; forms of solidarity: mechanical and organic).

The concepts of social capital, cultural capital and economic capital help not only in understanding the issues in Telugu journalism that this work deals with in the next chapters – patterns of recruitment, non-journalistic and journalistic practices in news production and various forms of exchanges and rituals prevalent in the field – but also in understanding the journalistic field in relation to the social, political and economic fields.

This conception of capital along with habitus and field helps in understanding the presence and role of caste associations (*sanghams*) and their representation in media, proliferation and celebration of family surnames as brand names in both the polity and the economy, provision of education and employment opportunities exclusively for certain castes, among a wide range of issues surrounding caste.

Ethnographic observations on the manifestation and articulations of caste in the semi-arid and industrialised Medak district appeared to be different from commercial crop and paddy-rich coastal river delta region of Krishna district. These regional and geographical variations are also crucial in understanding the social order following Cohn's (1987) suggestion that regions and regionalism are important to the study of Indian society. Cohn (1987, p. 130) writes:

> The relationship between the rise of regional élites and their role in selection and standardisation of symbols and values from the regional stock of symbols and values is a very complex one, relating to technology, education, access to civil and political roles, and the accidents of history and policy.

This observation is essential in understanding the political field that shares a dynamic relation with the journalistic field, which will be discussed in the following section. An idea about the political orders is as important as the social ones to understand the practices in the relatively less autonomous field of journalism.

Between the devil and the deep sea: a masculine sat-shudra game of thrones

During a discussion among stringers on the outcome of the General Elections in 2014, Sangareddy stringer MAK, who doubles as a photo-stringer for English language news agencies, stated, 'We can only choose between two Ramas to govern this country. One is "Ayodhya Rama" and the other one is "Bhadradri Rama". In the end, it is the same ruling castes and classes that grab political power'.[24] For him, 'Ayodhya Rama' is the aggressive muscular version of dominant Hindu ruler in the form of the BJP, while 'Bhadradri Rama' is a secular version of the dominant groups symbolising the Congress. Ultimately, it was Rama who rules the country. Stringers who took part in the discussion agreed with MAK, who explained that the power transfer was superficial and did not benefit the underprivileged castes and minorities even in the past.

This discussion alludes to the nature of parliamentary politics and social composition of politicians from village to national level in India. The transfer of power from one party to the other at the Centre, states and even *mandal* levels appeared to be a very cosmetic one, as influential castes take up leadership positions and key roles in both national and regional parties. Stringers belonging to the SC and OBC communities, who took part in the discussion, felt that despite having numbers (in terms of population and votes), their communities never got leadership opportunities in United Andhra Pradesh and even after bifurcations. 'Barring one instance in which Damodaram Sanjivayya (a Dalit), it was candidates belonging to the Reddy and the Kamma community, who ruled the state as Chief Ministers in AP. Now it is Velamas turn in Telangana', MAK said, while another stringer BYG pointed out that no one from the OBC category became Chief Minister before and after bifurcation of AP (Fieldnotes, 15 September 2014).

It is not just the state-level politics in which the Kammas and the Reddys dominate but even at the village panchayat elections as well. Persons from these communities command considerable influence in the villages and small towns. Kamma, Reddy and Kapu caste persons were in most cases referred to as *kammōru*, *reḍlu* and *kāpulu* in Gannavaram, Krishna district, respectively. Velamas in Sangareddy were infrequently addressed as *velama doralu* and often as *velmalu* or simply *velmās*.

Stringers and locals belonging to SC and OBC communities, while responding to my questions, addressed those influential caste groups as *agrakulālu* (upper castes), *dōpiḍidārulu* (exploiters) and *unnata kulālu/vargālu* (higher castes/classes) in Gannavaram, while in Sangareddy those caste groups were addressed as *patelōḷḷu*, *doralu* and *peddōḷḷu*.

Ambedkar's observations on these communities noted in *Thoughts on Linguistic States* were very perceptive. He observed, 'Take Andhra – there are two or three major communities spread over the linguistic area. They are either the Reddis or the Kammas and the Kapus. They hold all the land, all the offices, all the business' (1953/2014, p. 134).

What Ambedkar foresaw as perils for democratic functioning of the state way back in the late 1940s turned into a reality sooner rather than later. He went on to write:

> In a linguistic State what would remain for the smaller communities to look to? Can they hope to be elected to the Legislature? Can they hope to maintain a place in the State service? Can they expect any attention to their economic betterment? In these circumstances, the creation of a linguistic State means the handing over of Swaraj to a communal majority. What an end to Mr Gandhi's Swaraj! Those who cannot understand this aspect of the problem would understand it better if instead of speaking in terms of linguistic State we spoke of a Jat State, a Reddy State or a Maratha State.
>
> (1953/2014, p. 134)

Many decades later, Susan Bayly (1999, p. 287), while reflecting on this phenomenon on a pan-Indian scale, noted:

> The other crucial factor here was the creation from 1956 of the new linguistically defined state boundaries which were drawn up so that individual states became zones of high numerical concentration for the members of only one (or at most two or three) of the broad *sat-sudra* 'peasant' jati blocs. In Bihar, these numerically predominant cultivating populations are those whose members use the titles Koiri, Kurmi and Ahir-Yadav. Their counterparts in Karnataka are Vokkaligas and Lingayats; in Haryana and Gujarat the equivalent 'communities' are Jat and Kanbi-Patidar, while in Andhra most clean-caste 'peasants' identify themselves as Kammas or Reddis.

While Kammas, Reddys and Velamas 'attained' Sat-shudra status, sociologists labelled the Kapus of coastal Andhra as an intermediate agrarian caste (Chennur, 2019).[25] The Godavari-Krishna Kapus were numerically and economically strong, especially in the delta region of coastal Andhra, but were never able to compete with the Kammas and the Reddys in the political field.

The Kapus started a demand that they be included under the OBC quota after the bifurcation of the state under the leadership of a Kapu leader from East Godavari district, Mudragada Padmanabham. The bill was tabled in the AP Legislative Assembly and Council before sending it to the President of India for approval through the Governor of the state (GoAP, 2017). In Bourdieusian terms, the mobilisation strategy or scheme of action for Kapus to gain political recognition took the form of a social movement for reservations.

The Kapus in the Telugu-speaking states do not form a neat homogenous category, as they comprise castes such as Kapu, Telaga, Balija and Ontari among many other variants. The backwardness or forwardness of the caste varies from region to region. Sometimes, the status of Kapus in the list of state-wise lists of Backward Classes varies from district to district (Swamy, 2019). However, the Krishna and Godavari delta Kapus in Andhra Pradesh claim the status of Sat-shudras by tracing their lineage to Vijayanagara king Sri Krishnadevaraya and claim Kshatriya status.[26] Despite having economic status, numerical strength and cultural capital, the Kapus of the delta regions in coastal Andhra could never manage to get a chance to become chief minister of the then-United Andhra Pradesh (Table 2.7). This could be seen as one of the reasons why a Kapu leader from the Godavari region attempted to mobilise the community persons to fight for the cause of securing OBC status for the community.

Apart from the Telangana movement that kept newsworkers in both regions on their toes, another development that took place around the same time was the establishment of a new regional political outfit – the YSR Congress in 2011. This resulted in the conduct of by-elections as 18 Congress MLAs resigned from their positions and party to join the YSR Congress. Even though there were no by-elections for the Gannavaram Assembly constituency, the political atmosphere was tense due to the arrest of the YSR Congress supremo, Y. S. Jagan Mohan Reddy on 27 May 2012. This arrest was made a couple of weeks before the scheduled by-elections in Andhra, Rayalaseema and Telangana regions.

On that day, there was a state-level meeting of AP Union of Working Journalists (APUWJ) at Kanchikacharla. The speakers at the working journalists meeting from the morning were hinting at the possible arrest of the leader, which became a reality by evening. The timing of this meeting could not be missed as the accounts of *Sakshi* newspaper were frozen on 8 May 2012. The following day the paper printed a half-page with a headline – Black Day – in Telugu and two-line text that read: *sakshi patrika, sakshi TV accounts stambhimpacēsina CBI; kalālaku. gaḷalaku sankeḷḷu*! (CBI freezes Sakshi accounts; pens and voices chained!).

Many journalists attended the meeting, as the organisers promised that there would be elections for the office bearers of the district unit of the Union. Much to the shock of stringers and reporters from other newspapers, the meeting turned was no more than an expression of solidarity with the arrested leader. Many stringers predicted openly that the YSR Congress was going to take the place of Congress in the 2014 Assembly elections. (Field notes, Kanchikacharla, 27 May 2012), which turned out to be an accurate prediction, as the Congress Party was decimated in Andhra Pradesh.

This was one of the many instances that suggested the close relationship between the journalistic field and the political field. The union meeting instance was particularly presented to highlight the relationship at a larger level than that of the usual proximity or relationship that stringers maintained while going about their reporting work. On the same lines, 2 years later, I attended the inaugural meeting of the Telangana Union of Working Journalists (TUWJ) organised at the Exhibition Grounds, Nampally in Hyderabad on 9 March 2014. With the then-Chief Minister of the state resigning from the post on 19 February 2014 in protest against the Union government's decision to bifurcate the state in favour of Telangana, President's rule was imposed on 1 March 2014.

Telangana politicians, across parties, attended and spoke at the journalists' meet. However, the preferential importance given to the TRS President K. Chandrasekhara Rao by the Telangana journalist leaders was obvious and could not be missed. With some journalists publicly announcing their political ambitions, in the 2014 Assembly elections, some TUWJ leaders intervened to remind everyone that the meeting was about journalists' welfare in the soon-to-be-formed state and not an avenue to discuss electoral politics. Eventually, some journalists managed to get tickets from various parties to contest in both the 2014 and 2019 Assembly elections.

Having made these observations, I realised the need to gather details about the caste background of legislators who won from Gannavaram and Sangareddy constituencies to get an understanding of the political field, which seemed to share a considerable amount of affinity with the journalistic field.

Pertinent data was procured from senior editor and political analyst Kommineni Srinivasa Rao (2014a and 2014b), who publishes and updates a handbook comprising the details of candidates in both states, along with the data that I collected during the course of my fieldwork and Assembly archives of both states. The data suggested that the political field is an 'arena of the Sat-shudras' in both AP and Telangana. The provision of reservations in Assembly constituencies is applicable to SC and ST categories and not for persons from the OBC communities and women. In effect, in both states, open category Assembly and parliamentary seats are often won by persons belonging to castes such as Kamma, Reddy, Kapu and Velama.

The sheer number of women representatives in the Assembly from Seemandhra and Telangana regions before bifurcation in relation to the AP and TS Assemblies after bifurcation presented the masculine nature of the political field in the Telugu-speaking regions. The highest percentage of women representation was recorded in the 2009 Legislative Assembly since 2004. Apart from that elected house, the percentage of women representation was reduced to single digits indicating the masculine domination in the political field (see Tables 2.1 and 2.2). The situation worsened in the post-bifurcation scenario.

In order to highlight the male dominance in the field, I indicate the gender of the winning candidates in all the tables along with the caste and community details. What was striking was the meagre presence of women candidates in the state Assemblies (Tables 2.1 and 2.2) which reflects the

Table 2.1 Region-wise representation of women MLAs before bifurcation in united AP

Year	*Andhra+Rayalaseema MLAs – 175 (%)*	*Telangana MLAs – 119 (%)*	*Total – 294 (%)*
2004	13 (7.4%)	10 (8.40%)	23 (7.82%)
2009	19 (10.85%)	16 (13.44%)	36 (12.24%)

Source: AP Assembly archives

Table 2.2 State-wise representation of women MLAs in AP and TS

Year	*Andhra Pradesh – 175 (%)*	*Telangana – 119 (%)*	*Total – 294 (%)*
2014	18 (10.28%)	9 (7.56%)	27 (9.18%)
2019	14 (8%)	6 (5.04%)	20 (6.80%)

Source: AP and TS Assembly archives

Table 2.3 Accredited Telugu and English language print journalists in AP and TS

Language	*State*	*Editorial*		*Reporting*		*Total*	
		Female (%)	*Male (%)*	*Female (%)*	*Male (%)*	*Female (%)*	*Male (%)*
Telugu	AP	16 (6.3)	241 (93.7)	14 (5.7)	233 (94.3)	30 (6)	474 (94)
English	AP	7 (24.2)	22 (75.8)	2 (3.7)	53 (96.3)	9 (10.8)	75 (89.2)
Telugu	TS	65 (18.3)	290 (81.7)	29 (8.2)	325 (91.8)	94 (13.3)	615 (86.7)
English	TS	35 (26.7)	96 (73.3)	12 (10.3)	105 (89.7)	47 (18.9)	201 (81.1)

Sources: Compiled from GoT (2021) and GoAP (2021)

Note: Total number of state-level accredited journalists in AP and TS (all languages and media forms): 4,481
Andhra Pradesh: Male: 1,497 (94.9 per cent), Female: 80 (5.1per cent), Total: 1,577
Telangana: Male: 2,609 (89.9 per cent), Female: 295 (10.1 per cent), Total: 2,904

representation of women in the Telugu journalistic field (Table 2.3). While Table 2.4 presents the details of elected legislators from Gannavaram, Table 2.5 details the same about Sangareddy. Results of the latest Assembly elections held in Telangana, 2018 (Table 2.11) and Andhra Pradesh, 2019 (Table 2.10) clearly demonstrate that the MLAs from the Sat-shudra and forward castes can form a government in their respective states.

The situation of marginal communities in Telangana, where the incumbent TRS party won, appeared to be slightly better than their counterparts in AP, where YSR Congress party toppled the Telugu Desam party (TDP). The top-3 Sat-shudra caste MLAs (91 out of 175) in AP can prove their

Table 2.4 MLAs elected from Gannavaram – Caste and gender (1955–2019)

Year	*Name*	*Political Party*	*Caste*	*Gender*
1955	Puchalapalli Sundarayya	CPI	Reddy	Male
1962	Puchalapalli Sundarayya	CPI	Reddy	Male
1967	Velivala Sitaramayya	Congress	Kamma	Male
1968	Kakani Venkatratnam	Congress	Kamma	Male
1972	Tappata Sarojini Ananda Bai	Congress	Scheduled Caste	**Female**
1978	Puchalapalli Sundarayya	CPI	Reddy	Male
1983	Musunuru Ratna Bose	Congress	Kamma	Male
1985	Mulpuru Balakrishna Rao	TDP	Kamma	Male
1989	Musunuru Ratna Bose	Congress	Kamma	Male
1994	Gadde Rammohan	Independent	Kamma	Male
1999	Dasari Balavardhana Rao	TDP	Kamma	Male
2004	Muddaraboina Venkateswara Rao	Independent	Yadav (OBC)	Male
2009	Dasari Balavardhana Rao	TDP	Kamma	Male
2014	Vallabhaneni Vamsi Mohan	TDP	Kamma	Male
2019	Vallabhaneni Vamsi Mohan	TDP	Kamma	Male

Source: Rao (2014a); Fieldwork

Note: Congress (I) and Indian National Congress were listed as Congress for convenience.

Table 2.5 Details of MLAs elected from Sangareddy – Caste and gender (1962–2019)

Year	*Name*	*Political Party*	*Caste*	*Gender*
1962	Patlolla Ramchandra Reddy	Congress	Reddy	Male
1967	Narasimha Reddy	Independent	Reddy	Male
1972	Patlolla Ramchandra Reddy	Congress	Reddy	Male
1978	Narasimha Reddy	Independent	Reddy	Male
1983	Patlolla Ramchandra Reddy	Congress	Reddy	Male
1985	Patlolla Ramchandra Reddy	Congress	Reddy	Male
1989	Patlolla Ramchandra Reddy	Congress	Reddy	Male
1994	K. Sadasiva Reddy	TDP	Reddy	Male
1999	K. Satyanarayana	BJP	Scheduled Tribe	Male
2004	Turpu Jayaprakash Reddy	Congress	Reddy	Male
2009	Turpu Jayaprakash Reddy	Congress	Reddy	Male
2014	Chinta Prabhakar	TRS	Padmashali (OBC)	Male
2019	Turpu Jayaprakash Reddy	Congress	Reddy	Male

Source: Rao (2014b); Fieldwork.

Note: Congress (I) and Indian National Congress were listed as Congress for convenience.

majority in the house without any other community's support. In the case of Telangana, this category of MLAs (55 out of 119) will fall short of a simple majority by two seats even after taking support from three forward-caste MLAs. There are eight legislators from the Muslim religious minority out of which only one MLA was elected outside of Hyderabad hailing from

Bodhan in Nizamabad. In the case of AP, there were four Muslim legislators and all of them represent YSR Congress in the Assembly.

The caste matrix and composition of legislators are openly talked about not only in Telugu newspapers but also in English national dailies (Reddy, 2018, 2019). The political field in both AP and Telangana appeared to be a 'Sat-shudra arena' keeping Bourdieu's conception of these terrains of power as fields of combat sport between influential castes and how caste serves as a source of symbolic and social capital.

Some of the conditions that were considered 'essential and natural' to take part in the political field ('rules of the game') in these states clearly demand certain capital (money, credentials) and habitus, to which every person may not be entitled.[27] Interviews with stringers about the political field at both sites revealed that most of the time, an open or general category Parliamentary seat (Lok Sabha; lower house) is offered to business persons.

These candidates will have to 'take care' of the financial needs of the Assembly contestant from the same party falling under the Parliamentary constituency (see Tables 2.6 and 2.7).[28] In the case of Medak parliamentary constituency, there are seven Assembly constituencies including Sangareddy, and the number of Assembly constituencies in the case of Machilipatnam parliamentary constituency is the same, including Gannavaram Assembly constituency.

Table 2.6 Details of MPs elected from Machilipatnam – Caste and gender (1952–2019)*

Year	*Name*	*Party*	*Caste*	*Gender*
1952	S. Buchikotaiah	CPI	Kapu	Male
1957	M. V. Krishna Rao	Congress	Kapu	Male
1962	M. Venkataswamy	Independent	Kapu	Male
1967	Y. A. Prasad	Congress	Kamma	Male
1971	M. Nageswara Rao	Congress	Kapu	Male
1977	M. Ankineedu	Congress	Kamma	Male
1980	M. Ankineedu	Congress	Kamma	Male
1984	K. Sambasiva Rao	Congress	Kamma	Male
1989	K. Sambasiva Rao	Congress	Kamma	Male
1991	K. Peda Reddaiah	TDP	Yadav (OBC)	Male
1996	K. Satyanarayana	TDP	Kapu	Male
1998	K. Sambasiva Rao	Congress	Kamma	Male
1999	A. Brahmanaiah	TDP	Kapu	Male
2004	B. Ramakrishna	Congress	Kapu	Male
2009	K. Narayana Rao	TDP	Gouda (OBC)	Male
2014	K. Narayana Rao	TDP	Gouda (OBC)	Male
2019	V. Balashowry	YSRCP	Kapu	Male

Source: Rao (2014a)

Note: * Gannavaram village/*mandal*/town falls under Machilipatnam parliamentary constituency.

Table 2.7 Details of MPs elected from Medak – Caste and gender (1952–2019)*

Year	*Name*	*Party*	*Caste*	*Gender*
1952	N.M. Jayasurya	PDF	N.A.	Male
1957	P. Hanmanta Rao	Congress	Brahmin	Male
1962	P. Hanmanta Rao	Congress	Brahmin	Male
1967	S. Laxmi Bai	Congress	Yadav (OBC)	**Female**
1971	Mallikharjun Goud	TPS	Goud (OBC)	Male
1977	Mallikharjun Goud	Congress	Goud (OBC)	Male
1980	Indira Gandhi	Congress	Brahmin	**Female**
1984	P. Manik Reddy	TDP	Reddy	Male
1989	M. Baga Reddy	Congress	Reddy	Male
1991	M. Baga Reddy	Congress	Reddy	Male
1996	M. Baga Reddy	Congress	Reddy	Male
1998	M. Baga Reddy	Congress	Reddy	Male
1999	A. Narendra	BJP	Padmashali (OBC)	Male
2004	A. Narendra	TRS	Padmashali (OBC)	Male
2009	M. Vijayasanthi	TRS	BC-Kapu	**Female**
2014	K. Chandrasekhar Rao	TRS	Velama	Male
2014	K. Prabhakar Reddy	TRS	Reddy	Male
2019	K. Prabhakar Reddy	TRS	Reddy	Male

Source: Rao (2014b)

Note: * Sangareddy village/*mandal*/town falls under Medak parliamentary constituency. PDF = People's Democratic Front (a left-leaning political outfit). Telangana Praja Samithi (TPS) was floated by former CM Marri Channa Reddy during the first wave of Telangana agitation in 1969 and it was merged into Congress after the General elections in 1971.

This is the preferred scheme of operation by most of the political parties in picking parliamentary candidates for Lok Sabha. A cursory look at their profiles would reveal that most of them were into business before venturing into politics. A report compiled by the Association for Democratic Reforms (ADR, 2019, pp. 35–36) states that as many as seven candidates from AP and one from Telangana figured in the top-10 list of richest contestants in the first phase of General Elections conducted on 11 April 2019.

Various political parties seemed to have selected candidates for the Assembly constituencies on the basis of caste equations (*kulam*), money (*artha balam*) and muscle power (*anga balam*). Most of the time, it 'happened' that all the above forms of capital were wrested in the hands of males from certain castes in most parts of the country, while in the present case it was Sat-shudras. The list of chief ministers elected by the winning party in each term reveals the dominance of masculine Sat-shudras in the political arena from the inception. Out of the 16 chief ministers of United Andhra Pradesh, as many as nine of them were Reddys (all Congress), three CMs were Kammas, while a person each from Mala, Velama, Vysya and Brahmin castes were chosen for the top political post in the state (see Tables 2.8 and 2.9).

Table 2.8 Details of Chief Ministers of united AP – Caste, gender and region (1956–2014)

Term	*Name of CM*	*Party*	*Caste*	*Region*	*District of birth*	*Gender*
1956–1960	Neelam Sanjiva Reddy	Congress	Reddy	Rayalaseema	Anantapur	Male
1960–1962	Damodaram Sanjivayya	Congress	Dalit/Mala	Rayalaseema	Kurnool	Male
1962–1964	Neelam Sanjiva Reddy	Congress	Reddy	Rayalaseema	Anantapur	Male
1964–1971	Kasu Brahmananda Reddy	Congress	Reddy	Coastal Andhra	Guntur	Male
1971–1973	P.V. Narasimha Rao	Congress	Brahmin	Telangana	Warangal	Male
1973	Jalagam Vengala Rao	Congress	Velama	Telangana	Khammam	Male
1973–1978	Marri Channa Reddy	Congress	Reddy	Telangana	Atraf-i-Baldah	Male
1978–1980	Tanguturi Anjaiah	Congress	Reddy	Telangana	Hyderabad	Male
1980–1982	Bhavanam Venkatrami Reddy	Congress	Reddy	Coastal Andhra	Guntur	Male
1982–1983	Kotla Vijaya Bhaskara Reddy	Congress	Reddy	Rayalaseema	Kurnool	Male
1983–1984	N.T. Rama Rao	TDP	Kamma	Coastal Andhra	Krishna	Male
1984	Nadendla Bhaskara Rao	TDP	Kamma	Coastal Andhra	Guntur	Male
1984–1989	N.T. Rama Rao	TDP	Kamma	Coastal Andhra	Krishna	Male
1989–1990	Marri Channa Reddy	Congress	Reddy	Telangana	Atraf-i-Baldah	Male
1990–1992	N. Janardhana Reddy	Congress	Reddy	Rayalaseema	Nellore	Male
1992–1994	Kotla Vijaya Bhaskara Reddy	Congress	Reddy	Rayalaseema	Kurnool	Male
1994–1995	N.T. Rama Rao	TDP	Kamma	Coastal Andhra	Krishna	Male
1995–1999	N. Chandrababu Naidu	TDP	Kamma	Rayalaseema	Chittoor	Male
1999–2004	N. Chandrababu Naidu	TDP	Kamma	Rayalaseema	Chittoor	Male
2004–2009	Y.S. Rajasekhara Reddy	Congress	Reddy	Rayalaseema	Kadapa	Male
2009	Y.S. Rajasekhara Reddy	Congress	Reddy	Rayalaseema	Kadapa	Male
2009–2010	K. Rosaiah	Congress	Vaisya	Coastal Andhra	Guntur	Male
2010–2014	N. Kiran Kumar Reddy	Congress	Reddy	Rayalaseema	Chittoor	Male

Source: Rao (2014a, 2014b)

Note: Congress (I) and Indian National Congress were listed as Congress for convenience.

Table 2.9 Details of Chief Ministers of AP and TS – Caste, gender and region (post-bifurcation)

Term	*State*	*Name of CM*	*Party*	*Caste*	*Region*	*District of birth*	*Gender*
2014–2019	AP	N. Chandrababu Naidu	TDP	Kamma	Rayalaseema	Chittoor	Male
2014–2018	TS	K. Chandrasekhara Rao	TRS	Velama	Telangana	Siddipet	Male
2018–	TS	K. Chandrasekhara Rao	TRS	Velama	Telangana	Siddipet	Male
2019–	AP	Y.S. Jagan Mohan Reddy	YSRCP	Reddy	Rayalaseema	Kadapa	Male

Source: Rao (2014a, 2014b)

Table 2.10 Caste and category composition of MLAs in AP Assembly – 2019

Caste	*Category*	*No. of MLAs*	*Percentage (~)*
Reddy	SS	50	28.6
Kapu	SS	24	13.7
Kamma	SS	17	9.7
Balija	SS	2	1.1
Velama	SS	2	1.1
Vysya	FC	4	2.3
Kshatriya/Raju	FC	4	2.3
Brahmin	FC	2	1.1
Dalits	SC	29	16.6
Adivasis	ST	7	4
Turpu Kapu	OBC	7	4
Yadava	OBC	6	3.4
Koppula Velama	OBC	5	2.9
Setti Balija	OBC	4	2.3
Gavara	OBC	1	0.6
Rajaka	OBC	1	0.6
Kalinga	OBC	2	1.1
Reddika	OBC	1	0.6
Muslims	RM	4	2.3
Matsyakara	BC	3	1.7
Total		175	100

Source: AP and Telangana BC Welfare Association, Hyderabad

Note: SS = Sat-shudras FC = Forward castes; RM = Religious minorities.
MLAs party-wise break-up: Total seats – 175. YSRCP – 151; TDP: 23; Jana Sena Party (JSP) – 1.

Table 2.11 Caste and category composition of MLAs in TS Assembly – 2018

Caste	*Category*	*No. of MLAs*	*Percentage (~)*
Reddy	SS	40	33.6
Velama	SS	10	8.4
Kamma	SS	5	4.2
Brahmin	FC	2	1.6
Vysya	FC	1	0.8
Muslims	RM	8	6.8
Dalits	SC	19	16
Lambada	ST	7	6
Adivasi	ST	5	4.2
Munnuru Kapu	OBC	8	6.8
Yadav	OBC	5	4.2
Goud	OBC	4	3.4
Vanjara	OBC	1	0.8
Mudiraj	OBC	1	0.8
Perika	OBC	1	0.8
Lodha	OBC	1	0.8
Gangaputra	OBC	1	0.8
Total		119	100

Source: AP and Telangana BC Welfare Association, Hyderabad

Note: MLAs party-wise break-up: Total seats – 119. TRS – 104; All India Majlis-e-Ittehadul Muslimeen (AIMIM) – 7; Congress – 6; BJP – 1; TDP – 1.

Barring one or two CMs of united AP, everyone had at least one more member from his immediate or extended family in active politics. Most of them either passed on their political legacy or 'inherited' one. At the same time, there were many instances when persons from the same family were contesting against each other representing different political parties. But as a stringer in Gannavaram pointed out: 'In the end, the seat will remain within the family' (PCB, 28 May 2012).

This practice, which could be seen as a transmission of social capital, holds good cutting across regions in both states and parties even after bifurcation.[29] This practice of family politics or dynasty politics is not restricted to AP and Telangana alone (Balagopal, 1995, p. 2482; Elliott, 1995, pp. 133–152; Srinivasulu, 2002; Suri, 2002), as it was visible in almost all states and regions throughout the country (Vaishnav, 2015, 2017). For the present study, this practice is very much prevalent in the political field of both Sangareddy (Medak district) and Gannavaram (Krishna district). More importantly, there is a visible exertion of the dominance of the Sat-shudras in the political field at both locations.

The history of politics in United Andhra Pradesh, if political ideologies are kept aside, could be seen as an arena where the Reddys and the Kammas clash with each other. This situation concretised even after the bifurcation of the state. A sociological understanding of Telangana state politics reveals that the first-past-the-post system of elections provided an opportunity for a numerically weak Sat-shudra caste (Velama) to hold power in consecutive elections by patronising and appeasing all sections of society.

The social is clearly inscribed on the polity at various levels and even the economy, as most of these influential castes control the landholdings and businesses in these areas. Also, the triad of field theory concepts – field, habitus and capital – proved to be crucial in understanding the dynamic nature of society, polity and journalism at these locations. Where does that leave stringers, mostly from the OBC and Dalit communities, who are present at the bottom of the ladder, socially and professionally?

Notes

1 The Madigas along with the Malas and 58 castes belong to the Scheduled Castes (SC) category (Dalits) in Andhra Pradesh and Telangana. The Madiga community pioneered the sub-categorisation movement in India and have been demanding judicious split within the SC category reservation (affirmative action) on population basis for better opportunities in education and employment since 1972. The movement is a result of the lateral hierarchy extant within the Dalit community. For an understanding of the sub-categorisation movement, see Balagopal (2000, pp. 1075–1081; 2005, pp. 3128–3133).

2 From a Dalit-Bahujan perspective, Ilaiah (2009, p. 46) notes,

> Even the Communist school of thought, dominated as it was by the upper castes, deployed the *dappu* for political propaganda and cultural movements but never thought it important to attempt to bring about a change in the social value of the maker [of the *ḍappu* instrument] and the player.

3 Even as both DD and PCB belong to the SC category, DD occasionally bosses around with the latter due to his seniority. '*mā* PCB *gāḍu*' ('our' PCB 'fellow'), in this context, was a way of expressing a cordial relationship. However, this 'resigning to fate' expression emerged out of an incident that happened on the previous day, which will be discussed in detail in Chapter 4.

4 Both these authors did not endorse the archaic social stratification in their works. Studies that emerged out of the text-view time and again proved the ambivalent grounds on which present day's apparent social identities were based on in history.

5 I only mentioned some of the foundational works that were read for the present study. Jodhka (2018) provided an excellent empirical account of emerging and contemporary manifestations of caste in India delving into a range of issues including hierarchies, citizenship, economy, social mobility and mobilisations.

6 As per the list of state-wise Scheduled Castes updated up to 26 October 2017, there were 59 castes in Andhra Pradesh and Telangana in the category. For a complete list of castes, see: http://socialjustice.nic.in/writereaddata/UploadFile/Scan-0001.jpg (Andhra Pradesh) and http://socialjustice.nic.in/writereaddata/UploadFile/Scan-0026.jpg (Telangana). Out of these communities, most of the persons falling under the SC category that I interacted during fieldwork were from Madiga and Mala and one person from the Relli caste.

7 There is an evident symbolic violence in referring to the Dalits as *SC-STlu* or 'children of god'. Even as there were no persons from Scheduled Tribes (ST)

category in picture, forward caste members club SCs and STs as if they were one and the same. When it came to the utterance or reference *dēvuni biḍḍalu* (children of God), there was a palpable condescending pun involved in it. There were two observable reasons for this. They were: 1) Some of the Dalits follow Christianity and hence were labelled as children of God; 2) Dalits and STs and Adivasis were protected by law under SC, ST (Prevention of Atrocities) Act, 1989, which some influential castes found 'unaccommodating' (*paristhiti marī ibbandigā mārindi*) to use their language, which was discriminatory at least from the perspective of Dalits. 'Even if we talk *freely*, there could be a case against us', a stringer based in Gannavaram who hailed from the Kamma community said (Personal communication, 1 June 2012). In other words, 'talking freely' meant using 'upper-caste' language that appeared 'neutral' to them and was highly casteist and objectionable for many, especially for the Dalit communities. This was one of the problems, a majority of the Dalits had with the label – Harijans (People of God) – coined by Gandhi. Most of the time, it was the Shudras belonging to influential communities who used such expressions. At the same time, there was only one stringer from a Dalit background who did not belong to Madiga or Mala castes in both Krishna and Medak. He belonged to the Relli caste that falls under SC category. But fellow stringers in Gannavaram used to mock him as *konḍōḍu* (hillman). This was one of the reasons why the MRPS, Dalit and progressive intellectuals were arguing for sub-categorisation among the SC communities. See Balagopal (2000, 2005) and Gundimeda (2006).

8 This handbook provided lists of all Backward Classes (state level), Other Backward Classes (OBCs) and Most BCs. Galanter (1978, pp. 1812–1828) provides an exhaustive mapping of the career of OBCs from colonial times till late 1970s. His article continues to hold relevance, at least from the policy perspective, even in the wake of the recent reservations for the economically weaker sections under the OBC category.

9 It was interesting to note that the names of residential localities ending with 'Nagar' (which translates as city; space or abode for civilians) were most often inhabited by affluent and forward castes. The words *nagaram* (city), *nāgarikata* (civilisation), *nāgarikulu* (civilised persons or civilians) share a common root word: *nagar*.

10 Mudiraj, Vaddera and Golla/Kuruma (often used Yadav as last name) castes were classified under the OBC category.

11 Also known as Basavanna, Lord Basaweshwar along his wife Neelambika propagated the message of equality by raising their voice against gender and social discrimination by spreading *śaivam* in twelfth century A.D. The Lingayat saint's social philosophy and life story were documented by one of the earliest Telugu poets Palkuriki Somanatha (Rao and Roghair, 1990).

12 Karnataka was carved out of the Hyderabad State, Maharashtra (Bombay Presidency) and Mysore princely state. Even now regions in Karnataka are referred to as: Hyderabad Karnataka (Kalyana Karnataka), Bombay Karnataka and Mysore Karnataka. The Hyderabad-Karnataka region shares a border with Sangareddy district. North Eastern Karnataka Road Transport Corporation (*īśānya Karnataka sārige*) buses plying on NH-65 are a common sight at any given point of the day/night.

13 The Renuka Yellamma Temple located in the Fruit Research Station witnessed a huge gathering during the Batukamma festival, cutting across sections and castes in Hindu society to offer *bonalu* (cooked rice mixed with milk and jaggery/sugar offered in pots). Noticeably, women from well-to-do class offered *bonam* in sparkling golden yellow brass vessels, while devotees from modest strata offered in clay pots (ranging from reddish-brown to black).

14 These were important in understanding the social and religious fabric of Sangareddy (Medak) in particular and Telangana and India in general. As political scientist Kancha Ilaiah wrote an article in *Andhra Jyothi* newspaper blaming the ruling Telangana CM, K. Chandrasekhara Rao, for reviving Brahmanical *vaiṣṇavam*, furthering the ideology of the ruling BJP at the centre. This article, critically questioning the democratic nature (or the lack of it) of Hindu gods, triggered a controversy in Telangana. Subsequently, a case was filed against him for hurting the sentiments of a dominant religion. See *telangāṇa ippuḍu vaiśṇavāndhra* (Telangana is now Vaishnavandhra, 11 March, 2015, *Andhra Jyothi*) www.andhrajyothy.com/artical?SID=91482&SupID=26%20telangana%20ippudu%20vaishnavandhra%20-%20kanca%20ilaiah. Also, see: https://scroll.in/article/743651/kancha-ilaiah-neither-the-sangh-parivar-nor-the-telangana-government-can-arrest-my-pen

15 It is received wisdom in Telugu-speaking states (and in most parts of Tamil Nadu) that a *peta* was where commoners or public lived, while a *koṭa* (fort) is the house of rulers or administrators. Similarly, places ending with the suffix *-koṇḍa* (hill) housed the ruling community, while *-kal/gal, -kallu/gallu* (hillock) belong to the ruled. Suffixes *-kal/gal* [such as Jukkal in Kamareddy district, adjacent to Sangareddy district (old Medak district) and Wargal in Medak district] and *-kallu/gallu* [such as Guntakallu (Anantapur district), Kapugallu (Nalgonda), Orugallu is a variant of Warangal] in Telugu, Kannada and Tamil languages meant rock or stone or hillock. *Kallu* as a standalone word, meaning toddy in Telugu.

16 For a historical understanding of land-owning patterns on basis of caste-related power structures and modes of domination in Telangana region, see Thirumali (1972, pp. 477–482).

17 *Mārpēru* is a prefix to the name. If the person's name was Yadaiah, then the question would be which Yadaiah. Some of the markers were golla Yadaiah (Yadav), *gavaḷla* or *gaonḍla* Yadaiah (Goud), *kunṭi* Yadaiah (limp/physically challenged), *bakka* Yadaiah (lean), *bāyi kāḍa unḍē* Yadaiah (residing near the well), *cinna* Yadaiah or *pedda* Yadaiah (*cinna* here meant younger and *pedda* meant elder or older; age as a marker) and so on. Persons from the dominant and influential castes in the area such as the Reddy and the Velama were both referred to as *paṭēlā* or *paṭel sāb*. Brahmins were referred to as *bāpanōllu and bāpanaina* (singular) and a person from the Vysya (traders) community and any business person (regardless of caste) is referred to as *kōmaṭaina* (colloquially in absence of the person) and *sēṭhu* or *sēṭh* (respectfully in presence of the person).

18 It is a biryani variant in which finely cut buffalo meat cubes are used instead of the usual mutton or chicken. The name Kalyani comes from the Kalyani region (erstwhile Hyderabad Karnataka). Most working-class people consume this as early lunch before setting out for the day's work or very late in the afternoon (in-between work).

19 In a different context, Gundimeda (2009b, pp. 127–149) outlined the complex dialectical matrix of the food and caste hierarchies before constructing an argument around democratisation of the public sphere from a human rights perspective.

20 In mainland India, the word communal refers to community grouping on religious basis. On most occasions and instances, communal conflicts and clashes refer to friction and rifts between Hindu and Muslim religious groups. Newspapers reported that an objectionable online post resulted in communal clashes in the town injuring several persons and causing property damage. For more details on the incident, see https://timesofindia.indiatimes.com/city/hyderabad/Online-post-sparks-Sangareddy-riot/articleshow/12474746.cms and www.deccanherald.com/content/238435/communal-clash-medak-over-morphed.html.

21 At the time of fieldwork, Medak district was declared in the 'Red Corridor' – areas that had Maoist presence. However, the latest reports from the Union Ministry of Home Affairs removed the district from the list of Maoist-affected areas. See the updated list at https://pib.gov.in/PressReleaseIframePage.aspx?PRID=1562724.

22 For an understanding of fan cultures and movie stars in the Indian context, see Srinivas (2021) and Prasad (2009).

23 Nandamuri Taraka Rama Rao, popular as NTR Sr., was a thespian and Chief Minister of Andhra Pradesh. He was the founder of Telugu Desam Party (TDP), which came to power in the 1983 State Assembly elections.

24 Bhadradri or Bhadrachalam is a temple-town, where a Hindu tahsildar, Ramadasu, working under the Golkonda ruler Tana Shah built a temple, which was initially objected but later granted an official status. Bhakta Ramadasu story is often invoked in the Telugu-speaking states to invoke notions of secularism embedded in history.

25 The Telugu word *kapu* means protector or cultivator. They use the suffix – Naidu – in the East and West Godavari, Krishna and Guntur. However, in Rayalaseema region, the Reddys in their caste certificate usually are classified under Kapu community. Also, the title Naidu in Rayalaseema is used by the Kammas. Also, some Kammas along with Velamas, and Kapus shared the suffix – Rao. This sharing of titles and caste names suggested the similar or common roots that most of these land-owning and agrarian communities shared in the past.

26 The Kammas followed the same strategy during the late 1930s and wrote their history projecting themselves as Kshatriyas and have fallen from that grace (Chowdhary, 1939/1989, pp. 38–169). At the time of data collection in Vijayawada in 2012, controversy erupted between the Kapus, the Kammas and the Yadavas over a Telugu movie *Krishnadevaraya*, which was yet to be released. The Kapus and the Yadavas held press conferences in Vijayawada in their association offices (Field notes, Vijayawada, 10 September 2012). The release of the movie was delayed due to these controversies.

27 Social geographer, Jeffrey (2001, pp. 217–236), demonstrated the importance of caste dominance in the reproduction of social inequality in the context of Uttar Pradesh.

28 However, in case of reserved parliamentary constituencies, it is vice-versa. The MLAs contestants need to pool in resources for their party's parliamentary candidate.

29 At the same time, there were many instances when persons from the same family were contesting against each other representing different political parties. But as a stringer in Gannavaram pointed out: 'In the end, the seat will remain within the family' (PCB, 28 May 2012)

References

ADR [Association for Democratic Reforms]. (2019). *Analysis of criminal background, financial, education, gender and other details of candidates in phase I of Lok Sabha elections, 2019*. Retrieved from: https://adrindia.org/.

Ambedkar, B. R. (1916/2014). Castes in India: Their mechanism, genesis and development. In Moon, V. (Ed.), *Dr. Babasaheb Ambedkar writings and speeches* (Vol. 1, pp. 3–22). Bombay: Education Department, Government of Maharashtra.

Ambedkar, B. R. (1944/2014). Annihilation of caste. In Moon, V. (Ed.), *Dr. Babasaheb Ambedkar writings and speeches* (Vol. 1, pp. 23–96). Bombay: Education Department, Government of Maharashtra.

Ambedkar, B. R. (1948/2014). The untouchables: Who were they and why they became Untouchables? In Moon, V. (Ed.), *Dr. Babasaheb Ambedkar writings and speeches* (Vol. 7, pp. 256–277). Bombay: Education Department, Government of Maharashtra.

Ambedkar, B. R. (1953/2014). Need for checks and balances. In Moon, V. (Ed.), *Dr. Babasaheb Ambedkar writings and speeches* (Vol. 1, pp. 131–135). Bombay: Education Department, Government of Maharashtra.

Balagopal, K. (1995). Andhra elections: What happened and what did not happen. *Economic and Political Weekly*, 30(3), pp. 136–139.

Balagopal, K. (2000). A tangled web: Subdivision of SC reservations in AP. *Economic and Political Weekly*, 35(13), pp. 1075–1081.

Balagopal, K. (2005). Justice for Dalits among Dalits: All the ghosts resurface. *Economic and Political Weekly*, 40(29), pp. 3128–3133.

Bayly, S. (1999). *Caste, society and politics in India from the eighteenth century to the modern age*. New York: Cambridge University Press.

Bourdieu, P. (1986). Forms of capital. In Richardson, J. (Ed.), *Handbook of theory and research for the sociology of education*. Westport, CT: Greenwood.

Census of India. (2011). *Enumeration of scheduled castes and scheduled tribes*. New Delhi: Office of Registrar General, India. Retrieved from: https://censusindia.gov.in/census.website/sites/default/files/2022-05/SSDIV-ENG.pdf.

Chennur, S. (2019). Caste as social power: Sociological trajectory of an intermediate caste. *Economic and Political Weekly*, 54(7), pp. 38–46.

Chowdhary, K. B. (1939/1989). *Kammavāri caritra* (History of Kammas). Guntur: Kiran Publications.

Cohn, B. (1987). *An anthropologist among the historians and other essays*. New Delhi: Oxford University Press.

Elliott, C. (1995). Caste and faction among the dominant caste: The Reddis and Kammas of Andhra. In Kothari, R. (Ed.), *Caste politics in India*. Hyderabad: Orient Longman.

Dirks, N. B. (2001). Castes of mind: Colonialism and the making of modern India. Princeton, NJ: Princeton University Press.

Dube, S. C. (1967). *Indian village*. New York: Harper Colophon Books.

Dumont, L. (1999). *Homo Hierarchicus: The caste system and its implications*. New Delhi: Oxford University Press.

Galanter, M. (1978). Who are the other backward classes? An introduction to a constitutional puzzle. *Economic and Political Weekly*, 13(43/44), pp. 1812–1828.

GoAP. (2017). *The Andhra Pradesh Kapu (Reservation of Seats in educational institutions and of appointments or posts in the services under the State) Act, 2017*. December 2. Amaravati: The Andhra Pradesh Gazette.

GoAP [Government of Andhra Pradesh]. (2021). Consolidated media accreditations list. Amaravati: Information and public relations department. Retrieved from: http://ipr.ap.nic.in/.

GoT [Government of Telangana]. (2021). List of approved accreditation cards to Telangana journalists. Hyderabad: Information and publication relations department. Retrieved from: http://ipr.tg.nic.in/.

Gundimeda, S. (2006). *Brāhmaṇatva mālatvamā? mānavātma Ambedkaratvamā? vargīkaraṇa samasyapai carca* (Brahmanical Mala casteism or humanistic Ambedkarism? Discussion on the question of categorisation). Hyderabad: Rajyam Publications.

Gundimeda, S. (2009a). Dalits, Praja Rajyam Party and caste politics in Andhra Pradesh. *Economic and Political Weekly*, 44(21), pp. 50–58.
Gundimeda, S. (2009b). Democratisation of the public sphere. *South Asia Research*, 29(2), pp. 127–149. DOI:10.1177/026272800902900202.
Gundimeda, S. (2016). Dalit activism in Telugu country, 1917–30. *South Asia Research*, 36(3), pp. 322–342. DOI:10.1177/0262728016663270.
Harrison, S. (1960). *India: The most dangerous decades*. Princeton, NJ: Princeton University Press.
Ilaiah, K. (2009). *Post-Hindu India: A discourse on Dalit-Bahujan, socio-spiritual and scientific revolution*. New Delhi: Sage.
Jeffrey, C. (2001). 'A fist is stronger than five fingers': Caste and dominance in rural north India. *Transactions of the Institute of British Geographers*, 26(2), pp. 217–236.
Jodhka, S. S. (2018). *Caste in contemporary India*. New Delhi: Routledge India.
Kumar, M. A. (2015). Dalits preaching to Dalits: Lutheran modes of combating caste marginality in Andhra, South India. *Indian Anthropologist*, 45(1), pp. 61–73.
Omvedt, G. (2010). *Dalit visions*. Hyderabad: Orient Blackswan.
Prasad, M. M. (2009). Fan bhakti and subaltern sovereignty: Enthusiasm as a political factor. *Economic and Political Weekly*, 44(29), pp. 68–76. Retrieved from: www.jstor.org/stable/40279290.
Rao, K. S. (2014a). *Andhra Pradesh – prajā tīrpu* (people's mandate). Hyderabad: Prajasakti Book House.
Rao, K. S. (2014b). *Telangana – prajā tīrpu* (people's mandate). Hyderabad: Prajasakti Book House.
Rao, V. N. and Roghair, G. H. (1990). *Śiva's warriors: The Basava Purāṇa of Pālkuriki Somanātha*. Princeton, NJ: Princeton University Press.
Reddy, U. S. (2018). Reddys lead flock with 40 MLAs, next in line are BCs. *The Times of India*. December 13. Retrieved from: https://timesofindia.indiatimes.com/city/hyderabad/reddys-lead-flock-with-40-mlas-next-in-line-are-bcs/articleshow/67071245.cms.
Reddy, U. S. (2019). Two-third of AP MLAs belong to 3 upper castes. *The Times of India*. May 30. Retrieved from: https://timesofindia.indiatimes.com/city/hyderabad/two-third-of-ap-mlas-belong-to-3-upper-castes/articleshow/69572059.cms.
Robinson, M. (1988). *Local politics: The law of the fishes: Development through political chance in Medak district*, Andhra Pradesh (South India). New Delhi: Oxford University Press.
Robinson, R. and Kujur, J. A. (2010). *Margins of faith: Dalit and Tribal Christianity in India*. New Delhi: Sage.
Rudolph, L. I. and Rudolph, H. R. (1999). *The modernity of tradition: Political development in India*. Hyderabad: Orient Longman.
Shah, G. (1975). *Caste associations and political process in Gujarat: A study of Gujarat Kshatriya Sabha*. Bombay: Popular Prakashan.
Srinivas, M. N. (1959). The dominant caste in Rampura. *American Anthropologist*, 61(1), pp. 1–16.
Srinivas, M. N. (1960). *India's villages*. Bombay: Asia Publishing House.
Srinivas, S. V. (2009). Megastar: *Chiranjeevi and Telugu cinema after N. T. Rama Rao*. New Delhi: Oxford University Press.

Srinivas, S. V. (2021). Fan. *BioScope: South Asian Screen Studies*, 12(1–2), pp. 83–86. DOI:10.1177/09749276211026075.

Srinivasulu, K. (2002). *Caste, class and social articulation in Andhra Pradesh: Mapping differential regional trajectories*. Working paper: 179. London: ODI. Retrieved from: www.odi.org/sites/odi.org.uk/files/odi-assets/publications-opinion-files/2692.pdf.

Suri, K. C. (2002). *Democratic process and electoral politics in Andhra Pradesh, India*. Working paper: 180. London: Overseas Development Institute. Retrieved from: http://citeseerx.ist.psu.edu/viewdoc/download?doi=10.1.1.112.7227&rep=rep1&type=pdf.

Swamy, K. K. (2019). *A handbook on backward classes, scheduled castes, scheduled tribes & economically weaker sections* (Central, states of Telangana and Andhra Pradesh). Hyderabad: TEBCEWA.

Thirumali, I. (1992). Dora and Gadi: Manifestation of landlord domination in Telengana. *Economic and Political Weekly*, 27(9), pp. 477–482.

Vaishnav, M. (2015). *Understanding the Indian voter*. Washington, DC: Carnegie Endowment for International Peace. Retrieved from: www.jstor.org/stable/resrep12869.

Vaishnav, M. (2017). *When money pays: Money and muscle in Indian politics*. London: Yale University Press.

Webster, J. C. B. (2012). *Historiography of Christianity in India*. New Delhi: Oxford University Press.

3

AT THE BOTTOM OF THE LADDER

The stringer in the journalistic field

To put it concretely, the only field of service in which there is no discrimination against the Untouchables is scavenging. There is no need for discrimination in this field because the whole of it is made over to the Untouchables and there is no competition from the Hindus. Even here discrimination steps in the matter of higher posts. All unclean work is done by the Untouchables. But all supervisory posts which carry higher salary and which do not involve contact with filth are all filled by Hindus.

– Ambedkar, 1935/2014, pp. 108–109

Introduction

I reached Gannavaram before 9 A.M., earlier than usual to avoid travel in the heat. Both the 'shutter shops,' which served as workplaces for stringers to file stories, were shut. These shops were located on either side of the highway. The one located adjacent to Krishna Zilla Parishad Library was referred to as KP (stringer) point. Earlier, it used to be a public call office or public telephone centre with subscriber trunk dialling (STD) and international subscriber dialling (ISD) facilities. The other one located near the Gannavaram Mandal Revenue Office (MRO) used to be a photocopy centre before ARP (*Eenadu* stringer) converted it into his office on a rental basis. I went to the *grāmastula* viśrānta *gruham* (rest house for villagers) to read the newspapers. Usually, elderly people, who did not need to go for daily labour or any job, gather at this place and pass time reading the newspapers, watching television (when there's electricity), and having discussions on various issues.

This facility is provided to the villagers by a former Mandal Parishad Territorial Constituency (MPTC) member who 'retired' from active politics after the death of former Chief

DOI: 10.4324/b23313-3

Minister Y.S. Rajasekhara Reddy. DD (stringer) entered the building after seeing my bike parked outside. We headed out for a cup of tea near the MRO building. He was complaining about a bus driver who did not deliver his news items the previous day. 'Those were "important" items and our newspaper did not carry them,' he said. As he was talking about the importance of the items to get advertisements, especially with May Day (International Workers' Day celebrated on May 1) fast approaching, YSS (stringer) parked his vehicle and joined us for tea. Sipping his tea, he said, 'There's a small *panchāyati*[1] today at MRO office. Let's go there.' As we reached the premises of MRO office, there was a gathering of local residents (men and women). One middle-aged person greeted DD and YSS before walking towards them briskly with some papers in hand. He handed out a handwritten copy each to the stringers and asked if the content was 'okay.' He gave me a copy too. It was a written complaint they wanted to submit to the MRO against the construction of a cell phone tower in Sri Ram Nagar, a residential locality in Gannavaram, by a private mobile network, on top of a residential building in their colony owned by a Dalit.

The complaint, addressed to the MRO, read: 'We are not against the interests of the owner of the building. But we are against the construction and the contractor. The Sri Ram Nagar Welfare Association members are concerned about the health and environmental hazards that could result due to the location of the construction.' It was also mentioned in the complaint that the welfare association meeting was headed by a Dalit, who proposed the idea to stall the construction and a Muslim seconded it before arriving at a 'group conscience.' As the stringers were going through the copy of the complaint, another elderly person clad in a pristine white full-sleeved *khadi* shirt and white trousers approached them and asked, '*Māvāḍu inkā rālēdā*? (Hasn't *our man* reached yet?)' DD replied that the person in question must be on his way. The gathering was organised by this elderly person, who belongs to the Kamma caste, while the complaint was written as if the idea was proposed by a Dalit.

Upon asking, YSS told me that the *māvāḍu* ('our' man) in this context is ARP, the *Eenadu* stringer. Soon, CVR and SSS reached the office together on a bike, followed by ARP. The *Eenadu* stringer's entry at the location was noticed by everyone. A couple of locals along with the elderly person had a quick talk with him before the gathering met the MRO and submitted the complaint. Immediately after that, they went and submitted another copy to the sub-inspector of police. The elderly person posed for the camera, meeting the officials

> on both occasions. Women, who were present in one corner, the Dalit, who headed the meeting, and the Muslim, who seconded the decision, were not so prominent in the photographs published the following day.
>
> (Field notes, 26–27 April 2012)

The chances of such an incident being reported in any English-language newspaper are low. But Telugu dailies carried a report the following day.[2] The people who submitted the complaint to officials met with stringers after the news was carried in the zone pages and local tabloid district editions.

In this particular context, the interplay of hierarchy based on caste identity, building familiarity with stringers and 'appropriating' newspapers by the local gentry was striking. It was evident in the entire sequence: the positioning of a Dalit person in the front; projecting a Muslim by the local elite while lodging a formal complaint against the interests of another minority, a Dalit person; taking the lead on the ground and posing for the camera during the 'photo op', side-lining women and the minorities; referring to one particular newspaper stringer as *māvāḍu*.

These observations left me with more questions than answers about the social backgrounds of stringers and their relationships with other agents in the field, from local publics to officials. Certain patterns related to complex hierarchies and the agency of various newsworkers along with their relationships with the social, political and bureaucratic agents were becoming clear.

Coming back to the choice made of *māvāḍu* – by a person belonging to an influential caste (Kamma), while referring to a person from a different caste, usually, in Telugu *māvāḍu/manavāḍu* (our *man*), *manavāḷḷu/manōḷḷu* (our *men*) are used to refer to person(s) belonging to the same community based on caste, religion, regional, national and linguistic identities, depending on the situation. In this context, these commonalities did not hold any relevance. More importantly, at the time of this incident, ARP, who belongs to an OBC community, was working with the *Eenadu* and was sacked by the newspaper management on the basis of a complaint about his 'misconduct' reported by some locals to the bureau in-charge and editorial head. PCB, who belongs to the Madiga caste (a particularly marginalised Dalit/Scheduled Caste), replaced ARP. Soon after the replacement, the local gentry, who belong to Kamma caste, referred to PCB as *māvāḍu* on different occasions (Field notes, 4 May, 8 May and 22 May 2012). In the case of ANR, who worked for a medium-scale newspaper, belonging to the Kamma caste, the reference – *māvāḍu* – appeared to be self-explanatory.

The most likely commonality in question, which emerged logically, was that the owner of *Eenadu* newspaper, Cherukuri Ramoji Rao, is a Kamma. Even as the newspaper had a readership base cutting across sections and castes in Andhra Pradesh and Telangana, it is claimed by the Kammas with a sense of pride. The anticipation of the arrival of the *Eenadu* stringer by the locals need not be restricted to caste-based identity alone, as it was the most widely circulated Telugu newspaper not only in Andhra Pradesh but also in Telangana.

To understand the processes of local news production, one needs to know the social background of agents in the journalistic field, such as stringers, staffers, rural in-charges, bureau in-charges and editorial members. In this chapter, I present demographic profiles of stringers, staffers and editorial members, followed by a discussion on the processes of recruitment in the journalistic field. The demographic factors considered are: sex, education, age and experience, land owned, sources of income, religion, region and caste.

Social constitution of agents in the journalistic field

Before explaining the processes of recruitment, it may be useful to examine the basic demographic details of the agents (stringers, reporting and editorial staffers) like education, age, marital status and sources of income other than journalism.

Most professionals, such as engineers, doctors, lawyers and teachers, are required to have a corresponding professional education and/or certification. Even occupations such as police, army, civil services and bureaucracy require a certain degree or level of education, a prerequisite for the majority of government and private employment opportunities. Journalism from its inception never had any such requirement or mandatory eligibility for entry as a profession. The first Prime Minister of India, Jawaharlal Nehru (1954, p. 466), famously remarked, 'To some extent, politicians and newspapermen or journalists have much in common. Both presume to talk too much, to write too much, to deliver homilies; both, generally speaking, require no qualifications at all for their job'.

Most manuals and textbooks written by journalists (Bhaskar, 1981; Reddy, 2016; Rao, 2017) cite the names of veteran journalists to drive home the fact that there was no need for any specialised education to enter journalism. On similar lines, the prescribed literature/syllabus for training and educating journalists framed by the Press Academy of Andhra Pradesh does not mention educational qualifications required for any role in the field of journalism. However, educational qualification did play a crucial role in determining an agent's position in the journalistic field, as it helps gain what Bourdieu terms cultural capital. Out of the 42 respondents (including two English print reporters) in my study, 27 were stringers and 15 were editorial and reporting staffers. A total of 28 respondents had graduate and above-graduate-level education and 14 were not graduates.

Fewer than 50 per cent (13) of stringers had college education and there was a lone rural in-charge in Krishna district whose education was not even matriculation. Among the 13 stringers with only school education, 8 had studied till intermediate (10+2) and 5 only studied till tenth standard (see Table 3.1). It is the lack of formal education at the graduate level that hampered the career prospects of agents from marginal social backgrounds and they tended to enter the field as stringers. Most newspapers have their own in-house journalism schools and regularly roll out admission notifications for aspirants, who must be graduates below 30 years of age.[3]

These schools conduct entrance examinations for diploma courses with a duration ranging from 6 to 12 months. Often the minimum education standard prescribed in the admission notifications for these programmes proves to be barriers of entry for stringers. Notably, since these are private J-schools, the rule of reservations for persons belonging to SC, ST and OBC categories in education is not followed.

Most editorial and reporting staffers were at least graduates, except one, mentioned earlier, who was a rural in-charge. Two stringers, one each from Gannavaram and Sangareddy, were postgraduates (both M.Com.). A bureau in-charge from Krishna district, who did an M.A. in Entomology, enrolled for a Ph.D. in Lepidopterology (specialisation) but discontinued the programme to become a journalist in Telugu print media.[4] On the whole, only two respondents had Journalism education (a diploma course in Mass Communication and Journalism); one was working as the bureau in-charge of *Visalaandhra* and the other was the district edition in-charge of *Eenadu*. Both of them were working in Krishna district at the time of my fieldwork.

In the case of Telugu journalism, any person with language proficiency and journalism education would be offered a full-time position in small-scale and medium-scale newspapers. Such candidates were regarded as potential employees even in large-scale newspapers, as they may have to fulfil some additional criteria singular to each newspaper. During my interactions, the editorial staff said that they would not have the burden of having to train them, so they looked forward to recruiting such candidates. Even in the field, stringers with vast experience were humbled in the presence of young staffers who had a journalism degree.[5]

Table 3.1 Responses of stringers, reporters and editorial staffers regarding their education

Respondents' designation: Place	*Educational qualification*	
	Not a graduate	*Graduate*
Stringers: Gannavaram	10	8
Editorial and reporting staff: Krishna District	1	6
Stringers: Sangareddy	3	6
Editorial and reporting staff: Medak District	0	8
Total no. of respondents	14	28

Source: Fieldwork

For stringers, who usually did not have any formal exposure to journalism education, the Press Academy of AP and Media Academy of Telangana conducted workshops on a regular basis. As part of these workshops, stringers and reporters would be exposed to topics such as: press laws, ethics of journalism, code of conduct prescribed by the Press Council of India, personality development classes and the latest trends in the field around the globe.

Most stringers did not show interest in the workshops and instead relied on their higher-ups in the organisations or senior members in their peer group. Many stringers, reporters and editorial staffers who responded positively to these workshops were seniors in the profession and attended as local instructors or facilitators to those experts or professionals coming from Hyderabad or elsewhere. Most stringers felt that such workshops ate into their time and preferred not to attend (see Table 3.2). The average age of stringers, at the time of writing, was 44 years and 6 months, while the average age of editorial and reporting staffers was about 49 years. The age range among stringers was 33–56 and among editorial and reporting staff, it was 37–59.

Experience was another major criterion one needed to take into account in order to understand journalistic practice in the field. Statistically, it is difficult, at this point, to establish a direct relationship between age and experience with the influence a stringer had in the field. But, logically, the more experienced a stringer was, the more influential or prominent he was in the field. The average experience of stringers at the time of research in Gannavaram was about 10 years and for their counterparts in Sangareddy it was close to 13 years. On the whole, the average experience of stringers in both places, taken together, was about 11 and a half years. The range of experience of stringers among respondents was 1–26 years.

In the case of staffers, the average experience in Krishna district from the collected sample was about 18 years and in Medak district, it was about 19 years. The average experience of staffers on the whole was very close

Table 3.2 Responses from stringers and staffers about workshops conducted by the PAAP

Respondents' designation: Place	*Workshops attended*	
	Yes	*No*
Stringers: Gannavaram	3	15
Editorial and reporting staff: Krishna District	5	2
Stringers: Sangareddy	4	5
Editorial and reporting staff: Medak District	3	5
Total no. of respondents	15	27

Source: Fieldwork

to 19 years, at the time of data collection. The range of experience in both places for staffers was 9–29 years. It was very evident that a majority of staffers had relatively longer work experience than stringers in both places. The position as staffers, in both reporting and editorial departments, coupled with the work experience at the headquarters or organisation directly, gave them an upper hand over stringers in everyday newswork.

The data was tabulated after collecting details about their previous work experience (see Table 3.3). More intricate details were also collected about previous experience, presented in descriptions across this book. At the time of research, except for a couple of stringers (one each from Gannavaram and Sangareddy), all the stringers were married. Out of the total respondents in both areas, 37 had at least a two-wheeler (scooter/motorcycle) and 5 did not have any vehicle. One stringer in Gannavaram had two seven-seater autorickshaws, which he rented on a daily basis or sometimes drove himself. If stringers in the *mandal* needed to go collectively in case of any emergency, they hired or used his autos.[6] However, he did not have a two-wheeler.

Ownership of land was another crucial indicator of the efficiency and influence of a stringer or reporter in his area. Stringers would at least strive to secure a plot of land with an area of 60–80 square yards in the *mandal* in which they worked. The land-accredited *mandal*-level stringers were usually allocated as part of the government rural housing scheme for homeless persons below poverty line (BPL).

In Table 3.4, the land-owning patterns were tabulated for stringers who secured a plot through such government schemes and not pre-owned or ancestral property. This was the consideration for editorial and reporting staffers as well. However, they were allocated land through the journalists' housing scheme after taking membership in the Working Journalists' Housing Society.[7] Another important factor to ascertain the financial status of stringers was the source of income other than the job or profession of journalism. This was a descriptive category and will be dealt with at length in the following chapters while presenting the nature and repertoire of the work of stringers in the journalistic field.

Table 3.3 Responses from stringers and staffers about their previous work experience

Respondents' designation: Place	*Previous work experience*	
	Yes	*No*
Stringers: Gannavaram	12	6
Editorial and reporting staff: Krishna District	7	0
Stringers: Sangareddy	8	1
Editorial and reporting staff: Medak District	7	1
Total no. of respondents	34	8

Source: Fieldwork

Table 3.4 Responses from stringers and staffers on land ownership under journalists' housing scheme

Respondents' designation: Place	*Land owning*	
	Yes	*No*
Stringers: Gannavaram	14	4
Editorial and reporting staff: Krishna District	6	1
Stringers: Sangareddy	8	1
Editorial and reporting staff: Medak District	7	1
Total no. of respondents	35	7

Even as most stringers were responsible for collecting advertisements and generating circulation, the ones specifically mentioned in the category of advertising and publishing in this table are those with a specialised network or business concerned with collecting advertisements and running a publication. Most of these sources of income complemented their newswork and vice-versa in both Gannavaram and Sangareddy. The respondents who stated that there were no other sources of income were either from large circulation newspapers such as *Eenadu* and *Sakshi* or persons working in the local offices of political parties or informally as media publicists for local businessmen and contractors.

The most important factor in understanding the social backgrounds of agents in the field was caste. As mentioned in the previous chapter, almost all stringers were very open while talking about their own caste in relation to other agents.

However, many staffers (mostly those who did not fall under the reserved categories, General category) did not want to mention their caste and limited their response to identifying themselves as belonging to communities that did not enjoy the constitutional privilege of reservations in jobs or education given to lower caste communities.[8]

While responding to this particular query, staffers, especially those working as bureau in-charges and editors avoided the usage of the term *kulamu* (caste in Telugu) and referred to it as *sāmājika vargam* (social class). However, stringers referred to it as *kulamu* or caste without any inhibition. This phenomenon of senior journalists in a state of denial about 'caste' and specifically editorial persons who avoided – the word and the issue – by replacing it with *sāmajika vargam* reflect the dynamics in which agents operated in the hierarchical structure of the field.

Persons from influential castes considered *kulamu* a crude and rustic word and used the sugar-coated Telugu phrase *sāmājika vargam* instead. On the whole, *kulamu* or *jāti* was used to describe Dalits and OBC communities, to an extent. *Kulamu* became *sāmājika vargam*, while describing persons from influential castes by editors and bureau in-charges. Table 3.5 presents the

Table 3.5 Reservation category under which stringers and staffers belonged

Respondents' designation: Place	*Category*				
	General	*SC*	*ST*	*BC*	*Religious minority (OBC)*
Stringers: Gannavaram	3	5	0	8	2
Editorial and reporting staff: Krishna District	6	0	0	1	0
Stringers: Sangareddy	3	3	0	2	1
Editorial and reporting staff: Medak District	6	1	0	1	0
Total no. of respondents	18	9	0	12	3

Source: Fieldwork

Table 3.6 Religion of stringers and staffers

Respondents' designation: Place	*Religion*		
	Hindu	*Muslim*	*Christian*
Stringers: Gannavaram	16	1	1
Editorial and reporting staff: Krishna District	7	0	0
Stringers: Sangareddy	8	1	0
Editorial and reporting staff: Medak District	8	0	0
Total no. of respondents	**39**	**2**	**1**

Source: Fieldwork

data of the specific categories to which the agents belonged. Three respondents belonging to religious minorities – Christians (one) and Muslims (two) – availed reservation in the OBC category. Even as the respondents indicated that they belonged to the General category, it should be noted that it meant forward castes. However, there were no journalists from Scheduled Tribe (Adivasi) communities at any level at the time of fieldwork.

The demographic data collected from stringers suggested that a majority of them belonged to Other Backward Classes (13) and Scheduled Castes (8). Only six members from the General category were working as stringers. On the other hand, the presence of General category or forward caste members (12) working as staffers was very high in both districts. Only two members from BC (one each in Krishna and Medak) and a lone SC person were working as full-time or regular staffers in the places of research, of the 15 staffers interviewed at the time. Similarly, a majority of the agents were Hindus (39 out of 42) with a relatively insignificant presence of persons from religious minorities in the field (see Table 3.6).

These primary data sets, collected at the time of fieldwork, not only presented the social background of the agents in the journalistic field but also helped in understanding the recruitment process.

Recruitment and/in the journalistic field

A typical job notification for the recruitment of stringers for Telugu newspapers advertised in the local editions read as:

> Wanted contributors for _____ Newspaper (Logo)
> Brief description about the newspaper (two lines)
> Job description: Candidates need to have: interest in news reporting and Telugu language proficiency.
> Vacancies in the following centres:
> Candidates may contact over the phone or visit our office:
> Mobile number(s) and Address:

Most small- and medium-scale newspapers displayed the same template whenever there were vacancies. Notifications to fill up vacant stringer/part-time contributor positions in large circulation newspapers, apart from the usual 'interest in news reporting' and 'proficiency in Telugu', featured additional details such as eligibility conditions. There was no mention of a written test or interview. Mandatory eligibility requirements mentioned in notifications were (a) minimum education qualification: Degree; (b) knowledge of Telugu typesetting; and (c) must be residents in the advertised area or locality. Preference: Candidates with experience will be given preference and those who applied for the same positions earlier need not apply. Caveats: Candidates must bring their bio-data, certificates and proof of residence (driving licence or power or telephone bill) to appear for the written test at a specified time and location.

Upon coming across one such notification for the position of stringer/part-time contributor in one of the leading Telugu newspapers, I decided to appear for the written test to get a first-hand understanding of the recruitment process. The following is an excerpt from the field notes on the day of the written examination scheduled at 10 AM on a Sunday morning:

> I reached the newspaper office building located at Arundelpet in Guntur city, Andhra Pradesh at 9:30 pm. The newspaper office shared office space with a chit fund[9] company that belonged to the same business group. I 'dressed up' for the occasion wearing drab formal trousers, a plain off-white half-sleeve shirt, and leather sandals. I avoided my usual clothing to look like one of the 'aspirants'. By the time I reached the office, there was already a queue of candidates getting their certificates verified and filling forms before appearing

for the exam. I filled the job application form (in English) that asked for details: a) Full name, including surname; b) Educational qualification; c) Address; d) Area in the city that I wish to work for (within the specified vacant ones). Only after submitting the form did, I realise that everyone else had filled in the application in Telugu. The person who was overseeing this form filling procedure smiled at me after going through the details and said (in Telugu): 'You are supposed to write the exam in Telugu. I hope you know that.'

There were around 20 candidates at the venue. We were sent into the adjoining chit fund office, which had a larger room, comprising a cubicle workspace that could accommodate more than a score of employees. A middle-aged newspaper staffer was in charge of the examination and ordered us to either switch off our mobile phones or put them in silent mode. The candidates obeyed the instructions from him with military discipline. Once everyone was seated, there were no vocal sounds in the hall and the only noise one could hear was the muted vehicular traffic of a Sunday morning through the windows. We were handed question papers and specifically told not to write anything on them. The answer papers provided to write the examination were used newsprint (one-sided). The exam was for 25 marks and the duration given was one hour. There was a compulsory 10-mark question asking the problems faced by public in Guntur city and a five-mark question to which the candidate had to state his reasons for wanting to get into journalism. For the remaining 10 marks, there were objective questions such as: present cabinet ministers in the state government from Guntur, number of wards in the corporation, the who's who of the municipal corporation and district. There were a couple of questions about specific pages/sections of the newspaper to judge the reading habits of the candidate. I had a tough time giving my answers in handwritten Telugu. Moreover, I had no clue about the who's who of the Parliament, Assembly constituencies and Municipal Corporation despite being a native of Guntur, as I had left the place and have been residing in Hyderabad for more than a decade. I handed over the answer sheet and started interacting with my fellow examinees. They enquired about my details and reasons for applying to this job. I had to tell them that I worked as a reporter in Hyderabad (without giving more details) and was trying to look for opportunities in Guntur. Most of the candidates I interacted had prior experience of working as stringers in other newspapers. The reasons they stated for applying for this job was the brand value of the newspaper and the remuneration it offered. One aspirant said that he could not appear for this examination on earlier occasions as he did not have

> a graduation degree on hand. The examiners announced that the selected candidates would be intimated about the result over phone.
> (Field notes, Guntur, 15 April 2012)

> I waited for two days and did not get any call from the newspaper office. However, the following day, I showed up at the office in the morning and was told to visit them in the evening, as there were no staffers concerned. I headed to Krishna district and returned early to meet the newspaper staffers the same evening. The middle-aged staffer was present in his open-door cabin sorting out a pile of news reports on his antique-looking table. He recognised and greeted me instantaneously. After introductions, upon asking about my performance in the written test, he (SR) replied, 'The selection process for recruitment was over. You were over-qualified for this job.' He said that they knew about my background and casually asked me about the purpose of appearing for the exam and I had to reveal a part of my topic of research. SR, who was the edition in-charge of the newspaper's district edition, had some encouraging words for my research and said that he did not come across any such study in Telugu journalism. The edition in-charge revealed that the newspaper did a thorough background check of candidates before recruiting persons at any level in the newspaper. Before getting back to his work, in a very confident tone without looking into my eyes, he said, 'We would not be in this top position without taking such mandatory precautions while recruiting since the paper's establishment'.
> (Field notes, Guntur, 18 April 2012)

I did not realise the significance of two issues in the recruitment process of stringers: (a) the differences in the specifications of eligibility criteria for recruitment in the job notifications of small and medium-scale newspapers and the large-scale ones; (b) the mandatory background check procedure followed in the recruitment process in large-scale newspapers.

Recruitment patterns of stringers

In the year 1991, as India embraced neoliberal reforms initiated by the then Prime Minister P.V. Narasimha Rao-led Congress minority government, a significant development happened in Telugu journalism. The eight-decade-old *Andhra Patrika*, a newspaper established on Gandhian principles and a nationalist zeal, went out of press months before the Indian economy and administration did away with the permit-raj or licence-raj.

It was in the exact same year *Eenadu* established its journalism school.[10] That the advent of *Eenadu* newspaper served as a starting point for innovations in Telugu journalism was a notion everyone believes in and speaks about; on the contrary, it could be seen as the culmination of age-old traditions in the Telugu journalism field, for good or bad, when it came to the editorial policy, production and distribution of news and training and, more importantly for this research, recruitment of journalists and stringers.

Despite struggling to keep up with the pace at which *Eenadu* was functioning, it was in the 1990s that many newspapers had to go for colour pages and recruit stringers at the *mandal* (sub-district)-level. A majority of staffers and editors that I interviewed during my fieldwork were recruited in this period, along with some stringers in Gannavaram and Sangareddy, who remained in the same position at the time of my interviews with them.

The procedure for recruitment of stringers, on the face of it, appeared to be a simple case of 'hire and fire' policy put into use by the management of newspapers based on the performance of stringers in boosting circulation, increasing advertisement revenue and providing content. While these were definitely some of the considerations, there are many layers to the process of recruitment, especially with regard to the agents up in the order of hierarchy, along with the standing of a particular newspaper in the journalistic field. The data collected did not reveal any particular typology in the recruitment process of stringers as it did in the case of staffers. However, a close analysis revealed some interesting patterns.

At the time of research, I found that a majority of the newspapers with large and medium circulation figures followed a recommendation by the First Press Commission by placing an advertisement in newspapers (GoI, 1954, p. 194). However, it was a word-of-mouth-based announcement and recruitment in the case of small newspapers. There are variations in the notifications for recruitment of stringers based on the circulation of newspapers. This was evident in the content of the notifications published in newspapers that look for employees on a regular basis.

The data on the procedure for recruitment of stringers, reflecting their mode of recruitment for the first time when they sought employment, is tabulated in Table 3.7. The directly appointed candidates (5) became stringers either through personal contacts or through political party connections. While MMB and SSS of Gannavaram worked as 'apprentice stringers' (assistants to stringers) before becoming full-fledged stringers, another stringer, NS, from the same *mandal*, got into the field through recommendation by a local Communist trade union leader, who was his relative.[11]

Most experienced stringers did not need to write any exam to shift from one newspaper to the other. *Eenadu* and *Sakshi*, which were very particular about their recruitment procedures, subjected stringers to a written test. Gannavarm stringers, MMB and SSS, had small-time photography and videography studios in the *mandal* and used to accompany stringers of established newspapers such as *Eenadu* and *Vaartha* to take photographs whenever needed. After honing their writing skills and gaining experience,

Table 3.7 Mode of recruitment for stringers

Respondents' designation: Place	*Mode of Recruitment*		
	Written test and interview	*Interview only*	*Direct appointment*
Stringers: Gannavaram	9	6	3
Stringers: Sangareddy	4	3	2
Total respondents: 27	13	9	5

they joined as 'full-time' (in SSS' words) stringers in newspapers. In Sangareddy, while MPR of *Nava Telangana* (formerly *Prajasakti*) joined as a stringer through left-party connections, MKG of *Andhra Bhoomi* joined as a stringer without any test, as the management had an immediate requirement in the *mandal*.

The version offered by stringers who joined left-leaning newspapers was validated by the bureau in-charges who work in similar newspapers. *Prajasakti* staffer, VS, working in Vijayawada said:

> As and when the need arose, we recruited stringers in *mandals*. The procedure involved advertising the position in our newspaper. We scrutinise the profiles of interested candidates and inform our local party cadre or existing stringers in surrounding areas to know more about the candidate, if required. Once we get an approval, we select the candidates and put them on probation before finalising the recruitment process.
>
> (Personal communication, 23 September 2012)[12]

On the other hand, the candidates who said that they appeared for the written test and interview, in both *mandals*, had cut their teeth on 'big newspapers at the time of their joining'. They informed that they, subsequently, were never required to appear for such tests while migrating to other newspapers.

When asked about the changes in recruitment process in the field, 'veteran' stringer (*pramukha grāmīṇa vilēkhari*) or eminent rural reporter, as he was jovially referred to by his peers), DD, said that apart from big newspapers (*pedda patrikalu*), nobody followed any patterns in recruiting from the time he joined as a stringer (in 1988). 'If they (staffers and management) felt the need that the existing stringer should be changed, he will be replaced with a new one. Sometimes, they would not inform the stringer after firing him', DD revealed and reminded them that this was not a government position to give any warning or show cause notice (Personal communication, 8 May 2012, Gannavaram).

Bureau in-charge of *Andhra Prabha* at Sangareddy, VRK, echoed this about the recruitment of stringers. Stressing that the educational qualification of aspirants to become stringers did not matter anymore, he said:

> It (recruitment) was a major problem for us. In the past, even to recruit stringers, we scrutinised the educational qualifications, command over language, a deeper understanding of the society in general and the district and state in particular. The behaviour of the candidate was assessed in the interview. This is a thing of the past now. Also, recruitment (of stringers) used to happen at Hyderabad. Now we started recruiting stringers at the zone and *mandal* levels. This is the case with most newspapers. Nobody bothers to take educational qualifications into consideration while recruiting a stringer. About 60–70 per cent of stringers do not have any educational qualifications.
>
> (VRK, Personal communication, 10 October 2014, Sangareddy)

He did not mention the salaries of stringers, even when asked, but maintained that stringers got commensurate salary (*taginanta jītam vastundi*) in his newspaper. Notably, only newspapers that paid a definite amount to stringers had strict norms of recruitment.

After addressing the issues of minimum wage requirement for working journalists in their report, the members of the Press Commission (GoI, 1954, p. 196) suggested:

> It will obviously be impossible to prescribe standards of qualifications for different branches of the profession. But, as we are suggesting elsewhere, a provision being made for a minimum wage, it is obvious that in order to be entitled to that minimum wage, the entrants to journalism should have some minimum qualifications also.

Over a period of time, a majority of newspaper owners seemed to have succeeded in exactly reversing the suggestion. Since the management was not willing to pay minimum wages to stringers, they started going easy on educational qualifications, along with the other suggestions by the Commission. Some considerations suggested by the Commission members (GoI, 1954, p. 196) included 'psychological equipment of the candidate, his general aptitude for practising the profession of journalism, his flair for writing and nose for news'.

Many bureau in-charges told me that they checked if the candidate had the ability to write something about the issues and happenings in his own locality. 'What educational qualifications?' MMR counter-questioned with a frown, when asked about the criteria for recruiting stringers. Saying that this job (stringer) was not a civil service position, he said:

> Anyone who can write was allowed to work as a stringer for newspapers, if there was a requirement in a particular *mandal*. Newspaper organisations think like this: If there is a stringer in that particular area, our paper will reach all the nearby villages. The written test and interview they conduct are farcical affairs. Some stringers do not even know how to write. They (stringers) call their staffer over the phone and give strings of information about an issue. Sometimes, they grudgingly passed on that information, that too only when asked. It is the headache of the staffer to collect relevant and additional information and present it as a news story in the newspaper.
>
> (Personal communication, 9 October 2014)[13]

Many bureau in-charges and editorial staff felt that their role in the recruitment of stringers was getting minimised by the day and that the management, advertising and circulation heads had more 'say' in the process. DD, active in the working journalists' union as joint secretary of APUWJ-Krishna Rural unit, pointed out that these departments forced stringers to deliver newspapers, collect advertisements and assigned them many more non-journalistic tasks. 'If they (management) wanted stringers to do these kinds of work and that too with irregular salaries, how could they be particular about the qualifications of candidates at the time of recruitment?' he asked. He added that the owners of small and medium newspapers only assess if the stringer can meet their 'revenue targets', while recruiting (personal communication, 8 May 2012, Gannavaram).

On the whole, there was a clear disparity in the recruitment process and the responsibilities assigned to stringers between the big newspapers and the small and medium newspapers. In both states, apart from the 'Big-3' newspapers in each state, most newspapers did not pay, or paid very meagre amounts, to stringers and in an irregular manner. 'Anyone can enter this field now. There was no *hisab-kitab* (Urdu term for account ledger) in recruitment and payment in *cinna patrikalu* (small newspapers)', YPR concluded the interview saying.

Unlike small and medium newspapers, big newspapers paid great attention to the background of the stringer before recruiting him. Some stringers mentioned that both *Eenadu* and *Sakshi* were very particular about background checks and, especially, likened *Eenadu*'s background verification process to that of passport verification done by the police.

Elaborating on the recruitment policy of *Eenadu*, Krishna district editorial in-charge, GB said:

> If the performance in the written test and interview was satisfactory, we conduct a background check before recruiting. We do not recruit anyone with criminal cases, chit fund organisers, private money lenders, alcoholics, and gamblers (*pēkāṭa rāyuḷḷu*). Private school teachers, advocates, and literate farmers were given preference. Minimum education qualification was graduation. We do not compromise on this aspect.
>
> (Personal communication, 12 September 2012)[14]

These considerations appeared obvious if one tracks the history of the newspaper. Ramoji Rao established *Eenadu* after tasting success in the chit fund business (Margadarsi) and Priya pickles (agriproducts). Unlike English newspapers, greater preference was given to agriculture and agri-business-related issues in the newspaper and it achieved great success in creating space for advertisements for those areas (EQC, 1999, pp. 66–67).

Marketing representatives of The Margadarsi Marketing Private Limited (MMPL) were crucial in boosting the circulation of the paper (EQC, 1999, p. 137). The newspaper carved out a niche readership among farmers, small-scale agri-business persons at the zone level and had special columns written by experts on farming issues (EQC, pp. 66–67 & pp. 155–157). Many stringers who joined the newspaper after the launch of district editions were teachers.[15] *Eenadu*'s role in the anti-arrack movement in Andhra Pradesh was widely popular (EQC, 1999, p. 152).[16]

On similar lines, the Rural in-charge of *Sakshi* daily in Krishna district, NS, said that he handpicked stringers at the *mandal* level after personally cross-checking the background of selected candidates. However, stringers in both states suggested that persons belonging to the Reddy community were appointed as reporters, while the rest (non-Reddys) were offered positions as stringers.

Caste may not be the only factor for recruiting a stringer, as newspapers (regardless of their circulation size) focused on catering to immediate requirements but it seemed to have played a major role in journalists being able to climb up the professional hierarchy in newspapers.

Climbing up the professional ladder

Climbing up the professional ladder from stringer or sometimes trainee sub-editor without any salary to staffer and even higher positions was the most respected mode of getting employed as a full-timer in newspapers. In a bid to explain the gruelling journey from stringer to staffer, one experienced (19 years, at the time of research) stringer in Sangareddy, GG, likened this scaling up the professional journalism ladder to workforce in the construction field. He said:

> This field (journalism) is very similar to construction field, where *kūloḷḷu* (unskilled daily wage labourers) were picked up from the *aḍḍā* to construct a house. There will be a *beldar mēstri* (mason who handled hoe to plaster walls) and a *pedda mēstri* (head or supervising mason). The chances of a construction labourer reaching the position of *pedda mēstri* were very low. Similarly, it is very tough for a stringer to become chiefs of news bureau or senior-level editors in journalism. Most times, they became staffers and stagnated in that position.
>
> (Personal communication, 27 September 2014)

The point of the comparison was that stringers (generalists without any beat) were likened to daily wage labourers (unskilled), while the reporting staffers (a specific beat) were described as *beldar mēstri* (skilled labourer) and the editorial personnel were positioned as *pedda mēstri* (supervising mason). The news labour of stringers is often compared to manual labour at the sites of research and even in the journalists' union meetings.

At first instance, it appeared as if they are alluding to the hard labour in the construction industry, which is highly informal, as it is the case with stringers as well. But another way of reading the simile is the dominant Hindu outlook or the Brahmanical view of looking down upon manual labour as menial or lowly work, as opposed to valuing productive groups or classes. This reading is important to understand the possibilities and hindrances for stringers to climb up the professional ladder.

There were many legends and factual stories of individuals who joined as stringers and made it to the topmost positions in the field. This was the case with a majority of Telugu journalists and editors before formal Journalism education courses, along with in-house J-schools, began to function.[17] From Gannavaram *mandal*, Kommineni Srinivasa Rao who started his career as a trainee in *Eenadu* in 1978 and went on to become editorial board member in the same organisation before joining *Andhra Jyothi* in 2002, as chief editor. He played a crucial role in the setting up of a full-fledged news network of stringers for *Eenadu*. At the time of writing, he was serving as honorary editor (working) in Sakshi Television and also was active in digital journalism.

However, in this type of recruitment, caste and education (after joining the field) played a crucial role, many respondents revealed. The Bureau In-Charge of a leftist daily in Sangareddy, MMR, pointed out that those who made it big in the field after starting from scratch belonged to forward castes (personal communication, 6 October 2014). Noted Telugu journalist, M. Satish Chandar, was one of the most popular exceptions to the point MMR made. Born in a Dalit family, Chandar started his career as a stringer and went on to become chief editor of *Andhra Prabha* (2004–2006 and 2017–2017), having served in various capacities in different Telugu newspapers.[18] In Sangareddy, a literary Muslim, SAK, faced the same situation when he began looking for a job in journalism. Despite having published short stories and poems in Telugu newspapers, SAK was not offered a staffer position but had to join as a stringer to prove his mettle. He later worked as a staffer in various newspapers and quit working as a full-time reporter due to health reasons. At the time of writing, he continued to work in the field as a freelancer and ran a non-governmental organisation in Medak district.

Even as many studies suggest the lack of diversity or under-representation of persons from Dalit (SC), Other Backward Classes (OBC) and religious minority communities in Indian journalism, there was adequate representation from those communities at the *mandal* level as stringers in Telugu newspapers. In fact, persons working as stringers from SC and OBC communities in Gannavaram and Sangareddy were over-represented in terms of the constitutionally and legally sanctioned quotas of 15 and 27 per cent, respectively, for SC and OBC categories, in the government's education and employment sectors. General category candidates were relatively fewer but that is precisely because of the precarity of this employment.

It would be a gross mistake if one took these numbers of SC and OBC stringers to mean a democratisation of the journalistic field or that of the news media. There is no space to rationalise such a claim as they are *relegated* to the position of stringer, with no further growth, despite having considerable experience in the field. That would be to say that the almost-total SC composition of garbage cleaners and manual scavengers is a sign of democratisation. It is actually the opposite. Stringers complained that mediocre candidates belonging to forward castes were selected as reporters and opined that the forward caste candidates were backed by journalists already working in the field.

When asked about the reasons why he did not become a reporter despite having experience, a *Namaste Telangana* stringer in Sangareddy said that he did not have the 'network' or support system in the higher-ups of the field.[19] This was a clear response about the lack of cultural or network capital on the part of the stringer. More importantly, many stringers responded that they did not have 'proper support in the field' *fīlḍulō telisinōḷḷu lēru, saraina contacts lēvu, pedda* positions *lo manollu evarunnaru.* [We do not know any key persons in the field; do not have proper contacts; where are our people? There are no persons from our caste/community in the field] (Field notes, 8 May and 7 June 2012; 9 October 2014). They rationalised that this could be the reason for their lack of growth in the profession.

This *relegation* of persons from socially disadvantaged and marginal communities to the lowest rung appeared to be the 'doxa' of the field.[20] This was the experience even as they tried applying for full-time journalistic positions in a newly launched paper or a different media organisation due to what the Press Commission (GoI, 1954, p. 194) called 'parochial' considerations. It seemed as if the parochial considerations that the Commission stated more than half a century ago meant casteist and communal (both caste and religion) markers.

When asked why they continued to work in the field, most stringers I interviewed (experienced ones; not new entrants) said they had no alternatives. At the time of my fieldwork Sangareddy stringer MKG said:

> Without much knowledge we entered the field and got stuck here. Before we even realised, years passed by while trying to impress our bosses in the organisation and the local elite for survival. For good or bad, many like me continue this work.

He maintained the same even during my revisit to Sangareddy in January 2022. This situation or condition is what Bourdieu (2005, p. 471) talked about as 'doxa' – a realisation of the limited or restricted options available for the agents in the field with relatively lesser levels of capital (economic and cultural). This, however, does not mean that stringers have unconsciously accepted their position and are subservient to dominant agents within the field. As much as the dominant social, cultural and economic factors structure the perceptions and actions of the agents, the creative and ever-inventive strategies in the form of practices, regardless of the levels of capital, of the agents in order to endure and sustain in the field demonstrate their capacity to engage with dominant forces.

Going back to the ethnographic vignette on the construction of cell phone tower in Gannavaram presented at the beginning of this chapter, even though the influential caste persons gave importance to the *Eenadu* stringer overtly, the issue was not covered 'favourably'. Whereas, stringers from other newspapers ensured that it was given prominence and thereby, won the 'trust' of the locals on this particular occasion. Some of them even managed to secure advertisements to meet their revenue targets set for International Workers' Day by the managements and commission for themselves.

This capacity of strategising and manoeuvring to endure in the field (habitus) can be attributed neither to the social and economic conditions in which agents operate nor to their own dispositions and social backgrounds. It appears to be a category that emerges out of a dialectical relationship between the field and agents in the form of practices. It is these everyday practices that stringers engross themselves in that makes them believe in contesting and challenging the overarching forces of domination, however limited. Often, 'successful' stringers are the ones who are aware of their own position with respect to others within and outside the field and the limitations of their engagement and actions despite being *relegated* to the margins.

Sakshi stringer in Gannavaram belonging to the OBC category, YSS, said that he got disenchanted with the lack of growth and left the field for six years to join as a full-time worker in a national political party. The stringer said that he tried finishing his discontinued undergraduate degree in order to pursue law as a career option only to shelve the idea. He decided to return to the field when *Sakshi* was launched in 2008 and continued to work there.

During a conversation, in between 'assignments' for the day, YSS gave an analogy between the journalistic field and police department regarding appointments in the presence of an intelligence department inspector Ravi (name changed).

YSS: We (stringers) are not the only people suffering. The situation of constables in the department (police) was similar. I know constables who were happy when they got a government job and continued in the same position until retirement. Only lucky fellows got promoted as head constables. Take the cases of NS and DD. NS managed to get promoted as rural in-charge. But DD never got the chance. Even in the department, growth was not the same. Those who got recruited as sub-inspectors got very few chances to become superintendent of police (SP). Most of them stop at ASP (superintendent of police) level. Reporters and sub-editors who got direct appointments at the most became bureau-in-charges or district edition in-charges. That's the end of the road for them. Candidates with a Journalism degree who get appointed right after their education, like the *Eenadu* trainee reporter, who visited us the other day, are like Indian Police Service (IPS) officers.[21] In my experience, they (journalism graduates) continued to go up in the profession. That's the matter. What else did you want to research about this profession?

Me: What about those who worked as assistants to stringers?

YSS: [responding spontaneously]. Those unworthy fellows (*panikimālinōḷḷu*) were like orderlies and home guards in the department. They used to ask me how to become a stringer quickly. [He burst into laughter and looked for appreciation from Ravi and myself, as he 'fitted' the model with that of police to a T.]

Such an understanding, providing a 'sense of one's place' and 'organisation of the image of the social world' (Bourdieu, 2005, p. 471) and comprehending his own position in relation to others in the field and from other fields posed many more questions: why did stringers continue in the field, considering their position in it? How did they negotiate it on a daily basis? What were the ways in which they made it a form of sustainable livelihood? An understanding of the social and professional divisions in the field is a prerequisite before delving into these issues and concerns.

Notes

1 *Panchayati* is a term used for an issue related to the public or a public dispute. It is derived from Hindi, the root word being *pānch* (Five). 'A council (properly of five persons) assembled as a Court of Arbiters or Jury; or as a committee of the people of a village, of the members or a Caste, or what-not, to decide on questions interesting the body generally' (Yule and Burnell, 2008, p. 355).

2 Pointing out that the publication of such micro-level issues or incidents by language newspapers is a result of the localisation strategy employed by the newspaper organisation, Ninan (2007, p. 20) writes:

> In addition to more traditional notions of public space in small town and village India where both public issues and private scandal were discussed, you now had a newsprint-enabled and advertising-supported civic square where local gentry, local governance and local crime competed for attention.

She (p. 116) also suggested that the stringer 'became the local gentry's passport to figuring in the newspaper.' While the localisation strategy employed by the newspaper organisation was an undeniable reality on the ground, what captured the attention were the processes through which the strategy played out in the field.

3 *Eenadu* was the pioneer in taking up such an initiative in Andhra Pradesh and started the Eenadu School of Journalism in 1991 (Ramu, 1999, p. 126). Some schools (of large-scale newspapers) had a mandatory rule that successful candidates after completion of the course must work with the school's newspaper for 3–4 years. However, there was no such rule in case of medium and small-scale newspapers' journalism schools. Apart from these schools there were some more Hyderabad-based private J-schools, run by veteran and senior Telugu journalists, such as Rachana Journalism College, AP Journalism School among others.

4 He asked me to spell the word lepidopterology and made fun of me after I got the spelling wrong.

5 In one instance, a trainee reporter from *Eenadu* was assigned duty as contributor in Ramavarappadu (adjacent *mandal* to Gannavaram) in lieu of the regular stringer. During his visit to Gannavaram, he involuntarily commanded respect not only from *Eenadu* stringers but also from those working in other newspapers. This may be due to the fact that the trainee reporter could be their boss (higher-up) in the near future.

6 This auto proved to be handy for stringers to cover accidents on highways or when required to go to Gannavaram airport in case of a celebrity/state dignitary/politician's unexpected visit to Vijayawada.

7 This issue will be discussed in the following chapters in which it would be running theme along with the source of income of stringers other than the profession.

8 Accordingly, in order to maintain homogeneity, I tabulated the social background of the agents in terms of the category to which they belong, even as I collected specific caste information from the stringers and staffers.

9 According to the Andhra Pradesh Chit Funds Act, 1971:

> Chit means a transaction, whether called chit fund, chitty or by any other name, by which its foreman enters into an agreement with a number of subscribers that every one of them shall subscribe a certain sum of money or a certain quantity of grain or other commodity, in instalments for a definite period and that each subscriber in his turn, as determined by lot or by auction or by tender or in such other manner as may

be provided for in the agreement, shall be entitled to a prize amount, whether payable in cash, kind or any other article of value.

(GoAP, 1971)

This is a very popular mode of savings and borrowing by middle-class families in South India to purchase goods or properties.

10 A journalists' union leader GA said that the *Eenadu* group established this school anticipating the opening up of the satellite television market in the wake of neoliberal reforms. The union leader said that given his business acumen, chairman Rao would never leave anything to chance.

11 Gannavaram had strong left-oriented trade unions and political parties, which were active even at the time of research.

12 The Medak bureau in-charge of the same party's newspaper in Telangana (*Nava Telangana*), YP, shared the same process. Interestingly, while VS, of Vijayawada, did not rule out the possibility of the caste factor in recruitment, YP asserted that the caste background of the candidate did not matter at all while recruiting (13 October 2014).

13 MMR remarked, '*nāl-mukkala vārta mokhana goḍtaru*'. This literally translates as: 'They (stringers) throw bits of information on our faces'. This description was almost on the lines of what James Carey observed about how the emergence of new communication technology replaced the reporter with the stringer in the US context.

14 Gannavaram stringer, ANR, was selected in the written test and interview but was not offered a position in *Eenadu* after carrying out the mandatory background check, as he was a private money lender. Initially, he applied for a reporter's position and was rejected after they found out his business dealings. ANR tried to bargain for a stringer's job but was denied it despite having strong support from his community (Kamma) and political backing in the *mandal* (personal communication, 2 May 2012, Gannavaram).

15 See EQC (1999, p. 136) for one such case study of a school teacher turned contributor.

16 There was another take on the women-led anti-arrack movement supported by Telugu Desam Party's supremo and thespian, late N.T. Rama Rao. *Eenadu* carried a separate page – *sarai pai samaram* (War on liquor) – to educate the masses against the social evil of drinking. Jeffrey (2010, pp. 14–15), after gathering a version provided by freedom fighter and NTR admirer, Vavilala Gopalakrishnaiah, and *Eenadu*'s version, stated that such a 'campaign could not have happened without the newspaper revolution'. The point he missed, however, was the bitter media war between *Eenadu* and *Udayam*, the latter owned by a 'liquor baron' and Congress MP, Magunta Subbarami Reddy, from Ongole. A major part of the investment in *Eenadu*'s fiercest competitor *Udayam*, under the editorship of A.B.K. Prasad, came from the liquor business (Balagopal, 1992 pp. 2457–2461). Many considered that Ramoji Rao masterminded this campaign and successfully achieved results: (1) TDP's coming back to power in 1994 elections with its liquor prohibition policy; (2) *Udayam* was closed down after running into losses with no capital generated from the owner's liquor business which was shut down (see Donthi, 2014). *Eenadu* did not have any competition till *Sakshi* was launched in 2008. Earlier, *Vaartha* was seen as a potential competitor to *Eenadu* but lost out very soon due to various reasons, which are not needed here.

17 For profiles of such journalists, see Varadachari et al. (2011, pp. 27–136).

18 See http://satishchandar.com/?page_id=58. Chandar founded the AP College of Journalism churning out hundreds of journalists every year and also ran the Indian Institute of Political Leadership for the benefit of 'aspiring' politicians.

19 There seemed to be a well-oiled network in place for persons belonging to forward castes (Brahmins, to be precise) at the beginning of the twentieth century itself. During the 1920s, the founder of *Andhra Patrika*, Kasinathuni Nageswara Rao (referred as *pantulu gāru; pantulu* meant Sir in Telugu and *gāru* is a suffix used by Telugus as a mark of respect) employed students who approached him for help to pursue education in Madras, as sub-editors. Rajagopalrao (2004, pp. 72–73) noted:

> *Pantulu gāru* helped needy students who wished to study law and other courses in Chennapatnam (formerly Madras and now Chennai). He appointed them as sub-editors in *Andhra Patrika* and provided them accommodation in the office. He helped such students gain self-respect and self-sufficiency. The newspaper office was a *dharmasala* and functioned as the office of the Andhra Vidhyarthi Sangham (Andhra Students Association).
>
> [Translation mine]

The founder of the newspaper was a Brahmin and, in those days, it was a common practice for Brahmin boys or students to seek help from other Brahmin families or persons (sometimes even if they were unrelated or unknown) for education purposes. One of the famous such cases was that of freedom fighter, lawyer, journalist and first Chief Minister of Andhra State, Tanguturi Prakasam. Also known as Prakasam *pantulu,* he was one such needy Brahmin student. In his biography, he (1972, pp. 11, 22) wrote that his teacher Hanumanta Rao Naidu (a non-Brahmin) made special arrangements for his lunch in a Brahmin family during the course of his education, as Brahmins did not eat meals in non-Brahmin homes or eat 'outsiders' food. Prakasam pantulu became a celebrated barrister and even went on to establish a newspaper *Swarajya Patrika.* Other forward and agrarian castes from the Telugu linguistic community like the Reddys and the Kammas built such networks for themselves too (Upadhya, 1988, pp. 1433–1442). These were very important in understanding the nature of the field, as the who's who of the field – editorial or proprietorial – belonged to these castes and communities.

In Bourdieusian terms, these social and cultural relations provided the transfer of one form of capital to the other for dominant communities. This was not the case with the marginal and even intermediary castes and communities.

20 Wacquant (2008, 2015) and Bourdieu and Passeron (1990, pp. 141–167) deploy the concept of relegation which is based on ethno-racial and class dispositions of agents in the context of ghettos and education, respectively. While keeping the spirit of that conceptualisation intact, I use it to highlight both exclusionary and enclaving strategies based on the caste and sex backgrounds of stringers in their professional space, which often gets legitimised as 'normal' or 'taken for granted'.

21 IPS officers were recruited at Union (central) level, while the state police get appointed locally. There was a huge variation in the recruitment procedure of police between the state and central cadre. Home guards and orderlies were recruited at the district level. Throughout the country, orderlies and home guards were at the lowest rung of the hierarchy in the department and many a time subjected to carry out menial jobs. Jauregui (2013, pp. 643–669) addressed the issue of caste and ranks in the police department in her ethnographic study. For more information on the issues surrounding the orderlies and home guards: See www.thehindu.com/news/national/tamil-nadu/high-court-frowns-upon-use-of-orderlies-by-police-officials/article23297013.ece, https://timesofindia.indiatimes.com/city/hyderabad/Cook-wash-clean-babysit-Day-in-life-of-a-home-guard/articleshow/53193976.cms

References

Ambedkar, B. R. (1935/2014). Problem of discrimination in Untouchables or the children of India's ghetto. In Moon, V. (Ed.), *Dr. Babasaheb Ambedkar writings and speeches* (Vol. 5, pp. 108–111). Bombay: Education Department, Government of Maharashtra.

Balagopal, K. (1992). Slaying of a spirituous demon. *Economic and Political Weekly*, 27(46), pp. 2457–2461.

Bhaskar, R. A. (1981). *Journalism: caritra, vyavastha*. Hyderabad: Udyama Publications.

Bourdieu, P. (2005). *Distinction: A social critique of the judgement of taste*. Abingdon, Oxon: Routledge.

Bourdieu, P. and Passeron, J. (1990). *Reproduction in education, society and culture* (Tr. by Richard Nice). London: Sage.

Donthi, P. (2014). Chairman Rao: How Ramoji Rao of *Eenadu* wrested control of power and politics in Andhra Pradesh. *The Caravan: A Journal of Politics and Culture*. December. Retrieved from: www.caravanmagazine.in/reportage/chairman-rao.

ECQ [Eenadu Quality Cell]. (1999). *Eenadu: pātikeḷḷa akshara yātra*. Hyderabad: Eenadu Quality Cell.

GoAP [Government of Andhra Pradesh]. (1971). *The Andhra Pradesh chit funds Act, 1971*. Retrieved from: www.ap.gov.in/Acts%20Policies/AP%20Chits%20Fund%20Act%201971.pdf.

GoI. (1954). *Report of the first press commission (Part – 1)*. New Delhi: Government of India Press.

Jauregui, B. (2013). Beatings, beacons, and big men: Police disempowerment and delegitimation in India. *Law & Social Inquiry*, 38(3), pp. 643–669. DOI:10.1111/lsi.12030.

Jeffrey, R. ([2000] 2010). *India's newspaper revolution: Capitalism, politics, and the Indian-language press*. New Delhi: Oxford University Press.

Nehru, J. (1954). The modern newspaper. In *Jawaharlal Nehru's speeches* (Vol. 2). New Delhi: Publications Division.

Ninan, S. (2007). *Headlines from the heartland: Reinventing the Hindi public sphere*. New Delhi: Sage.

Prakasam, T. (1972). *Nā jīvita yātra* (My life journey) (Vol–I). Madras: Emesco.

Rajagopalrao, C. V. (2004). *Andhra Patrika caritra* (History of *Andhra Patrika*). Hyderabad: Press Academy of Andhra Pradesh.

Ramu, S. (1999). *Saṁsthāgata śikshaṇa-nāṇyataku rakshaṇa* (Institutional training – A safeguard for quality). In ECQ (Ed.), *Eenadu: pātikeḷḷa akshara yātra*. Hyderabad: Eenadu Quality Cell.

Rao, B. K. (2017). *Mīre jarnalisṭ* (You can become a journalist). Vijayawada: Pallavi Publications.

Reddy, K. S. (2016). *Jarnalisṭu karadīpika* (A handbook for journalists). Hyderabad: Vemana Publications.

Upadhya, C. (1988). The farmer-capitalists of coastal Andhra Pradesh. *Economic and Political Weekly*, 23(27–28), pp. 1433–1442, pp. 1376–1382.

Varadachari, G. S. (Ed.). (2011). *Mana pātrikēya velugulu*. Hyderabad: Veteran Journalists' Association.
Wacquant, L. J. D. (2008). *Urban outcasts: A comparative sociology of advanced marginality*. Cambridge: Polity Press.
Wacquant, L. J. D. (2015). Revisiting territories of relegation: Class, ethnicity and state in the making of advanced marginality. *Urban Studies*, 53(6), pp. 1077–1088. DOI:10.1177/0042098015613259.
Yule, H. and Burnell, A. C. (2008). *The concise Hobson-Jobson: An Anglo-Indian dictionary*. London: Wordsworth Editions.

4

'LIFT IRRIGATION, TORTURE AND KISMET'

The wayward fortunes of stringer's newswork

Sipping *chai* in front of a roadside café located opposite the Sangareddy 'Zero Milestone', GG, with more than 8 years of experience as a stringer, declared on a Monday morning (29 September 2014): 'No matter what we write, news is decided by the ignorant desk person placed above us. I thought that they would publish it on Sunday or Monday. *Bardāsht aitaledu*' (I'm not able to tolerate this).

> GG had written a special story on a specially-abled (deaf and dumb) person from a village in Sangareddy, who fought all odds to complete his intermediate education along with vocational training and was placed in a chain hotel group in Hyderabad. GG told me that the specially-abled attended a job fair organised at an educational institute for persons with special needs in Hyderabad on September 23. He said that this job fair was part of the international week for the deaf and dumb and he was going to file a story which he thought would be a genuine 'human interest' story.
>
> (Field notes, Sangareddy, 25 September 2014)

The story was not carried and GG was upset as he believed it was a 'success story', which might have inspired persons with similar disabilities in the immediate locality and beyond. He also pointed out that lack of space was not the reason, as the newspaper he works for carried reports filed from Hyderabad in the Medak district edition. GG came to the conclusion that his story was 'spiked' without reason and he was annoyed with the distant and anonymous editorial person.

More than with the person concerned at the desk, GG seemed to be livid at himself for not being able to comprehend the logic of the rejection of his special story by the editorial staff. He told me that the bureau in-charge cleared the story and sent it across to the desk for publication. This was a regular affair with stringers. In the case of Medak, there was no chance of direct contact or establishing a relationship with the person concerned in the

DOI: 10.4324/b23313-4

editorial section for feedback or to check the status of the news item. The job of the bureau in-charge and rural in-charge ends after sending the story to the head office located in Hyderabad, where the pages are made.

GG's disappointment was not unusual as this happened on a number of occasions to stringers during my fieldwork in Gannavaram. In Gannavaram, unlike in Sangareddy or Medak, there was a district edition centre for all Telugu news dailies located in and around Vijayawada. Sometimes, stories filed by stringers get 'picked' or 'lifted' by reporters working in the edition centres. However, most stringers in both Gannavaram and Sangareddy complained that their stories were lifted by either reporters or rural in-charges without giving them any credit.

The following is an excerpt from my field notes about one such instance on an exceptionally long Friday in the field along with stringers at work in the blazing hot sun in Gannavaram:

> SSS, a stringer working for a top Telugu daily, noticed that streetlights were switched on during the day in Buddhavaram, Kesarapalli, and Chinna Avutupalli villages for two consecutive days. He managed to meet the electricity lineman near the MRO's office and enquired about it. The stringer learnt that due to a technical snag, the electricity lines had become direct and they were not able to turn off the power supply. He met the assistant engineer (AE) from the local electricity office and got this confirmed. The stringer even put a headline *Gannavaramlō pagaṭi velugulu*! (Lights during daytime in Gannavaram!). The pointers for the story were catchy too. They read: *Adhikārula nirlakshyam* (careless officials); *Vṛdhā avutunna vidyutcakti* (wastage of power). He emailed the story to the edition centre along with photographs of the streetlights taken in the morning with an alert stating that more reports would follow soon.
>
> (8 June 2012, Gannavaram)

The story did not appear in the Gannavaram zone page the following day (Saturday) and SSS was confident that the desk would take it on Sunday (10 June 2012), which also did not happen. However, much to our shock, the story appeared as the anchor story on the front page of the district tabloid on Tuesday with a Vijayawada dateline. While SSS's story focused only on Gannavaram, the reporter who wrote the published article gave an overview of the situation in the entire district, with quotes from Machilipatnam (headquarters) and Vijayawada electricity officials.

By the time I reached the reading room on Tuesday morning, fellow stringers already started pulling his leg saying that the district reporter had indulged in 'lift irrigation'. Lift irrigation was a common expression among stringers and reporters in Telugu journalism for when a story gets picked up by either another reporter from the same paper/news organisation or by another newspaper and is carried without any credit to the stringer.

When reporters cannibalise stories filed by stringers in the same organisation, the latter is deprived of credit in both financial and literal terms. The story published with a different dateline means a loss of money for stringers and at the same time the 'credit' for his news story idea goes to someone else. SSS called up the rural in-charge who replied that he was not on duty on that particular day and advised him not to make it a big issue. When I asked him about the possibility of taking this issue to the bureau in-charge or editorial in-charge, as he had enough proof of having filed the story and sent the photographs in emails, the stringer said: '*Vāḍi* torture *vaddu ippuḍu*' (I do not want to face any 'torture' from the reporter now).

There were also instances when the bureau/rural in-charges gave a 'bare news report' (spot report) idea and helped stringers come up with a comprehensive news article. In one such instance at Sangareddy:

> A stringer of the second largest circulating Telugu daily reached its office before lunchtime, while I was interviewing the bureau chief, to file a news report about an abandoned girl child near a temple at Angadipet in Sangareddy *mandal*. After going through the report, the bureau chief took some time off from the interview. He sat the stringer down and told him that the story was much bigger than a single column report. He suggested that the stringer go through all of last month's newspapers to find out whether there were more such cases (they totalled 10) and asked him to come up with a broader report taking responses from the local Integrated Child Development Services (ICDS) officer, doctors, and *anganwadi* workers. The single column news item turned into a special story after the bureau chief gave final shape to the rough item filed by the stringer. It was marked 'Checked and Cleared' by him (usual practice) and sent to the desk based in Hyderabad through email. He turned towards the stringer who was standing next to him all this while, and said, 'This is how you need to convert news into special stories.' The three of us broke for lunch.
>
> (Field notes, 1 October 2014)

The following day, the special story on abandoned girl children was carried on the front page of the Medak district edition, occupying four of the six columns that constituted the half page alongside a two-column standalone picture of Goddess Durga during the *Bathukamma* festival. The story flowed into the second page of the edition, occupying another four columns (2 October 2014) with another box column prominently carrying a quote by the ICDS officer.

The aforementioned observations highlight the interactions between agents occupying different positions and performing roles demanded by those positions in the professional hierarchy within the organisation. In the instance of the 'human interest' story, an unquestionable and inaccessible editorial desk holds the decision-making power on whether or not to carry a story filed by a stringer, even if it is cleared by the reporting head concerned.

In the case of the stolen ('lift irrigation') story, there is a clear and visible preference for the reporter over the stringer so much so that the latter is not in a position to claim his right over the poached story. Observations in the field revealed that this sort of practice is common with stringers who email their stories to the desk directly as opposed to passing on the handwritten stories to bus drivers who dispatch them to the bus stop nearest to the edition centre. Along with such 'malpractices', there are 'healthy' practices when seniors at work guide, shape and train stringers to file better stories, as in the case of the stringer who got the opportunity to convert a tiny spot news report into a special story with his own date and credit line.[1]

Understanding journalistic roles in local news production

> *Tāḍini tannēvāḍu untē vāḍi talanu tannēvāḍu inkōduntāḍu* (If there's someone who reached the top of a palm tree, there's always someone else who can scale even greater heights).

This proverb was uttered by a stringer when I asked him about the roles and functions in his organisation and how he deals with them as part of his daily work. The context in which he mentioned the proverb encodes a meaning to the effect that 'If there's someone smart, there is always someone else who can outsmart her/him'. The stringer was hinting that it was the only way to survive in the field. What was implicit in his response was the hierarchical nature of the roles.

Journalistic practice involved the conflation of multiple hierarchies, the strategies of agents in their respective social spaces and the division of labour, implicitly based on the background of the agents in the journalistic field. While there was an apparent relationship between the dispositions of the agents and the positions they occupied in the field, the dynamics between agents, structures and strategies involved in the process of news production changed on a daily basis and sometimes depending on the news event as well.

Responding to a question on the existence, functioning and boundaries of a field, Bourdieu points out:

> [T]he field as a structure of objective relations of force between positions undergirds and guides the strategies whereby the occupants of these positions seek, individually or collectively to safeguard or improve their position, and to impose the principle of hierarchisation most favourable to their own products. The strategies of agents depend on their position in the field, that is, in the distribution of the specific capital.
>
> (Bourdieu's response to Wacquant, 1989, p. 40)

This chapter elaborates on the issue of *relegation* not only in positions but also in practice before presenting the multiple forms of hierarchy within and outside of the field, crucial to understanding local journalistic practice. In doing so, the positions occupied by agents in social space, their social capital and professional roles are mapped in order to locate them in a relatively less autonomous journalistic field. In the process, this chapter attempts to address the question: what hierarchies are in operation in the production practices of native language journalism in the Telugu-speaking states?

The aforementioned incidents highlight the roles and the relationships among the various agents in a newspaper organisation. The selection and rejection of articles mentioned earlier do not have any apparent political (realpolitik) overtones or ideologically or monetarily driven intentions.[2] These descriptions mention not only the roles in news production but also the weight those roles carry, along with some arbitrary understanding or doxa ('rules of the game') present in the field. Interestingly, the Press Academy manual addressed this issue to educate stringers in understanding the nuances of the field and outlined a code of conduct they should maintain in the profession. A part of the manual (Chakradhar, 2011, p. 19), which appeared like an excerpt from the Code of Hammurabi, reads:

> Ensure that you are in the good books of desk persons so that they may consider your stories for publication. As a stringer, you need to maintain a cordial relationship with the staff reporter too. Having an amiable relationship with staff reporters and the desk workers is highly beneficial.

The textual description of the relationship between various agents in form of a suggestion in the manual is enigmatic, to say the least. Understanding the roles and responsibilities of various agents as division of labour in newswork emerged from field observations and interviews. Even as there are various designations within the reporting and editorial sections of newspapers based on experience, there is not much variation in the nature of their work. While designations in the reporting section include reporter, senior reporter, chief reporter, rural in-charge and bureau in-charge, in the editorial section, they were sub-editor, senior sub-editor, chief sub-editor, deputy news editor, news editor, and district edition in-charge.

Most newspapers have a functional mechanism in place to address the issue of a weekly off for staffers, as there is always a second-in-command to substitute for the top roles in the latter's absence. In the editorial section, especially in Krishna district, allocation of *mandal* and zone pages to sub-editors is based on a rotation policy, so that there is no possibility of a nexus between the page in-charge and the stringers in the various *mandals* of the district.[3]

In the case of the reporting section, at least one person among the bureau in-charge, the rural in-charge and one chief reporter must be on duty to ensure that there are enough stories to bring out the district edition.[4] In case of an extreme situation in which all the reporting staffers are absent, the editorial section carries reports from the nearby district/edition centre with a bare minimum of local reports (mostly press releases) to ensure that advertisement commitments are honoured. Before dealing with the issue of roles and relationships among the agents in the journalistic field, the nature of roles and responsibilities of stringers, reporting and editorial staffers are presented in a tabular form (see Table 4.1).

Even as Jeffrey (2010, p. 147) points out 'the line between a stringer and a staffer could blur', there is a huge difference between the work culture and organisation of the two at the mofussil or district edition level. After probation or training (for a period of 3–6 months), every reporting staffer is given a specific territory and beat. While a territory could comprise legislative and administrative regions or units, such as: metro (city), Assembly constituency, parliamentary constituency and district headquarters, among others, the beat for reporting staffers could involve covering issues related to politics, crime, agriculture, health, education, business, lifestyle, the district collector's office, municipal corporation, sports and the courts of law.

While the Vijayawada and Krishna district editions of Telugu dailies had almost all of these beats and territories for reporters (in some cases more than one dedicated reporting staffer for crime and political beats), Sangareddy and Medak districts had reporters handling more than one beat. Even as the total area of erstwhile Medak district was bigger than Krishna district and both have two parliamentary constituencies each, the presence of a large city like Vijayawada within the district limits warranted having separate urban and rural editions.

The stringer and the staffer: roles and responsibilities

Table 4.1 The stringer and the staffer: Roles and responsibilities

Stringer	*Reporting staffer*	*Editorial staffer*
• Not salaried (*precariat*) • Diurnal • Field • Workplace: No • No by-line • Part-time • Zone page (a leaf in district tabloid edition) • Generalist (no beat) • Credibility • Handwritten reports/email/WhatsApp • Writing • Facts, quotes, pictures for stories • News incident, event, press conference • Qualities: Dynamic, objective, gregarious • Feedback: Sources, peers, locals, and readers • Weekly off: No • Duties: News gathering, reporting; coordinating with staffers, bureau in-charge, editorial, advertising and scheduling department, and management; procuring advertisements; boost circulation • Role: News gatherer cum photographer, newspaper circulation agent, ad revenue generator • Mode of payment: Credit line account, commission from advertisements	• Salaried (*salariat*) • Diurnal • Field and office • Workplace: Office • By-line (exclusive stories; occasionally) • Full-time • District edition (tabloid), main edition • Beat (Specific) • Credibility • Email/WhatsApp/news writing software • Writing • Facts, quotes, assigning duties • News incident, event, press conference, special story • Qualities: Dynamic, objective, gregarious • Feedback: Sources, peers, editorial staff • Weekly off: Yes • Duties: News gathering, reporting, writing special stories, monitoring stringers (bureau and rural in-charges) • Role: News gatherer, aggregator, supervisor • Mode of payment: Salary account	• Salaried (*salariat*) • Nocturnal • Desk (office) • Workplace: Office • No by-line • Full-time • Zone/District/Main editions • Specific pages • Honesty • WhatsApp/Email/news writing and page design software • Rewriting, editing, sourcing • Prioritising, highlighting, playing down stories • Language, layout, grammar • Qualities: Patience, prudence, clarity • Feedback: Peers, senior staffers, readers • Weekly off: Yes • Duties: Editing, translating, designing, coordinating • Role: News processor • Mode of payment: Salary account

Source: Field notes and interviews

Senior reporting staffers are expected not just to carry out their own responsibilities but also to oversee the work of junior reporters and ensure that they are performing their duties. These senior or higher-level reporting staffers (city/district/rural bureau in-charges) also assign duties for a particular day to the reporters. The reporters are expected to complete these tasks along with covering their beat, for which they are solely responsible. From the point of view of reporting staffers, the physical space in which the administration and assignment of reporting activities take place is referred to as office (workplace) and the bureau is the organised work process of a particular beat. Each reporter literally has a 'bureau' (computer table) of their own or at least shares it with one more reporter, taking turns at the time of filing reports.

This organised workspace (office) and work process (beat and bureau) are things to which a stringer does not have access. The workplace, residence, office and space of operation are indistinguishable. Work culture becomes part of the social surrounding or the world of everyday life. Unlike reporters who return to their offices to file reports, stringers do not have that facility.[5] In Gannavaram and Sangareddy, stringers gossip, hang out, kill time, invite local elites to discuss and file reports from the same place (like the media point or rest house discussed in earlier chapters).

However, this is not the case with editorial staffers, as each of them has a niche (cubicle) of their own in the office.[6] Within the editorial section, they too have designated and assigned pages to deal with for the night. Editorial staffers do not have direct contact with either stringers or reporters and even if they need clarification on copy, they have to go through 'a proper channel'.

This involves informing their superior who is 'privy' to talk to the reporting bureau in-charge or rural in-charge, who in turn contacts the stringer or reporters. Many senior editorial staffers expressed that this bureaucracy is necessary to avoid a 'nexus' or 'give and take' between page sub-editors and stringers or reporters. Some pointed out that the bureau or rural in-charges or senior reporters have a better understanding of the news event (history and context) than them and they do not want to take a chance. However, in emergency situations or in the case of developing stories, editorial staffers are allowed to call stringers in order to take input or information directly before the edition is put to bed.

Having considered the differences in the nature of the work of reporters, stringers, and editorial staffers, conceptions of time and space in the editorial and reporting (including stringers) departments need recognition. In most of the descriptions of newswork in manuals for journalists (Rao, 2011; Reddy, 2011; Rammohanarao, 2011), this aspect is ignored.

A glance at any print morning daily reveals that there are two different time zones in it. It may not appear loud enough to grab the attention of newspaper readers but it is evident and crucial to understanding the logics of time and space. The news event or incident happens at a particular time of the day and the stringer/reporter files the story at a different time of the day (say, by evening) with the date and place of reporting, dateline and credit line, respectively. For the desk person, the workday begins by changing the date on the top corner of the page (in most dailies) she/he edits to the following day and the location happens to be the location of edition centre, regardless of the locations from where news was reported and the pages, such as zone, district, metro, nation, world, edit, op-ed, sports and movies.

In effect, there is a narrative about newswork that unfolds in the gaps between when an incident happens, the time it becomes a report filed by a stringer or reporter (interactions/negotiations with agents from other fields) and the time it is finally printed (interactions, negotiations, communication between stringers, reporting and editorial staffers).

These multi-layered interactions and negotiations among agents within and outside the field are crucial in examining relations of production in the journalistic field. This understanding also helps gauging the scope and limits of the roles of agents operating within the field.

Understanding relations of news production between agents

A major complaint on part of stringers was the lack of opportunity to write a story the way they perceived it. They were well aware of the social and political relevance of events that took place in their immediate surroundings. They not only were aware of their environments but also had a good understanding of the backgrounds to events. But they had little opportunity to write new articles and report comprehensively on events.

Most stringers charged that reporters and rural or bureau in-charges did not allow them to write full reports and they were given the responsibility of gathering sidelights or trivia, denying them the task to report on events or issues that had broader social significance, as perceived by them. Stringers pointed out that some reporters regularly picked up stories filed by them and got them published on a Vijayawada dateline without any credit.

Stringers in both states complained that while reporting and editorial staff restrict themselves to journalistic work, newspaper management personnel 'assign' and put additional non-journalistic work on stringers. They said that the management dictates terms on what and what not to report about certain businessmen, politicians and political parties, based on 'advertisement interests'.

Stringers in Medak district pointed out that because parts of the district are industrial hubs, stories on some companies and firms that flout norms are repeatedly rejected. In Krishna district, a 'nexus between politicians, real estate businessmen, and the newspaper management' was obvious. They informed me that newspaper management and firms have a 'very good understanding'.

Since there was no direct access to the desk, it was management who had the final say in the publishing or rejection of stories, rather than reporting heads.

In Krishna district, stringers said that some reporters shared a good rapport with local politicians and businessmen and ensured that there was no negative reportage about local elites. They also said that desk and management ensure that there are no reports filed against a particular political party. Some stringers suggested that there was a heavy 'caste-based bias' (in favour of Sat-shudra) involved in the selection or rejection of reports in Gannavaram. This caste-based gatekeeping is evident and will be discussed further in the section on the logic of journalistic practice.

Explaining the ways to avoid hardships in the profession, stringers in both states (especially experienced ones) indicated that there are no problems for them if they follow and adhere to what management and reporting heads tell them to do, pointing out that 'caste, money, and political power decide news' in their respective locations. The caste background of a stringer comes to the fore whenever local politicians, businessmen and bureaucrats among others complain about them to the newspaper management, after which they are usually sacked.

Stringers revealed that on most occasions they restricted their roles to merely sending strings, pieces of information and details in their reports so that the desk persons stitch them into a news story, which sticks to the editorial and management policies of the newspaper. They even pointed out that this way of reporting created problems locally, as some politicians questioned why their statements were distorted in the story. They said that it was the responsibility of stringers to strike a balance between local elites or news sources, rural or bureau in-charges and management.

Elaborating on the caste question, stringers from Dalit and OBC communities explained that reporters and reporting in-charges belong to influential castes (both Sat-shudra and Savarna) in society and in the journalistic field. They (stringers) averred that the reporting and editorial heads routinely edged out stories that highlighted the neglect of marginalised communities by the government, officials, police and politicians. Stringers alleged that even though there was ample space in district editions, desk persons preferred to publish items from nearby cities (Hyderabad or Vijayawada datelines) instead of taking such items. When asked about the reasons behind the rejection of such articles, stringers said that some of the questions posed to them by reporting or editorial heads were: 'How many people from that community (caste or tribe) read our newspaper? What is our circulation in that village?'[7]

At the same time, some stringers and reporting heads from both locations revealed that the *kismet* (fate) of a story making its way to the printing press was not determined keeping the number of readers or the organisational or professional (unprofessional) structure in mind. Instead, the track record (habitus) of stringers as observed by editorial staffers became one of the factors while selecting or rejecting special stories.

Editorial staff stressed that the news organisation's principles and editorial policy come before individuals in daily journalistic work. Most indicated that in case stringers deviate from it (the policy), they initially try to 'get them into the groove' (*dārilōki teccukunṭāmu*); then warn them if they persist in deviating from it. If stringers still do not get editorial and management policies even after repeated warnings, they are fired, editorial persons in Krishna district said.

Most editors said that they reminded stringers to write stories keeping the editorial policy as well as readership base in mind. They said that they took the help of bureau and rural in-charges and reporters to learn about the background of the stringer who filed the reports for that day. Editorial staffers said that they pose a set of questions to themselves before selecting a story or spot news event for publishing. These include (a) Who is filing the report? (social backgrounds and history of the stringer); (b) What is the relevance of the news report on that particular day?; (c) Was there any possibility of vested interests on the part of the stringer in filing the story (especially negative ones against the local elite)? They also indicated that they acquired the knowledge of assessing the nature of a report (whether or not it was manipulated) over a period of time in the job or role of an editor.

Rural in-charges in both states expressed that the decision-making power regarding the selection of stories is vested in the hands of sub-editors. In case the editorial staff express any doubts regarding stories, they said that they cross-check the veracity of the news item through their own sources from the locality where it was filed. They said that with decades of experience in the field, they develop their own networks across the district and most of them stated that they could easily identify the intention and motive of a stringer in filing certain stories.

Bureau in-charges too maintained that the stringers have many vested interests as they did not have proper salaries. They pointed out that this was the main reason why they file certain stories seeking monetary and non-monetary[8] benefits, setting aside the 'professional ideal of serving the public'. Stressing that monitoring stringers was a 'necessary evil', rural in-charges maintained that the lack of such a mechanism would not only put the reputation of the newspaper at stake but also result in the 'degradation of the noble profession of journalism'.

A way of monitoring stringers at the *mandal* level was by prominently highlighting a helpline mobile number on the *mandal* or zone page, asking the public to inform them about civic issues and related problems they face in their locality. Through this medium, locals, along with officials, businessmen, and small-time political leaders forward their complaints about local stringers too. In most dailies, this was handled by management personnel who informed the editorial or reporting heads about the misconduct of the stringer(s) working in their newspaper.[9]

Some news organisations seemed to have a training system in place for sub-editors to understand the editorial policy of the newspaper, the 'taste' of the readership base and, above all, the relevance of the report. Editorial heads said that 'common sense' and a 'nose for news'[10] came before any other criteria while selecting or rejecting news filed by stringers or reporters. As a part of the training system, some organisations had a practice in which sub-editors were required to file news reports once or twice in a month so that they understand the issues and problems faced by reporters and stringers. Such measures were in place for top-circulation newspapers and those with a long standing in the field. Editorial heads said that these measures helped in building a better relationship between the editorial and reporting sections of the newspaper.

Editorial heads also pointed out that there were some editors, reporters and stringers who formed a nexus and abused the newspaper by publishing stories based on their whims. They said that working in tandem with management personnel, they monitored such issues on a regular basis with the help of their own 'sources' at the *mandal* and district levels. Editorial heads said that with this mechanism, they also monitor the efficiency of stringers who are often callous about their duties and miss out on stories of importance to the newspaper and often avoid reporting, on purpose, on certain issues in order to protect influential persons in their localities in exchange for monetary benefits.

All these observations raised questions on a range of issues and categories, from monitoring the workforce and editorial policy and control to the bureaucratic structure within the organisation; from gatekeeping, socialisation among newsworkers to, more importantly, the division of labour in the news production process. Given the 'generalist' role of a stringer, mentioned in Table 4.1 while discussing the roles and responsibilities of agents, it is important to map the relations not only between agents within but also outside the field.

Strategies employed by stringers differ significantly from those of other agents (reporting and editorial staffers) due to the very nature of their work, that is, not having a specific beat, a regular salary from the organisation, location of work (social setting), of which they are an intrinsic part. The position stringers occupy in the structure of the journalistic field and in the social setting or field needs to be ascertained along with their modes of engagement with other stringers, local elites and the public in order to understand news production practices in the local journalistic field.

Based on my ethnographic observations during fieldwork, a map of the relations is presented in Figure 4.1, with the stringer at the centre. This map portrays the relations between stringers, reporters, bureau/rural in-charges, management personnel and editorial staffers along with the district edition in-charge.

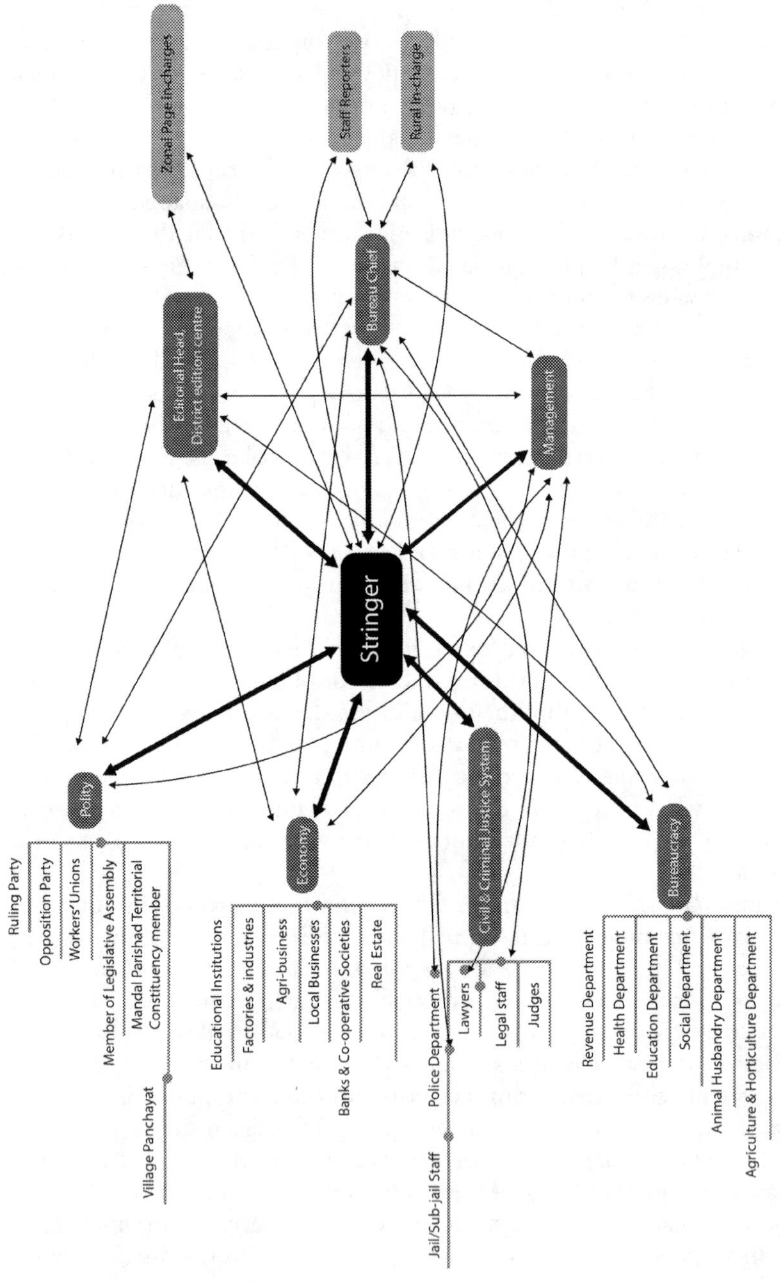

Figure 4.1 A mapping of news gathering and production relations

Source: Author.

The two-way arrow indicates the interactive relationship between agents, while the one-way arrow suggests a top-down relationship, usually the case with offices of either district edition in-charge or bureau chief (reporting head) of the district. In these cases, the stringer on his own cannot interact with the top brass of the newspaper for which he works. At the same time, anyone calling from the 'office' (mobile number or landline) means the stringer is going to hear 'his master's voice' (bureau or editorial in-charge).[11]

Interactions between agents from economic, legal and police, political, and bureaucratic fields at the local level and agents within the journalistic field sometimes situated in the district headquarters, do exist. Most of these relations with the other fields from the headquarters are maintained to monitor and ensure control over stringers by reporters, reporting in-charges and the newspaper management. In case of any complaints about stringers, local elites approach reporters and rural in-charges and inform them about the 'behaviour' or 'character' of the stringer.

Interactions between stringers and agents from other fields take place not just for journalistic purposes but for advertisements, circulation and allied non-journalistic purposes, which include conversion of capital in Bourdieu's sense.[12] The map laying out the interactions and exchanges between agents within the field and other fields of power attests to the relatively less autonomous nature of the journalistic field, as discussed in Chapter 2.

Hierarchies and structures: reproduction in the journalistic field

One of the quintessential elements of Telugu newspapers is the hierarchical organisation of news items in pages which, in most cases reflects the editorial policy of a particular paper. The lead story (banner item) on the front page has a visibly bolder and bigger font to make the story prominent, with the placement of the remaining stories on the page depending on the editorial team's or editor's selection.

Even as there is an increasing trend to use flashy pointers to highlight the important elements of the news stories along with graphics, the text of the news is written on the lines of the good old inverted pyramid model. While this is the case with the writing style, the structure of the workforce of journalists (both editorial and reporting) at the district edition level reflects a pyramid with editorial in-charge at the top followed by bureau/rural in-charges, editorial and reporting staffers.

Essentially, the world of stringers in mofussil areas appears to be a rigidly hierarchical one. It was palpable in the language and expressions they used, not only when they talked about their work but also in their descriptions of persons in their immediate life-worlds. Very often they used expressions such as 'The boss is always right', *peddōḷḷu* (influential people), *pedda sāru* (person commanding respect), *Peddā-cinnā tēḍā teliyaḍam mukhyam*

('Realising the importance of a person is essential'; *pedda* and *cinna* also mean big and small), and *Evaḍu cēsē pani vāḍu cēyāli* ('Know your limits while going about work'), among others. More importantly, recognition for a stringer in the locality in which he operated was based on the newspaper for which he worked, that is, the political affiliation of the newspaper.

Work hierarchies: water is not 'holy', unless it be poured into the conch

The very constitution of the bureaucratic structure of any given newspaper or media outlet reflects the hierarchical nature of the work. It appears to be very obvious and doxical, keeping in mind the functions each part of the structure are 'assigned' or supposed to deliver. If one looks at the structure of the news organisation based on the functions (expected results), a major part of it appears to be a flat or lateral hierarchy. The basic fact is that newswork is the result of teamwork and it cannot be accomplished without the contribution of each and every individual involved in the process, ranging from the editor-in-chief to the sub-editor; from the chief of news bureau to the stringer; from the publisher to the printer in the factory; from the advertisement scheduling department to the image scanner of advertisements; from the circulation manager to the newspaper boy who delivers the product at the doorstep.

Theoretically, this appears to be universal. But the nature of hierarchy in the Telugu language newspaper is far more complex.[13] The complex hierarchical nature of news organisations was felt only in the journalistic practices in the field.

A bureau in-charge of a Telugu daily in Sangareddy, VRK, in a personal interview, narrated how he landed the position (he was a senior reporter based in Hyderabad) thanks to a news item he wrote for his newspaper in the mid-2000s. According to him, he visited Medak district on some personal work and happened to see that the wooden doors of some *pucca* houses were missing. VRK said:

> Out of curiosity, I enquired about it. Women started revealing the extortionist strategies of microfinance companies' personnel in recovering the loans that the women took. As they failed to pay the instalments, the agents of companies started taking away household items and it reached a point where there was nothing left to take from the homes and, finally, they took away the doors. I noted down all the details and filed a report, which was published on the front page. My editor and the chief of the news bureau encouraged me to write a series of articles on the adverse effects of microfinance institutions in rural Medak.
>
> (10 October 2014, personal communication, Sangareddy)

At the same time, stringers working in both mofussil and urban areas have access to a mine of information about the local public, the elites, institutions and local happenings. Stringers interact with drivers (chauffeurs), domestic helps and even security guards (watchmen) of local politicians on a daily basis, during lunch hours or innumerable *chai* (tea) breaks. They literally keep an eye (surveillance or *nigāh*) on local people and places of importance and acquire much secret information.[14]

English news daily reporters, PLR and RS, in Vijayawada, admitted that they rely on 'credible and trustworthy' stringers on most occasions to write about incidents and developments in interior parts of districts, as such places are beyond their reach and their reporting workforce is miniscule when compared to the networks of Telugu newspapers. English daily reporters said that they develop rapport with stringers over a period of time and sometimes the hard way, not catching factual errors in their reportage. However, they acknowledged their dependency on stringers in the news-gathering process for certain stories from the hinterland.

However, a stringer usually cannot convert this information into a news article and on many occasions, even when a stringer hints at a developing story, it does not get its due. In one of the many such instances:

> PSR wrote a 'special story' on the state of affairs with cotton farmers during Kharif (autumn) season. Apart from the usual reporting, he did the 'legwork' showing cotton farmers tangled in a web of debt from private moneylenders despite generating a good yield before the harvest season. His main point was that the delay in the sanctioning of loans prompted farmers to borrow from private money lenders at high interest rates. The stringer gave a catchy headline with rhyming agrarian words: *puttaḍi telangāṇalō cittaḍi avutunna patti raitu* (Cotton farmers swamped in golden Telangana). He emailed the story along with mugshots of the farmers to the desk in-charge. He was visibly upset with the way his story was treated by the desk, as he was not pointing fingers at anyone specifically (not highlighting names of money lenders or officials) and only presented the state of affairs. I managed to meet him on Monday in Sangareddy after three days, as he was busy travelling to villages for this story.
>
> (Field notes, 25 August 2014)

The story never saw the light of day during my fieldwork period, which lasted for close to four months and came to an end by the third week of October 2014. However, by the last week of the month, almost all newspapers carried stories about the plight of farmers and their debt-ridden lives despite the government's plan to implement the loan waiver scheme, announced as part of their election promise.

Finally, a revised version of PSR's story along with a ground report on a farmer suicide case was published on the front page of the Medak district tabloid edition of his newspaper on 24 October 2014, followed by a big front-page article in the main edition filed by a special correspondent (*pratyēka pratinidhi*) from Hyderabad and an editorial on 26 October 2014.[15] By this time, due to the influx of stories in all newspapers in various languages, including English language dailies, the National Human Rights Commission (NHRC) intervened and took up the issue.[16]

It appeared as if the information or news stories filed by stringers at the village or *mandal* levels did not have value in themselves until a staffer picked up the story or a correspondent from the headquarters filed a story on the same issue. In the field, such occurrences were regular affairs and suggested that the information a stringer collected acquired *legitimacy* and *sanctity* only when filed by a reporter before finally getting *consecrated* by the desk. In the process, the stringer is 'invisibilised'.[17] This process indicates that professional standing in the field is a necessary condition for the news story to make its way to the edit table before finding a place in the printed newspaper the following day.

When asked about the difference between the ways in which a stringer and a reporter file the same event based on the same information, an experienced stringer in Gannavaram YSS remarked, '*basic-gā śankhamlō pōstēgāni tīrtham kadannaṭṭu, adantē*' (Basically, it is like the way how water does not become holy unless it is poured into a conch. That's the way it is).[18] While the remark ends on a casual note *adantē* (that's the way it is), the unwritten rules of the game based on which the journalistic field operates are clear. This resignation to one's own position (doxa) could be seen as a sign of maturity and it comes with experience.

While this appears to be an emic perspective, Bourdieu, while elucidating the sociology of cultural production, applicable to journalism, makes an important observation about these unconscious strategies that take place in the field. He notes:

> All relations among agents and institutions of diffusion or consecration are mediated by the field's structure. To the extent that the ever-ambiguous marks of recognition owe their specific form to the objective relations (perceived and interpreted as they are in accordance with the unconscious schemes of the habitus) they contribute to form the *subjective* representation which agents have of the *social* representation of their position within the hierarchy of consecrations.
>
> (Bourdieu, 1993, p. 133) [Emphasis original]

The visible predominance of the editorial and reporting staffers over stringers who fall outside of the organisational structure is evident. This superiority and highhandedness of the former is often overtly expressed. When reporters from headquarters or edition centres visit mofussil areas to cover some high-profile visit or event, stringers are given specific instructions to 'just' accompany them; they are reduced to the role of acolytes.[19]

In one instance, in Gannavaram, the president of the then Opposition party (BJP), M. Venkaiah Naidu, visited Gannavaram village. His visit was announced earlier and reporters from Vijayawada rushed to the airport. I was with PCB (who is relatively inexperienced in the field), as he was interacting with a senior reporter from the Vijayawada centre.

The latter casually asked PCB if he had any particular question in mind to which he replied: I want to ask him (Venkaiah Naidu) about the party's stance on the bifurcation of Andhra Pradesh. The reporter immediately snapped: 'Over action *cheyagāku. Avannī mēmu cūskuntāmulē gāni nī pani nuvvu cūsko*' (Do not try to be over smart. Stay within your limits and mind your own business). Shortly, during the media interaction organised at a local BJP leader's home, the reporter asked the same question to the former BJP president to which he got a curt reply: '*Telangana gurinci māṭlāḍatāniki idi saraina samayam, sandarbham kādu sōdarā*' (This is not an appropriate time and occasion to talk about Telangana issue, brother) [30 April 2012, Gannavaram airport].

The following day, a single-column brief appeared on the inside pages of the main edition filed by the reporter mentioning that the BJP president was in Gannavaram. In effect, PCB was reminded of the 'limits of his actions' (scope and role) in the field. Also, in effect, along with the routine news item getting published from Vijayawada dateline, the professional hierarchy is reproduced unconsciously among the agents involved as in this particular instance. Even his peers made him *understand the rules of the game* in their own way by mocking PCB.[20]

Given the fact that there is no training or journalism education for stringers, incidents such as these help them learn the rules (official and unofficial; written and unwritten) by which the field operates. Having examined the professional hierarchies present in the field, the following section addresses social hierarchies, inseparable from professional ones crucial to understanding the news production process.

'Caste feeling': the ubiquity of social hierarchies

One rarely misses a chance to enquire about the caste background of a person in the delta region of Andhra Pradesh. This defines relationships at the workplace, educational institution and place of residence. The question of caste in Telangana is not as important as it appeared to be in the delta region at first glance but this is misleading as identity markers such as caste, region and religion are as ubiquitous as in other parts of the Telugu-speaking regions.

These identity markers become crucial in the news production process at individual, organisational and societal levels.[21] For stringers especially, both in the organisation and also in the localities in which they operated, social identities matter the most right from the time of recruitment to upward mobility in the profession. The very fact that editorial staffers, as part of their daily work, probe into issues such as who is filing the story and what could be the motive behind the story testifies that the social background of the stringer (or sometimes even reporters) is considered before copy is 'subbed' and cleared.[22]

Social background is, if not the defining, definitely a foundational principle in understanding the working hierarchies of a news organisation or the field itself. The inverted pyramid model of journalism overlaps or gets superimposed by a caste, region and religion based social pyramid (see Graph 4.1). The very fact that a stringer was part of his community, social setting, village, occupation (for subsistence) and also part of the journalistic field by working in a particular news organisation suggests a dynamic interplay of hierarchies and identities at various levels. Comprehending and laying out these struggles at the individual, organisational, field and societal level forms the primary objective of field theory as a meso-level of analysis in understanding journalistic practices.

During interactions and in recorded interviews, editorial and reporting staffers talked about the social and *(im)moral* backgrounds of stringers as matters of fact and said that 'stringers need to be tamed', 'they are unscrupulous' and 'unethical' (MMR, 9 October 2014, Sangareddy; VRK, 11 October 2014, Sangareddy; NS, 17 September 2012, Vijayawada). Even in the existing academic literature, senior journalists labelled stringers as 'corrupt', 'uncontrollable' and 'blackmailers' and as people 'known to file stories that are either untrue or inaccurate' (Jeffrey, 2010, p. 147; Rao and Malik, 2018, p. 6).

On the face of it, the barrage of terms and expressions uttered by mid and entry-level journalists echoed ethical concerns, apart from the talk about the falling standards and morals in the field. But a sociological understanding entailed recognition of the *caste and class nature* of these pronouncements on the part of not only editorial staffers but also reporters.

An understanding of the roles of agents in the journalistic field (Table 4.1) and field dynamics (Figure 4.1) reveal the voluminous amount of journalistic and non-journalistic work with which a stringer has to engage on a daily basis. On most occasions, responses from the editorial and reporting staffers would be: 'He's supposed to do it'.

This phenomenon was what Bourdieu theorised as 'misrecognition', a concept closely linked to the aspect of symbolic violence in a given field. For Bourdieu, it is a process in which agents, in this case, staffers, fail to engage with or acknowledge the existing nature of social reality of which they are a part or take the 'rules of the game' for granted in fields of power (2000, pp. 142–143). In a way, agents occupying privileged positions in the field need only to go about their work adhering to the 'rules of the game' which in turn ascribe legitimacy to the already dominant. Existing hierarchies and multiple layers of domination are reproduced in a manner that both the dominant and the dominated are made to believe that it is happening in their best interest but for the betterment of the field itself.

The manner in which some of the salariat class agents in the field talked about stringers appeared even more problematic during my fieldwork in Vijayawada (Krishna delta version of Telugu). Their 'casual' remarks when asked about the heavy workload on stringers from different departments in their organisation – *mari cēyaka*? *Castāḍā*? Or *evaḍi kōsam cēyaḍu* (What else can he do? Isn't he supposed to do the work?) – show their attitude towards stringers.[23]

The division of labour in the form of professional hierarchies in the organisation resulted in forming both solidarities and hostilities among agents. Most stringers suggested that belonging to the same caste or community as that of rural in-charge or bureau in-charge was beneficial in the field. Even some of the reporting in-charges admitted the presence of favouritism on caste lines in the field but claimed it was not the case in their organisations.[24] Social hierarchies coupled with professional hierarchies play crucial roles in journalistic production.

As mentioned earlier, when stringers attempted to report some human-interest story or a burning issue about a development in a remote village or underprivileged areas, reporting in-charges spike the story stating that the newspaper does not sell there or that there is no readership in that village or area.[25]

Regardless of the justification that a newspaper is a commodity and a news organisation a capitalist enterprise, the omission of certain news stories about regions and spaces amounts to what Gerbner (1972) terms symbolic annihilation. He writes, 'Representation . . . signifies social existence; absence means symbolic annihilation (p. 44).[26]

When asked about these issues, the most articulate response was from DD, a Gannavaram stringer:

> Journalism is a field that excels at maintaining double standards. The profession is about fighting in democratic spirit against social evils. But this field is rampant with 'caste feeling'. To survive in this profession, we have to shut our senses and do what is required. Had I not followed this principle, I would not have been able to continue in this profession for close to three decades.
>
> (Personal communication, DD, 11 May 2012, Gannavaram)

An aspect he did not mention was his own stagnation in the lowest rank of the field for more than two decades, at the time of research. In order to present the dynamics and struggles between agents in the field, I present a visual representation (Graph 4.1) amalgamating the various hierarchies in operation. The issue of relegation becomes evident.

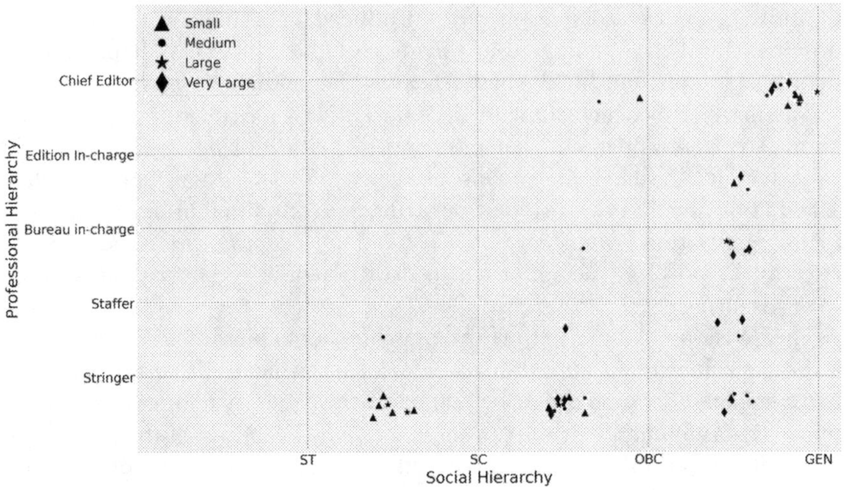

Graph 4.1 Social, professional and newspaper hierarchies in the field (Relegation)
Source: Author.

Scheme: On the *Y*-axis, the professional hierarchy of the agents is taken, which comprises the rank of the agent, along with experience in the field. On the *X*-axis, social hierarchy is taken, which comprises the social identity of the agent along with education. Triangle, circle, star and diamond shape-points represent small-scale, medium-scale, large-scale and very large-scale newspapers, respectively. Some values are very close to each other and overlap as the agents share commonalities in the parameters considered in this particular representation. In addition to the journalistic agents, whose profiles were dealt with in Chapter 3, I included editors-in-chief and chief editors of Telugu newspapers in this biplot to present a broader picture of the field.

Analysis: Agents belonging to Scheduled Tribe category are completely absent in the field at both Gannavaram and Sangareddy. There were no persons from the SC and OBC communities working in the editorial sections of newspapers. Even outside of the sample of profiles I collected as part of the research, senior and old-timer journalists expressed that SCs and OBCs were absent at that level in mainstream Telugu dailies. Agents from these communities occupying the positions of staffer/reporter and bureau/rural in-charge were also fewer compared to the general category (Sat-shudra and Savarna) and most of them relegated to the position of stringers. Agents belonging to the general category are seen spread across all professional positions in the field. The precedence of agents from the general category to emulate is lacking for persons from marginal communities. Needless to add, it becomes more difficult for them to climb up the professional ladder compared to general category agents. This is a clear case of possession of 'social capital', in the form of a professional network within the field.

Hierarchies of newspapers and ownership patterns

Often hailed as vehicles for enlightenment and as heralds of change in hagiographic descriptions of them, newspapers have hierarchies of their own. The ranks are usually based on market logics (readership, availability and circulation), the sheer volume of the newspaper (the number of pages and special editions or pull-outs) and political affiliations.[27]

The reproduction of the social order in the journalistic field becomes obvious when one looks at newspapers categorised by the public on the basis of caste and region, at least in the Telugu-speaking states. As part of a semi-structured interview, I carried out in Sangareddy, the lone Dalit bureau in-charge in Medak district gave an overview of the hierarchies in newspapers as follows:

> There is a visible hierarchy among newspapers in terms of circulation and political affiliation. Similar to that of caste in society, which is discriminatory in nature, there is a distinction of small or big newspapers in the field. Along with that, affiliation of a newspaper to the ruling party or opposition or politicians is an important factor in this profession.
>
> (1 October 2014, MPR, Sangareddy)

The conflation of caste, class and political orders was evident in the description and without recognising this, it is not possible to understand journalistic practices. Along with the local elites, even bureaucrats and locals refer to newspapers as *cinna patrika* or *pedda patrika* (small or big newspapers) based on their circulation. What was missing in the description was the regional aspect of the newspapers. At the peak of the Telangana movement, media houses were divided along lines of regional identity.

Even the state (governing body) classified news dailies on the basis of circulation, which is essential for two purposes: a) deciding on government advertisement rates; b) allotment of accreditation cards to working journalists. This classification holds good for both states, as the logic of classification is as per the recommendation by the Registrar of Newspapers of India (GoAP, 2006; GoT, 2016). As per the classification, 'Big Daily means Newspaper having circulation above 75,000 per day; Medium Daily means Newspaper having circulation between 25,001 to 75,000 copies per day; Small Daily means the Newspaper having a circulation up to 25,000 copies per day' (GoT, 2016, p. 2) [Uppercases retained as in the original].

Newspaper ownership details

Table 4.2 Newspaper ownership details

Newspaper (Year of establishment)	*Owner/promoter/ director*	*Caste*	*Political affiliation*	*Other business interests*	*Region(s)*
Eenadu (1974)	C. Ramoji Rao	Kamma (*Sat-shudra*)	TDP	Finance, hospitality, food process units, media, film city, shipping, school education	AP & Telangana, Delhi, Mumbai, Bengaluru, Chennai
Sakshi (2008)	Y.S. Bharati	Reddy (Sat-shudra)	YSR Congress	Cement, real estate, power, infrastructure and media	AP & Telangana, Delhi, Mumbai, Bengaluru, Chennai
Andhra Jyothi (1945; relaunched 2002)	Vemuri Radha Krishna	Kamma (Sat-shudra)	TDP	Power project, real estate, media	AP & Telangana, Bengaluru, Chennai
Vaartha (1996)	Girish Kumar Sanghi	Vysya (Savarna)	BJP; former Congress	Textiles	AP & Telangana
Andhra Prabha (1938)	Mootha Gopalakrishna	Vysya (Savarna)	Janasena (Present); Former Congress, former TDP	Infrastructure, oil field services, logistics, sewing threads, media services	AP & Telangana
Andhra Bhoomi (1960)	Deccan Chronicle Holdings Ltd.	Reddy (Sat-shudra)	Former Congress	Not available	AP & Telangana
Surya	N. Surya Prakasa Rao	Koppula Velama (OBC)	Former TDP, former Congress	Infrastructure, housing, film Production	AP & Telangana
Namaste Telangana (2011)	D. Damodar Rao	Velama (Sat-shudra)	TRS	Broadcasting and marketing	Telangana
Prabhata Velugu (2018)	Dr. G. Vivek VIL Media Pvt. Ltd	Mala (Dalit)	BJP; Former Congress; former TRS.	Manufacturing, investment, finance	Telangana
Prajasakti (1981)	CPI collective	–	CPI	Publishing	AP
Nava Telangana (2015)	CPI collective	–	CPI	Publishing	Telangana
Visalaandhra (1952)	CPI(M) collective	–	CPI (M)	Publishing	AP
Mana Telangana (2015)	CPI (M) collective	–	CPI (M)	Publishing	Telangana

Source: Shaw (2017); Damodaran (2008); Jeffrey (2010); Murthy (2003); Venugopal (2009, 2011); Simhadri (2017); APSEC (2006).

For the purpose of the present study, I classified newspapers following three aspects: (1) the number of pages dedicated to local news (some newspapers had two pages, while others had one or half a page; yet others did not have a dedicated page for *mandal*-level content); (2) the number of publishing centres or edition centres (this aspect covers the scale of newspaper); (3) the standing of the parliamentary political party to which a newspaper is affiliated. These are tabulated in order along with relevant details in Table 4.2.

The details presented in Table 4.2 serve as overtures in ascertaining the 'institutional habitus' of the media organisations or the varying capacities of the media firms in converting journalistic capital (a subset of cultural capital) into social and economic capital and vice-versa.

How is the hierarchy of a newspaper related to news production or what effect does the scale of newspaper (*cinna* [small] or *pedda* [big]) have on the newswork of a stringer? One oft-heard piece of advice to rookie reporters from seniors is: 'News stories do not land at your doorstep. You have to chase them'. But in the case of stringers or reporters working in very large and large newspapers, news stories did land at their doorstep – 'the-come-and-give-your-news principle' – in mofussil areas (Ninan, 2007, p. 119). Even if they missed a development or some interesting story of the day in the immediate locality, stringers working in smaller newspapers often brought the issue to the notice of the stringer working in the big dailies.

This seemed to be mutually beneficial for them, as the *cinna patrika* (small newspaper) stringer's story gained acceptance and legitimacy when a *pedda patrika* (big newspaper) stringer filed the same story with minor changes. On the face of it, this appeared to be working in favour of the *pedda patrika* stringers. But this phase appeared to be ephemeral and would not work in the longer run, unless he did not do his legwork, as there was a danger of losing his job to the same stringer who earlier was helping him.

Working in a *pedda patrika* could have its own negative impact as the stringers are perennially under the watchful eyes of locals, government officials, political leaders and the public. A single wrongdoing results in the loss of the job. Also, locals who own the newspaper thinking that it is their community or caste person's newspaper immediately reach out to the headquarters and complain about the stringer if he does not report in their favour or does not agree to report in a manner that appeases them.

There were some benefits for stringers working in *cinna patrikas* too. News items related to charity, social service and garlanding of statues of eminent persons on their birth and death anniversaries among others, which appeared in the news-briefs column or single column in *pedda patrika* had chances of finding a three-four column space along with photographs in the case of a *cinna patrika*. Despite their smaller readership and visibility, paper cuttings from these small newspapers had their own afterlives, as the donors or local politicos who took part in such programmes were seen displaying those news items in their offices.[28] They seemed to have a shelf life even in the digital age.

Cultural and social aspects along with the dominant political economy indicators determine the ownership patterns of Telugu newspapers. Bourdieu (1998, p. 39) writes:

> Journalism is a microcosm with its own laws, defined both by its position in the world at large and by the attractions and repulsions to which it is subject from other such microcosms. *To say that it is independent or autonomous, that it has its own laws, is to say that what happens in it cannot be understood by looking only at external factors. That is why I did not want to explain what happens in journalism as a function of economic factors.*
>
> [emphasis mine]

The majority of the newspapers are owned by persons belonging to Satshudra category (5), followed by Vysyas (Savarna category; 2). Persons belonging to SC and OBC communities own one newspaper each.[29] The leftist newspapers did not have any specific caste affiliations. There was only one woman running a mainstream Telugu newspaper.

Having considered the dispositions of the agents, the positions they occupied in the journalistic field and the official and unofficial rules of the game, of which certain agents are sometimes forcefully made aware, along with the relations between agents at various levels, there seems to be a visible correlation between the journalistic practices within the field and the social order, 'which is based on the principle of graded inequality' (Ambedkar, 1935/2014, p. 101).

Already privileged agents occupy higher positions in the field and taking it for granted as if it were 'natural' in an overt manner and further indulge in symbolic violence under the garb of ethical and moral concerns. With graded inequalities reproduced, the inscription of social order on the journalistic field is clearly visible as bold letters of the banner item's headline in newspapers.

For the sake of analysis, I laid out the structures, which in reality operate in a latent manner. This is similar to the aspect of relegation which the agents feel is *natural* and forms the unwritten *rules of the game* (doxa). In this chapter, I have attempted a mapping of the relations between the dispositions and professional roles of agents that delineate the relationship between habitus, forms of capital and the field.

One might be led to believe that this is a static hierarchy with little scope for manoeuvre. Journalistic roles and hierarchies are not located in the field like the interior of the largest matryoshka doll, which symbolises a hierarchy of order of magnitude, where each doll contains smaller ones. Agents in each role function in a dynamic way with other agents and forces that influence the journalistic field.

As much as agents internalise the externalities, they externalise their own internalities in a way that the spatial relationship between the dispositions and conversions of capital, from one form to the other, is dynamic as opposed to visibly top-down functional hierarchies and vertical social hierarchies. Capturing this simultaneity is essential to understanding the crux of the logic of local journalistic practice, dealt with in the following chapter. While explaining the logic of practice in the field, I present the repertoire of stringers and agents in the field by taking into account both journalistic and non-journalistic work.

Notes

1 Credit line specifies the location of the news item and at the same time confers the monetary and authorship credit to the stringer/reporter. Based on the length of the report and photograph used, a corresponding amount of money is credited to the stringer's account based on this credit line.

2 At a theoretical level, it is possible to see the political in all the aforementioned incidents on the lines of disability (marginalised), bureaucratic misadministration (politics of efficiency/inefficiency), and gender discrimination (abandonment of *female* infant), respectively.

3 One district edition in-charge likened this policy to that of public sector banks and insurance companies in which employees are transferred from one location to the other or at least from one branch to the other on a regular basis to avoid fraudulent activities while issuing loans or clearing claims (VS, personal communication, Vijayawada, 23 September 2012).

4 The editor in-charge of a leading Telugu daily, CBRP, informed me that they encountered such a problem in 2008, when almost the entire reporting staff, including stringers and a majority of editorial staff resigned *en masse* and joined a newly launched newspaper. He said that with a bare minimum workforce, they continued to bring out the district edition till they recruited new staff, with most of the editing and page layout work done at the headquarters located in Hyderabad till then (CBRP, personal communication, 17 September 2012).

5 This holds true for most English daily reporters working in mofussil areas too. For instance, two such reporters working for separate English national dailies converted a room in their home into their office or workspace.

6 The editorial staffers in Vijayawada during my fieldwork make themselves feel at home by eating at their workplace and sharing food. They have their own sets of friends within the same office with whom they have tea or smoking breaks.

7 These queries were confirmed by desk and reporting in-charges while explaining about their nature of work during the interactions and interviews.

8 They hinted those non-monetary benefits could include getting a licence for fair price shops, concessions or discounts from small-time businessmen, gaining political benefits and so on.

9 At the time of research, only the mobile number was given. Soon, most newspapers provided contact information on WhatsApp, which also served as a platform for locals to send photographs and video clips about the civic issues they face in their localities.

10 These expressions were in English during the interactions and recorded interviews in both states.
11 In the cases of Medak and Sangareddy, a call from the Hyderabad office often rattles stringers and reporters alike. A call from head office always means emergency work or something of top priority. This is the same with English dailies where I worked.
12 Non-journalistic interactions and exchanges will be discussed in the following chapter.
13 Comparing the hierarchies in the work cultures of English and Hindi dailies in Lucknow, Ursula Rao (2013, p. 33) notes that 'the flat hierarchies and substantial independence for journalists in the English press contrasts against the elaborate hierarchies and networks of patronage in the Hindi-language organisations'.
14 Even state government intelligence department constables or inspectors cross-check the veracity of their own pieces of information with those of the stringers before filing daily reports in Gannavaram and Sangareddy. These intelligence department persons were required to cover three to five *mandals* each, unlike a stringer who at the maximum covers two *mandals* or two newspapers. In the case of Gannavaram, the intelligence officers were more concerned with the political developments and movements of the Opposition leaders, while priority was given to Maoist and communal issues in the case of Sangareddy. More importantly, any press releases (handwritten) by banned Maoist organisations and their allied front organisations are duly passed on to bureau in-charges or sometimes sent directly to the head office in Hyderabad instead of filing from local datelines to avoid trouble from the local police.
15 The headline for the story filed by PSR was: *Bangāru Telangāṇa anṭe.. raitula balavanmaraṇālenā..?* (Does golden Telangana mean farmers' suicide?). The headline for the editorial was: *Raitu atmahatyalu . . . parishkāram ekkaḍa?* (Farmer suicides . . . where's the solution?).
16 For reports on the farmers' suicides issue in English dailies and websites, see: www.thehindubusinessline.com/news/national/farmers-tribe-to-knock-nhrc-doors-with-more-data-on-suicides/article23155909.ece; www.newindianexpress.com/states/telangana/2014/nov/26/2014-686838.html; www.thenewsminute.com/telanganas/177. Here, I am not suggesting that these reports were 'picked up' from Telugu dailies or stringer reports.
17 This aspect of stringer's role being 'invisibilised' is akin to Bourdieu's commentary on the gay and lesbian movement (Bourdieu, 2001, p. 119).
18 In temples, *tīrtham* (holy water) is offered to devotees in a conch or shell which is placed at the idol's feet in the *sanctum sanctorum*, considered auspicious by the Hindus. This is a Brahmanical expression often used in political, bureaucratic and journalistic circles to refer to either consecration or to mean 'from the horse's mouth'.
19 Even the handbooks written for the benefit of stringers prescribe a second fiddle role in relation to reporters (Chakradhar, 2011, pp. 19–21).
20 Once the battery of stringers returned from the airport to the usual media point to file stories, ANR (controlling his laughter) told PCB, '*ērā cinnā, Gannavaram grāmīṇa vilēkharigā unṭū front page story rāsi dillinē upeddāmanukunnavā? Anta scene ledurā*' (What champ, being a Gannavaram rural reporter do you want to rock Delhi by filing a sensational story on the front page in the main edition? We do not stand a chance). This mocking went on till PCB left for the day [Field notes, 30 April 2012, Gannavaram].
21 While presenting the 'working hierarchies' in Hindi-language journalism, Ursula Rao (2013) suggests, 'Three principles govern relationships at *Hindustan* and *Dainik Jagran*: 1) formal and informal designations 2) performance 3) seniority'

(p. 31). The last two principles are obvious. However, by formal and informal designations in the organisations, she means those who have rank and file and those who do not.

22 Based on her survey in the Hindi heartland, Ninan (2007, p. 121) notes:

> When stringers did the reporting themselves, many complexities coloured their output. How well he reported had to do with whether or not he also collected advertising, what his caste and professional background was, why he had come into the profession and how much gumption he had as an individual.

23 This is a loaded and discriminatory expression in the Krishna delta version of Telugu. The expression suggests that it is the end of him if he does not accomplish the task.

24 As mentioned earlier, often editorial and reporting staffers were in denial of caste. Even when some of them talk about it, they mention that it exists in other organisations but not in theirs.

25 Some newspapers in both regions give strict instructions to stringers not to report on issues in certain villages and areas for various reasons.

26 Tuchman (2000) furthers this argument in her essay on women's representation in the mass media in the US context.

27 The phenomenon of newspapers aligning with a political party existed since India became independent and has a well-documented history that begins during the struggle for freedom. In independent India, the issue of political party ownership was discussed in the First Press Commission report (GoI, 1954, pp. 265–312). A staunch Nehruvian, Chalapathi Rau expressed his concerns about the same, when he noted:

> The Congress with twenty-nine newspapers commands only a circulation of 27,483, the Communist Party with twenty-five newspapers commands a circulation of 82,920 and the Socialist Party has a few newspapers with little circulation.
>
> (Rau, 1965, p. 71)

28 One budding politician from Fasalwadi area of Sangareddy has a well-documented archive of paper clippings about his participation in political events from 2001 (the year of the establishment of the TRS). Some big newspaper clippings rest on his office desk between a royal blue *makhmal* (velvet) cloth and broken-but-fixed transparent glass.

29 *Prabhata Velugu*, owned by Dr G. Vivek Venkatswamy, was established on 5 October 2018 and was not operational during my fieldwork. It is included in order to not miss out on a crucial detail about emerging ownership patterns in the Telugu newspaper industry.

References

Ambedkar, B. R. (1935/2014). The Hindu and his belief in caste. In Moon, V. (Ed.), *Dr. Babasaheb Ambedkar writings and speeches* (Vol. 5, pp. 100–102). Bombay: Education Department, Government of Maharashtra.

APSEC [Andhra Pradesh State Election Commission]. (2006). *PROFORMA-VI(B) – Declaration of election results for ZPTCs in West Godavari, Andhra Pradesh*. Retrieved from: www.apsec.gov.in/ELECTIONRESULTS/ZP%20ELECTED%20RESULTS%202006/West%20Godavari.pdf.

Bourdieu, P. (1993). *The field of cultural production: Essays on art and literature*. New York: Columbia University Press.
Bourdieu, P. (1998). *On television* (Tr. by Priscilla Parkhurst Feguson). New York: The New Press.
Bourdieu, P. (2000). *Pascalian meditations*. Stanford: Stanford University Press.
Bourdieu, P. (2001). *Masculine domination*. London: Polity Press.
Chakradhar, G. (2011). *Vilēkhari – vyatitva vikāsam* (Journalist – personality development). Hyderabad: Press Academy of Andhra Pradesh.
Damodaran, H. (2008). *India's new capitalists: Caste, business, and industry in a modern nation*. New York: Palgrave Macmillan.
Gerbner, G. (1972). Violence and television drama: Trends and symbolic functions. In Comstock, G. A. and Rubenstein, E. (Eds.), *Television and social behaviour, vol. 1: Content and control* (pp. 28–187). Retrieved from: https://web.asc.upenn.edu/gerbner/Asset.aspx?assetID=2584.
GoAP. (2006). *Government order No. 96: State and district level press accreditation committees and media accreditation rules, 2005*. Hyderabad: Information and Public Relations Department. Retrieved from: http://ipr.ap.nic.in/New_Links/G.O.Ms.pdf.
GoI. (1954). *Report of the first press commission (Part – 1)*. New Delhi: Government of India Press.
GoT. (2016). *Government order No. 239: Telangana media accreditation rules, 2016*. Hyderabad: Information and Public Relations Department. Retrieved from: https://ipr.telangana.gov.in/GOMSNO-239.pdf.
Jeffrey, R. ([2000]2010). *India's newspaper revolution: Capitalism, politics, and the Indian-language press*. New Delhi: Oxford University Press.
Murthy, R. (2003). *Rural reporting in India*. Hyderabad: Prajasakti Book House.
Ninan, S. (2007). *Headlines from the heartland: Reinventing the Hindi public sphere*. New Delhi: Sage.
Rammohanarao, N. (2011). *Telugu patrikala bhāṣa* (language of newspapers). Hyderabad: Press Academy of Andhra Pradesh.
Rao, S. and Malik, K. K. (2018). Conversing ethics in India's news media. *Journalism Practice*, pp. 1–15. DOI:10.1080/17512786.2018.1491321.
Rao, U. (2013). *News as culture: Journalistic practices and the remaking of Indian leadership traditions*. New York: Berghahn Books.
Rao, V. H. (2011). *Grāmiṇa vilēkharulu – vārtā vanarulu* (rural reporters – news sources). Hyderabad: Press Academy of Andhra Pradesh.
Rau, M. C. (1965). *Fragments of a revolution: Essays on Indian problems*. London: Pergamon Press.
Reddy, C. V. N. (2011). *Prabhutvam – patrikalu* (State – newspapers). Hyderabad: Press Academy of Andhra Pradesh.
Shaw, P. (2017). Who wants own Telugu news channels? *The Hoot*. Retrieved from: http://asu.thehoot.org/media-watch/media-business/who-wants-to-own-telugu-news-channels-10046.
Simhadri, S. (2017). *Kulam nīḍalō abhivṛddhi rājakīyālu* (Development politics in the shadow of caste). Hyderabad: Bhumi Book Trust.

Tuchman, G. (2000). The symbolic annihilation of women by the mass media. In Crothers, L. and Lockhart, C. (Eds.), *Culture and politics*. New York: Palgrave Macmillan.

Venugopal, N. (2009). *Media nāḍi* (Pulse of Telugu media). Vizianagaram: SK Publications.

Venugopal, N. (2011). *Media scan*. Viziaanagaram: SK Publications.

Wacquant, L. J. D. (1989). Towards a reflexive sociology: A workshop with Pierre Bourdieu. *Sociological Theory*, 7(1), pp. 26–63. DOI:10.2307/202061.

5

NEVER THE *SŪTRADHĀR*?

The logic of local journalistic practice

> *Mēmu e ātalō pātradhārulamē kāni sūtradhārulu kāmu* (We are mere role-players in this play, not the narrators or showmen).
>
> – Sangareddy stringer, MAK & Gannavaram stringer, CVR

Having considered the roles, multiples hierarchies and structures which consistently reproduce graded inequalities, this chapter attempts to answer two questions: (a) how do these men, located on the margins of the field, operate? (b) What are their strategies to work around these societal and organisational structures? It is only for the sake of developing an understanding, I make a distinction between journalistic and non-journalistic practices, which otherwise get blurred in the field. I present the journalistic practices to delineate the mode of local news production and then describe the repertoire of stringers and their pursuits to maximise their resources to unveil the counter-tendencies that operate in the field.

Events, newspaper logics and journalistic practices

The following events that took place during my fieldwork present operational logics of newspapers and journalistic practices, influenced by political and social factors from within and outside the journalistic field.

Event 1: partisan bias and local reporting practices

Context: A meeting was organised by the district education officer (DEO) inviting all *mandal* education officers, teachers, teacher MLCs (Members of Legislative Council), teachers' union leaders and mediapersons for consultation purposes on the 'rationalisation' of government primary schools in the district on 30 September 2014 (Tuesday).

The DEO made an announcement about this meeting following the directive issued by the district collector. This meeting was held a week ahead of

 DOI: 10.4324/b23313-5

the scheduled day for public grievances, a regular monthly affair in the districts organised at the district collector's office in Sangareddy.[1]

> Only two stringers turned up for the meeting organised at 3 p.m. (post-lunch); one from *Namaste Telangana* and the other one from *Eenadu*. As we were having *chai* outside the office premises, an *Andhra Bhoomi* stringer joined us and took the details from the two stringers. Apart from the Sangareddy municipal council meetings in the morning (followed by lunch), there was nothing great for the day, the stringers felt.
>
> (Field notes, Sangareddy, 30 September 2014)

Barring one or two news dailies, every newspaper highlighted its political affiliation even in what was supposed to be a report on a consultation meeting held by an important official in the district. While *Eenadu* and *Namaste Telangana* reported the official version of the story,[2] The *Andhra Bhoomi* stringer merely mentioned that a review meeting happened on the issue.[3] Except for *Sakshi* and *Andhra Jyothi*, the rest carried the same content with a change of names of leaders and political parties opposing the initiative. While *Sakshi* mentioned that 'various teachers' unions and student bodies opposed the move', *Andhra Jyothi* carried a news item from Hyderabad stating that a 'former TDP MLC from Medak district met the education minister at Telangana Secretariat on Tuesday to discuss the matter'[4] [This particular leader joined the ruling party in a week's time].

Left-leaning dailies *Prajasakti* and *Visalaandhra* reported more or less the same content, opposing the move. However, while the former highlighted the Telangana State United Teachers' Federation leaders, affiliated to the CPI, the latter took the School Teachers' Federation of India and Student Federation of India (SFI), both affiliated to CPI (M), as the lead for the story.[5]

District leaders of the Telangana Tribal Students' Joint Action Committee (TTS-JAC) and Dalit-Bahujan Front (DBF) were prominently featured in *Surya* and *Vaartha*.[6] *Andhra Prabha* carried a report with a Hyderabad dateline quoting the ruling TRS party leader, Ramulu Naik, who, in the report, ensured that the interests of tribal students were the priority. Apart from that paragraph, the rest of the report remained more or less like the rest of the newspapers.[7]

In Telugu journalism, it is almost an accepted practice that news dailies often report of an event or development by giving a political hue that favours the political party to which they are affiliated to or support. Even in Gannavaram, often when there is a *dharna* (protest) or *rāstarōko* (road blockade) especially during the *Samaikhyandhra* movement (against the bifurcation of Andhra Pradesh) on the highways, stringers used to take photographs and quotes from leaders belonging to the political party their newspaper favours. Even readers are aware of these journalistic practices and political affiliations of newspapers.

But Event 1 raises a question which is of utmost importance in understanding local journalistic practices: why is it that even in the case of events or developments in remote places, the political and social affiliations or interests of the newspaper management are reflected? When asked about this, responses from stringers and editorial staffers were starkly different, if not diametrically opposite. Editorial staffers expressed that stringers do not have any sense of news and are often clueless about pitching the story in a 'publishable format'. Krishna district editorial staffer of a leading daily, GB, said:

> While editing local news stories, we (desk) do not tamper the details provided by stringers. Even cub reporters have this misconception [that editors are spin doctors]. We only give a news form to the information gathered by them. Many of them do not even know how to write the lead paragraph of a report or story.
>
> (Personal communication, 12 September 2012, Vijayawada)[8]

Stringers, on the other hand, pointed out that there is a constant pressure and insistence from editorial and reporting heads to give preference to certain people (communities or groups) and perspectives (ideologies). '*Em rāśina* story *āllaku naccina tīrlanē vastadi. Konni konnisārlu spotkiboi* report *jēshuḍu* waste' (No matter what we report, the story gets published as per the editor's wish. At times, it is a waste of time to do spot reporting), a Sangareddy stringer GG said (personal communication, 27 September 2014, Sangareddy).

Stringers at both sites of research stated that in case they questioned the changes made by the desk, they would have to face disciplinary action such as not carrying reports filed by them, purposely changing datelines of special stories (to Hyderabad or Vijayawada edition centres) so that they (stringers) do not get credit and also lose lineage for payments among others. More than monetary loss, stringers are concerned about the loss of credibility when either reports are not carried or changed datelines, which sometimes have other repercussions. Unlike in metros and cities, locals have direct access to stringers in mofussil areas and often question them the following day in case of any perceived misreporting or a report which is not published as promised by the stringer.

Event 2: stringer on a delegated task

Context: The management of one of the top leading Telugu dailies, owned by the influential Kamma caste (Sat-shudra), decided to come up with an advertorial supplement as part of the anniversary celebrations of the district edition. This coincided with the inauguration of a new office building and printing facility. For this purpose, they delegated the task of writing a '*manci*' (good) story on an old age home to the newspaper's Gannavaram rural stringer, who belongs to the Dalit community, in two days (Field notes, Gannavaram, 19 April 2012).[9]

> The following day, I accompanied the stringer to the old age home located in Telaprolu village by 9 A.M. The intention was to finish the task in one hour and proceed to Davajigudem, where a state government programme was scheduled to start at 10:30 am. However, the watchman denied us entry, even as the stringer showed his card. The stringer tried reaching the person whom he was supposed to meet and finally managed to enter. I was told to wait outside the building premises. He returned after interacting with the person(s) for more than half an hour. On our way to Davajigudem, he was explaining that it was about elderly couples whose children reside in the USA and this place is providing a comfortable stay for them, unlike in their villages, where they used to reside. It was also about the facilities provided in the old age home, emphasizing its proximity to Gannavaram airport.
>
> He did not see any story as he was of the 'opinion' that the role of newspaper is to highlight issues such as poverty and discrimination. More importantly, he pointed out that the elderly person was very rude towards him throughout the interaction and did not even let him see some parts of the premises, which he felt was discriminatory. The stringer recalled that he was treated in a better manner when he was working as a videographer before joining journalism. He told me that he was not going to file the story. [More than the younger lot, elderly persons in villages speak highly coarse and discriminatory language. Also, the locals, especially elderly, influential caste persons assess the caste of a person based on their looks.]
>
> (Field notes, 20 April 2012)

> The following day he got a dressing down by the management person as well as by the rural in-charge for not working on the advertorial item and missing out on a detail, considered very important by the editorial, in the press conference held by a local TDP leader. The newspaper management assigned the task to a trainee reporter from Ramavarappadu. The Gannavaram stringer was told to accompany the person and learn from him, as the trainee was a product of the in-house J-School.
>
> (Field notes, 22 and 24 April 2012)

During my interaction with this particular newspaper's editorial staffers in Vijayawada, I learnt that they are trying to cater to the 'tastes' of the Telugu diaspora in the United States. Apart from that, Gannavaram was experiencing a boom in real estate due to the separate state demand and some were trying to project Vijayawada as the capital of Andhra Pradesh, in anticipation of the state bifurcation.

The stringer's response to the entire episode, during my interview, was revealing. He said: '*Paper vāḷḷadi, endukanṭe* owner *vāḷḷōḍu kabaṭṭi. Kāni panicēsē mēmu maṭuku eppaṭiki bayaṭivāḷḷmē*' (They (influential castes) feel the paper is theirs because the owner belongs to their caste. But people working in the newspaper are always considered outsiders by them) [personal interview, 24 May 2012, Gannavaram].

The stringer clearly communicated his thought that people from his own community (Dalit, Madiga) were *relegated* not just in the social order but also in the profession, which could be seen as an experience of symbolic violence. However, the stringer learnt about various types of articles in newspapers from the trainee, who explained to the stringer the differences between news reports, spot news, features, conference reports, and advertorials, among others.

Some staffers in Sangareddy and Gannavaram delegate tasks or duties to stringers in such a manner that their reputation ('image', in stringers' parlance) remains intact, while the latter bear the brunt. If the cultural literacy of agents makes one realise the rules of the game, the work of this sort of *conditioning* by the hierarchical structures in the field on their habitus seems to make them believe that it is indeed their position in the field, as if there were no other options.

Event 3: symbolic annihilation

Context: 'Ambedkar's statue was demolished by someone. Go to our spot (villagers' rest house) directly. Our people are there', ARP stopped me on the highway near his *dhaba* and broke the news. By the time I reached there, the regular set of stringers had already assembled there along with some elderly locals who were busy talking about the incident and politics in Andhra Pradesh (Field notes, Gannavaram, 9 May 2012).

The statue was located at the centre of the Gannavaram village. The incident occurred as part of a series of cases in which Ambedkar statues were desecrated, starting in the month of January 2012. Members of a fact-finding committee visited Amalapuram of East Godavari district to probe into the 'politics fuelling the continued desecrations and the vested dominant caste interests protecting the accused' (Round Table India, 2012a, 2012b). The convenor of Dalit Stree Shakthi, G. Jhansi, who was part of the committee, stated that this could be due to the 'conflicts between Dalits and the Kapus that run as a constant undercurrent'.

She also said:

> Four statues were first desecrated in Amalapuram, and then another in Dhavaleswaram. The next one was in Medchal in Ranga Reddy district. Yes, it was not confirmed, only a finger was reportedly damaged. Then there was the Jalalpur incident in Nizamabad. The last known desecration was in Siddhantam in West Godavari district, where one finger and an ear were damaged.
>
> (Round Table India, 2012a)

Most stringers present at the reading room-cum-rest house in Gannavaram were aware of the desecration episodes. They tried to reach some politicians concerned but were unsuccessful. More importantly, they also were talking about the by-polls in both Andhra and Telangana regions of United Andhra Pradesh, scheduled in the month of June (Field notes, Gannavaram, 9 May 2012).

The following day, only two newspapers reported the incident. Following are translations of the full reports published in district tabloid editions. These two were the only ones to shed light on such an important issue at a crucial time in AP politics.

> *Tractor ḍhīkoni . . . dvamsamaina Ambedkar vigraham*
>
> (Ambedkar statue demolished in tractor collision)
>
> Gannavaram, Newsline, May 9: The Ambedkar statue installed at the road divider located near the Mandal Revenue Office was demolished after being hit by a hay-laden tractor on Wednesday, according to the locals. The statue was installed at the Gannavaram – Agiripalli roads and buildings highway about a year ago by local TDP leaders. At that time, they were not given any approval by the police and revenue officials.
>
> TDP leaders, SKMM Kalam among others, rushed to the spot soon after learning of the incident. They shifted the demolished statue within minutes fearing backlash from Dalit organisations. Local YSR Congress leaders demanded a police probe into the incident. However, police officials remained silent over the issue.[10]
>
> *Ambedkar vigraham kulcivēta*
>
> (Ambedkar statue vandalised)
>
> Gannavaram, Pra.Vi., May 9: Unidentified miscreants vandalised the Ambedkar statue located at the local revenue office in the early hours on Wednesday. Tension prevailed in Gannavaram village for a brief time due to this incident. Local political leaders reached the spot soon and shifted the debris of the statue to the villagers' reading room nearby, according to locals. Dalit community leaders demanded action against the miscreants. No case has been registered.[11]

The words 'observer', 'chronicle', 'mirror', 'express' and 'times' are often associated with reputed dailies and tabloids to reflect the character of the medium. This seems to be a case where the primary purpose of a newspaper, which is to report, took the backseat. Anyone who wishes to do a media construction of an important issue such as the desecration of Ambedkar's statues in 2012 may not be able to find sufficient material related to this incident in the daily newspapers. However, some stringers sent their reports to Dalit periodicals published from Vijayawada and Guntur, respectively.[12]

While NMR and KP sent their reports to Dalit magazines, another experienced stringer, DD, then vice-president of local chapter of the Union of Working Journalists, sent the report to *Krishna Zilla Journalist*, a bi-monthly magazine run by the union (Field notes, 15 May 2012 and 18 May 2012). Apart from belonging to Dalit Christian backgrounds, some common factors with these three stringers were their exposure to wider journalistic field that helped in circumventing the rigid organisational structure, grit to report the event that concerns the community to which they belong and the penchant for documenting and archiving information, something they have picked up while on the job as stringers for years, about an extremely sensitive issue.[13]

It was difficult to ascertain the reason behind the omission of this report filed by the stringers. Most of them even gave written copies to RTC bus drivers or faxed the items. The irrefutable presence of casteism in the news production process, which consciously or unconsciously favoured 'trivial' news items while even a 'bare mention' of an attack on the icon of a marginalised community was denied 'space', is evident.

Those who vandalised the statue for political reasons must have had a problem with the statue being located at the centre of the town/*mandal* and desecrated it to make a caste-supremacist, non-verbal statement that the icon belongs to labour colonies or SC colonies or simply put in the *velivada* (Dalit ghetto), a socio-spatial zone of relegation (Wacquant, 2008, pp. 243–247).

The omission of the filed news report was a message to Dalit-Bahujan stringers to 'teach' them the hard way that the newspaper medium was not theirs. As Gerbner (1972) suggests, omission means symbolic annihilation; in this case, it happened to be reportage on desecration of the statue of an icon. Is it a case of editorial judgement or caste-bias from the editorial desk or management? How do stringers negotiate or resist such highhandedness on the part of the editorial or reporting staffers working from the district edition centre offices?

The three events discussed present the scope and intensity of the channels of domination in the journalistic field. They suggest that the aspects of caste, class, gender, region and ability, usually seen as markers of an individual's identity, appeared to be the modes and channels through which power operates in relationships between the dominant and the dominated. However, this only presents a partial portrait of the complex field of stringers.

If the tendency in the journalistic field is to *relegate* agents based on their dispositions and possession of various forms of capital, does it make stringers disenfranchised and left with no option but to continue carrying out faceless and unpaid newswork in a perennially hopeless state?

The 'field out there' presents stringers engaging in a complex array of practices through which they negotiate and moderate the internalised or *doxical* rules and norms with their willed actions. These practices seem to operate as a counter-tendency to the hierarchically organised social and professional relations through which stringers not only engage in everyday struggles to endure the power structures but also shape and tinker with them despite the limited material and non-material resources available to them. These tendencies and counter-tendencies operate in simultaneity in the field, which makes it difficult to divide structure and agency.

Closely linked to the issue of *relegation* is the aspect of *delegation*, which is 'the ability of the dominant to exist and to act at a distance through the agency of representatives, deputies and employees' (Bourdieu, 2018, p. 110). In a way, delegation is how agents occupying powerful positions (editorial and reporting heads) in the journalistic field get the 'dirty' or 'lowly' work done by those agents occupying fringe positions like stringers. Experiences in the field suggest that developing an understanding of structure and agency as mutually exclusive, neat categories is erroneous. The malleability of structures and ductility of agency is understood only when one looks at the inseparability of journalistic and non-journalistic work in the field which will be addressed while elaborating on the aspect of *delegation* and the conversion of capital in this chapter.

Journalistic capital, non-journalistic work and repertoire of stringers

In this section, I present how journalistic capital of stringers converts into economic capital or gets utilised in augmenting social capital, while providing details of their repertoire and descriptions of non-journalistic work. While relations of domination/discrimination could be witnessed in journalistic work, capillaries of affirmation and resistance, though in a limited manner, could be noticed in the non-journalistic work of stringers in the field.

Whether due to the acquisition of linguistic capital by way of working in newspapers for a long period of time or simply due to the accumulation of worldly wisdom needed to perform tactical manoeuvrings in their immediate locality of operation, stringers operate as 'mediators' between the government administration, local politicians and the local public.

There has been a considerable body of research in political science and public administration that seeks to understand the role of '*pyraveekars*' (fixers) and 'small-time political fixers', while focusing on rural institutions or the functioning of the state at the ground level (Reddy and Haragopal, 1985; Manor, 2000). Writing in the mid-1980s, Reddy and Haragopal (1985, p. 1149) noted:

> In rural India the gap between the administration and the people is filled by the 'middleman' or 'the fixer' – the *pyraveekar*, as he is familiarly called. It is a matter of common knowledge that the *pyraveekar* has come to play an important role in the public affairs of rural India.

They explain: '[T]he word *pyraveekar* was derived from the Persian word *pyrov*, which means follower or one who pursues, and *kar*, which refers to work. *Pyraveekar*, therefore, means one who follows up work' (p. 1149). Manor (2000, p. 187), while updating this understanding, pointed out:

> These people are middlemen (and nearly all are still male) who serve as crucial political intermediaries between the localities (*sic*) and powerful figures (bureaucrats and, especially, politicians) at higher levels. . . . They also provide critically important assistance to politicians, especially but not only at election time.

My ethnographic observations revealed that many stringers carried out tasks similar to the ones performed by the *pyraveekars* and small-time political fixers. The experienced ones, especially, seemed to have their own way of dealing with various groups by showering adages and proverbs, with liberal doses of wordplay, upon them, along with working for politicians as publicists. Based on these observations, I present some of the roles played by stringers while carrying out non-journalistic work.

The stringer as petty *pyraveekar*

The combined Medak district with its headquarters at Sangareddy before its administrative reorganisation was relatively large in area. For any official work in the district collectorate, the Sessions Court and with either the member of Legislative Assembly (MLA) or the member of Parliament (MP), most villagers and town dwellers in the erstwhile district had to visit Sangareddy. On the other hand, Gannavaram, the host *mandal* for the entire Assembly constituency, had visitors from nearby and remote *mandals* and villages to submit their grievances to the MLA or the Mandal Revenue Officer (MRO).

It was the stringers who facilitated meetings between the villagers and local officials or politicians. Generally, the grievances were about including their names in the list of beneficiaries of government schemes, applications for farmer loans and issues in their locality, among other works in panchayat and revenue offices. Given the lack of awareness about the administrative and bureaucratic functioning among the villagers and non-local town people, stringers function as mediators and bridge the gap between the public and officials.

Stringers have time and again proven to be the persons through whom to approach officials, especially as they know how to pursue the matter 'through the proper channel' or the 'formalities' and are aware of the 'paperwork/documentation' required. These were the common words and phrases used by stringers and the public in both Gannavaram and Sangareddy. There was a difference between the dictionary meaning of these phrases and words and the functional meanings they have acquired.

For government officials, a stringer, a known face, is a safe bet while for the public, he helps avoid bureaucratic red-tape. Stringers seemed to have acquired the know-how of the functioning of officials. For instance, they know when (it is time) to approach an official keeping the circumstances such as presence/absence of higher officials or vigilance officers or local elite who inform higher officials in case of any misdoings or malpractices in the office.

Whether in Sangareddy or Gannavaram, the scope of the *pyravee* (pursuit) was minimal, as for 'bigger' work, beneficiaries or parties concerned would have to go either to Hyderabad in the case of Sangareddy or Vijayawada or Machilipatnam in the case of Gannavaram in Krishna district. But the stringers were well aware of such networks and were part of a network of real *pyraveekars* (who called themselves 'social workers') in their respective areas.

Initially, stringers in Gannavaram would leave me behind when they went about these *pyravees*. After taking me into their circle of confidence, they started talking about this work. Stringers stated that they were only 'small fish' whereas the big fish were in Vijayawada (city) and Hyderabad (the then AP Secretariat) to whom they did not have much access. It was the same case in Sangareddy, with a slight modification in terminology. While Gannavaram stringers referred to this kind of work as *panchāyati* (settlement) or *dukāṇam pani* (shopping), Sangareddy stringers mentioned it as *cinna* issue or 'small settlement'.

Mostly, these petty *pyravees* included getting income and caste certificates, ration cards, *ex gratia* amounts (announced by governments) and registering names in government schemes. People approached stringers generally through known contacts from other parts of the districts and sometimes they were from among staffers of the newspaper establishments in which they worked. Usually, stringers did not take any cash from the individuals for doing these petty *pyravees* but did not mind if they offered to buy them some snacks and tea in the shops located outside these government offices.

In Gannavaram, there were verbose, melodramatic responses from stringers while rejecting any cash favour for the work they did, while in Sangareddy and most parts of Medak district, stringers' curt responses would generally be: 'Leave it. No need to give' [with gentle authority] or 'No need [to give anything]. Don't stay here after sunset. Head home'. These authoritative expressions are tough to translate into English and arise not only due to the favour they did for the individual(s) but also out of care.

The maximum amount that the stringers took from beneficiaries who received lump sums was in the hundreds (less than one thousand Indian rupees) and even this pittance varied from case to case. However, stringers would give a patient ear to individuals who visit MLAs, MPs, MROs, and District Collectors (especially during the meet-the-collector/MRO monthly calendar programmes), as they could turn out to be valuable resources to file district-level news reports on issues that local publics face.

The stringer as local political publicist or go-to guy

Despite the ubiquitous social media platforms and messaging services, one noticeable feature in villages and small towns (even in urban spaces) was the presence of flex posters and vinyl banners. There is a new banner in the market and other public places for every festival, local event and meeting and during visits of high-profile politicos. Stringers engaged in a range of activities as part of political campaigning for local leaders, such as helping in designing banners, photography, placement of the banners and writing and proofreading the content.

A majority of stringers give 'briefings' to local politicos and sometimes even write their speeches, in case of birth and death anniversaries of various iconic leaders, before they file a report on it for newspapers. Only local persons who hang around with newsmen and politicians are able to witness this 'ventriloquist act' by the stringers. Many stringers extended these services to local 'cable' television agencies, making advertisements for them during festivals. These abnormally loud broadcast advertisements would be inserted in commercial breaks in locally operated Telugu entertainment and film channels.

While the legislative and parliamentary constituency members or contestants usually got their publicity campaign material prepared in cities such as Hyderabad and Vijayawada, it was the second-rung leaders and 'youth wing' cadre of respective parties who approached stringers for assistance. When asked (informally) if they get any monetary gains from the publicity work, stringers in Medak said that they maintained a *khātā* (account) with local politicos, while Gannavaram stringers said that it was based on 'understanding'.

This local publicity was a collective activity for stringers, as some of them own photo/video studios, others were good at writing and proofreading and yet others know how to convince aspiring politicians as part of marketing strategy. Both in Gannavaram and in Sangareddy, stringers either worked in key positions or owned local cable TV franchises.

This was one area where the limited journalistic capital of stringers was visibly converted into economic capital and sometimes even added to their existing social capital. Despite the collective nature of this publicity work, some senior stringers acted as public relations personnel for local politicians. It was not only to local politicians or aspiring politicians that stringers suggested some publicity tips but also to the local elite (who wanted to gain some popularity by taking up some civic issue or doing charity work), trade union leaders, government, and aided schools' teachers, among others.

Occasionally, stringers offered advice on the 'timing' of protests by locals, politicos and trade union leaders. Stringers had knowledge about the times and venues of VIP visits on a particular day in nearby localities of importance, such as central and state government institutions and the airport and alerted people to stage a protest or *dharna* accordingly, to gain visibility. At the same time, stringers also cautioned these groups when not to protest. For instance, when the district police promulgated Section 30 of the Police Act, 1861, there would be a ban on public protests, gatherings, and political and religious rallies (Field notes, Sangareddy, 2 October 2014).

On the whole, while the conversion of journalistic capital into economic capital was explicit in this description of the non-journalistic work by stringers, implicitly, they added a considerable amount of social capital. The work helped them acquire relatively 'elevated statuses' as personae indispensable to certain sections of the population in their immediate surroundings. More importantly, this was the brighter side of the picture. They would face negative consequences from local politicians if they did not do a balanced walk, as sometimes stringers were sandwiched between their proximity to local leaders and the professional directives laid out by newspaper establishments or suggestions/orders from desk persons.

To avoid this dissonance, experienced stringers preferred to work in small or medium-scale newspapers where there was not much professional and institutional pressure and, at the same time, 'freedom' to engage in non-journalistic work using their professional identity.

For novice stringers, this was a tricky situation. While the bureau and rural in-charges along with desk staffers saw this non-journalistic work as obsequiousness on the part of stringers, not engaging in such work even after local politicians, government officials and elites insisted would lead them to be seen as headstrong. Often, local leaders complained to the head office about such non-cooperative stringers resulting in loss of jobs. The non-journalistic work was also noticeably precarious in nature, as more than three complaints against a stringer were good enough for the managements of leading dailies to fire them.

The stringer and the journalistic *illusio*

Playing this risky game in the journalistic field, characterised by unwritten and unstated rules, was one of the crucial factors in deciding the standing of the stringer among his peers. Understanding these rules entailed what Bourdieu (1990, p. 66) refers to as developing a 'feel for the game'. Often, it was lack of or poor understanding of these that made the job precarious.

Staffers who supported their managements pointed out that stringers continued to work in the field without fixed wages because they had their means of earning using their position and doing non-journalistic work in the villages and *mandals*. 'Stringers use their influence to avail government schemes and benefit from various facilities provided by the government to journalists such as housing schemes, basic health facilities and free travel passes', CBRP, the Krishna district bureau head of a Telugu daily, said (Vijayawada, 17 September 2012). He added that stringers often indulge in 'unethical practices', take money from politicians and live off small-time businesspersons. The majority of staffers in both districts offered similar reasons for stringers' engaging in these practices. There was a palpable discomfort on the faces of editorial and reporting heads when asked about the nature of the work of stringers during interviews. While referring to stringers, often from a moral pulpit, they used adjectives such as 'corrupt', 'immoral', 'unethical', 'illiterate' and 'third-class'.

But this rationale appeared to be based on economic aspects and overlooks the social positions stringers occupy and the cultural capital the job provides. Having considered the dispositions (belonging to lower social and economic strata) and the habitus of stringers in the journalistic field, working as a local newsman resulted in acquiring a considerable amount of cultural capital, which would not be possible otherwise. It seemed that stringers continued to carry on newswork and non-journalistic work for the following reasons: (a) to secure identity in their immediate surroundings; (b) to gain better recognition and access; (c) to augment existing social and cultural capital.

Stringers, wherever they went about in their *mandals*, were always greeted by the public and well-received by village officers, police and even politicians. They also freely walked into the houses of the local elites, inaccessible to the common public. The usual hierarchies among stringers based on their own habitus and the newspaper for which they worked mattered. Considering the social status of stringers vis-à-vis the local elite, entering the houses of the latter is still considered a 'privilege' in villages and small towns:

> After joining a newspaper, most stringers get a press identification card, which gives them access to many places. They also start brushing shoulders with politicians and businesspersons. Even a medical doctor or an engineer from any caste background does not enjoy

> this status in villages and *mandals*. We (stringers) get used to this after sometime and cannot imagine leading a normal life.
> (Sangareddy stringer, PR, Interview, 4 October 2014)

It was precisely why stringers in Gannavaram and Sangareddy expressed that journalism had become an intense obsession and their willingness to take part in the social games even if those games are unfair with unfavourable rules. Many of them after getting fired from a newspaper tried to get the same job in another newspaper as they could not quit the field/game. Some stringers even offered 'donations' to a fellow stringer to share the dateline.

Bourdieu's (1998, pp. 76–77) concept of *illusio* is 'the fact of being caught up in and by the game'. This 'journalistic *illusio*' (for the present purposes) along with the cultural capital associated with journalism provides a plausible explanation for why stringers continue in the precarious local journalistic field. Moreover, the disposition as a local reporter helped them consolidate and build various forms of capital and facilitate the conversion of one form of capital into the other.

The rationale for stringers to continue in the profession and the strategies they resort to in their everyday life will become more obvious if the existing practices in the field, in the form of rituals and unwritten codes, are considered. By discussing these aspects, the following section also provides nature of the journalistic field (heteronomous and thereby highly influenced by fields of power).

Decoding non-journalistic practices: codes, rituals and gift-exchanges

Telugu newspaper stringers meet with officials and local elites on most occasions over a cup of tea, one of the codes they follow in both fieldwork sites. The moment stringers enter any government office and reach an employee's desk, they are offered a seat and a cup of tea. This happens if both parties are on good terms. In case the officer or employee was not in a mood to interact, or livid with stringers for writing anything against him, tea was not served, indicating that they may leave.

Sometimes stringer(s) attempts to persuade the official that the article against a particular employee or the office was published without their knowledge and so on. But, on the whole, serving a cup of tea signified amicable terms between the two parties and vice versa. It was not only the tea but also a shared meal that had its own code and an embedded message, depending on the time of the meal. It also appeared that a meal was an intrinsic part of journalistic practices and news production in both AP and Telangana.

The gregarious nature of reporters makes it impossible to imagine them carrying a lunch or tiffin box with them. Almost every reporter is with her or his peers or at least in public places from the time they step outside their home to carry out newswork till they call it a day. This was the case with stringers in small-town spaces with the exception of alcohol, as drinking was considered *haram* before 'sunset'. But given the physical proximity to various agents from other fields in small towns, unlike in urban spaces, stringers had these socialising activities over breakfast (before work) and dinner (after work). Often, like the news-gathering process, these meetings were collective in nature and not on a one-on-one basis.

In their interactions, stringers revealed that they met a local politician or an influential person over breakfast either to discuss the plan to be executed, if any, or received 'feedback' on an article that is published on that particular day. I accompanied two stringers for a couple of *nāshta* (breakfast) meetings with second-rung political leaders at their residences in Sangareddy at the time of by-poll for a parliamentary constituency in August 2014. The local leaders gave the itinerary of political campaigning and 'briefed' the stringers about the issues to be highlighted to ensure media coverage.

Having a meal (breakfast, lunch and dinner) is part of the 'work culture' and an accepted code in both states at the time of fieldwork (Table 5.1). However, some local elites did not entertain them, as they had a 'direct link' with the bosses at edition centres or the head offices of newspapers, leaving stringers in a disgruntled state. While *nāshta* sessions happen occasionally in Telangana, breakfast meetings between stringers and parties concerned took place on a regular basis in AP. Lunch arrangements would take place between assignments in a coordinated fashion after talking to those who wished to meet stringers to discuss local matters, almost on a daily basis.

In case there were more than two persons or sets of people who wanted to meet a stringer or a group of stringers, they would politely ask the party

Table 5.1 Types of meal, code and actual practice

Type of meal	*AP Code*	*Actual practice*	*TS Code*	*Actual practice*
Breakfast	Tiffin (breakfast; vegetarian)*	Feedback session	*Nāshta* (breakfast; vegetarian and meat)	Agenda setting
Lunch	Meals	Working lunch	Lunch	Working lunch
Dinner	Dinner (vegetarian and meat)	Reciprocal or appreciative gesture as well as casual	*Dāwat* (feast; vegetarian and meat)	Reciprocal or appreciative gesture as well as casual

Source: Fieldwork

Note: *The word tiffin in coastal Andhra means breakfast on regular days and supper on Saturdays. Also, a majority of stringers in both states did not eat meat as a part of their meals on Saturdays and some avoided it on Thursdays for religious reasons.

to re-schedule the meeting to the following day or some other time. It is not the case that stringers would leech on individuals for lunches; rather, it is a basic courtesy and concern locals exhibit, possibly emerging from agrarian or semi-agrarian culture (no return favour was expected).

During my fieldwork, I observed stringers in both districts visit a government school at least once a month to check the implementation of the midday meal scheme and attendance (or absence) of teachers along with state-run social welfare hostels. It appeared that this ritual of visiting schools and hostels was one of the humane sides of stringers who sometimes even mildly intimidated the persons concerned saying that they would inform the *mandal* or district education officer of any lapses. Acts such as these, as a part of their everyday work, gave stringers a sense of moral authority and command over others.

Dinner was not a regular feature and seemed relatively exclusive. Only experienced stringers had the tact and skills to persuade local elites and politicians for a dinner meet. Though I did not attend such meetings, I was around when such events were being planned. They would casually begin a conversation by saying: 'Sir, how come you stopped taking care of us?'; 'Salute . . . how come brother [respectfully] you don't turn your head toward the poor [us]?)'. The manner in which they put across their interest made it difficult for the other person to respond negatively. Novices and relatively younger stringers are excluded from such meetings and the reason given by seniors was to the effect that the former did not know where to draw a line between liberty/familiarity and respect. Stringers had their own language, shared values, and customs, rituals, norms, and practices that constituted the rules of the journalistic game. Among stringers themselves, as much as the caste factor was reproduced in the organisational hierarchy, it was the knowledge of these unwritten rules that decided the inclusivity and exclusivity of certain social events with people from the creamy section of their locality.

Certain material and non-material exchanges in the world of local journalism were routine. Writing a favourable news item in order to procure an advertisement for the newspaper seemed to be a normal affair for stringers. Even the broad and general principles of classification of places and situations were based on favours either in cash or in kind. The intersection of religion, caste, power and ideology permeates the various codes and phrases that stringers frequently use.

For instance, stringers referred to attending a protest or press meet organised at local offices of the communist and other national parties as *śivālayam* (temple of God Siva), while in case of parties where influential caste persons (local leaders) were at the helm of party affairs, it was often called *rāmālayam* (temple of Hindu god Rama). Stringers, unlike in the case of dominant regional parties, did not receive any pecuniary gains for attending press meets organised by national parties. The analogy seemed appropriate from the perspective of stringers, as the *prasādam* (sacred food offered in temples) at the Shiva temple was *vibhūti* (holy ash, which is inedible) and *vaḍapappu* and *pānakam* (*Lens esculenta* soaked in water and a jaggery-based beverage laced with black pepper; both are delicacies) in the case of Rama temple on special occasions, and a variety of other rice-based items on normal days.

Such utterances, expressions and exchanges pointed out the influence of the dominant religious culture in turn had on the journalism practitioners at the sites of research. They also provide the specific logics of substantiating their own positions in the field (doxa).

At the time of fieldwork, I noticed that individuals (donors) placed their hands below while offering money to stringers and reporters and the latter would receive it from above. I observed this peculiar way of money offering in Gannavaram and Vijayawada. It recurred in Sangareddy on several occasions. The striking element of the transaction was the positions of the donor or giver and the receiver. The hand positions were not even on an equal plane but in a reversed manner to the 'normal' way of donor having the upper hand.

In effect, this appeared to be contrary to popular expressions in Telugu and Hindi languages, respectively: '*iccēvāḍidē paicēyi*' or '*denewale ka hāth upar hi rahtā hain*' (The donor's hand is always on top; an expression used in all major religions to promote the concept of charity or giving). Essentially, this meant that even while receiving, the journalists had the upper hand, indicating the prominence bestowed on their professional status.

The recreated graphic of placements of hands (Figure 5.1) captures the *bodily hexis*[14] of stringers and influential persons and more importantly, the dynamic conversions of social, economic and journalistic capital from one form to the other. There is little scope to celebrate the agency and social elevation they receive due to their professional identity, as their scope is minute and limited to a *mandal* unit in which they work in relation to owners of newspapers or even journalists in high-profile designations, platforms and in all possible kinds of spaces.

It is important to track this dynamic sense of the stringer both in his own mind and in the minds of those around him. The purpose and motive of a stringer's work was brilliantly described by a Gannavaram stringer, YSS who said: 'In this profession, completion of a task should give either job satisfaction or else *jēb* [pocket] should be satisfied)'. Another stringer belonging to a religious minority community in Sangareddy mentioned that he felt secure with a 'press ID card' and red uppercase 'PRESS' sticker on his bike.

Almost all bureau in-charges and editorial heads informed that they get the stringer into the groove by teaching them journalistic ethics and ideals in training programmes on a regular basis, which most of the time stringers skipped. A Gannavaram stringer, CVR said, 'They [journalist-instructors from Hyderabad] unnecessarily target us. Most of the big reporters polish

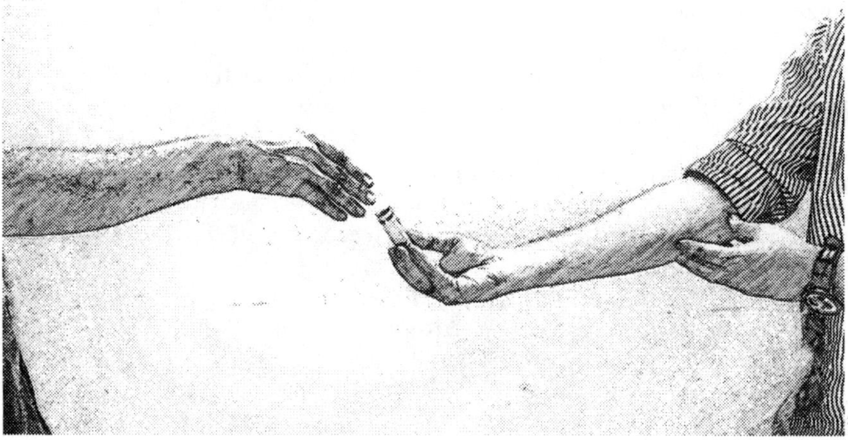

Figure 5.1 Illustration capturing the bodily hexis of a stringer (left) and donor (right) Caption: Journalistic capital or the donor's hand reversed

Source: Author.

off the meat in the food surreptitiously and put a garland of bones around our neck. We look like food-thieves in everyone's eyes' (personal communication, Gannavaram, 22 May 2012).

Another experienced stringer in Sangareddy used a similar food metaphor when he said, 'Newspaper owners and reporters swallow *rasgulla* [a juicy Bengali/Odia sweet] and go unnoticed. But we will be seen and heard chomping *murukku* [an inexpensive south Indian snack that crackles]. For the public, they are gentlemen and we are fraudsters' (1 October 2014). These metaphors by stringers allude to what Shaw (2017) notes about the crass-commercialisation of media industry in the Telugu-speaking states by indicating the multiple business interests of media owners.

Stringers expressed what they know and felt in their own language and terms. Neither the Press Council nor media educators from press academies understand ground realities when they talk about media ethics and norms during the training workshops.

In my ethnographic account of the stringers and the manner in which they employed journalism as a mode of subsistence by doing both journalistic and non-journalistic work, I was able to contextualise the lives of the stringers who blur the boundaries of what constitutes journalistic work. It appears that a field-based research component, with a specific focus on the cultural aspects of news production and media research on ethics, norms and practices would be fruitful in sharpening policy recommendations.

There is a case to be made to recognise the role of non-journalistic practices that take place on the ground if one were to ascertain the autonomous (of the lack of it) nature of media, which has considerable significance in a democratic setup.

Attention to the relations between agents within the journalistic field and also with agents from other fields of power allowed me to discuss the conversions of various forms of capital and how they feed into each other. The elaborations on codes, everyday rituals and patterns of gift exchanges provided an understanding of the nature of this journalistic field and its relations to the political, bureaucratic, and economic fields revealing its heteronomous character.

A Sangareddy stringer PR during my revisit to the field, invoked an agrarian metaphor when asked how he sustains this highly difficult role. He said, 'Our role is similar to that of a farmer, who does not know anything but to farm even if the crop fails' (5 January 2022). The Sangareddy stringer was stripped of the role in a top Telugu daily but managed to join another. His expression was uncannily similar to that of his counterpart in Gannavaram in the interview recorded on 12 May 2012. This metaphor also demonstrates how stringers get caught up in survival games in the field (*illusio*).

Conclusion: being stringer, never *sūtradhār*?

I have attempted to understand the logic of local journalistic practice based on the quotidian practices of stringers by discussing some of the many events that I came across during my fieldwork related to their journalistic and non-journalistic work. In doing so, I used some terms that emerged from the ground and were uttered by stringers and reporters in the field.

As mentioned in the epigraph of this chapter, one of the ways stringers understand their own work is by using dramaturgical terms, such as *pātradhārs* and *sūtradhārs*. When broken down, *pātra* means role; and *dhār* means to wear. *Pātradhār* means the one who gets into the character or role in a play/drama. On the other hand, *sūtra* or *sūtr* means principle or formula.

In theatre arts, the *sūtradhār* means the narrator or impresario of a play or simply someone who directs and comments on the action. There is a hierarchy associated with these two terms. *Sūtradhār* is usually privileged over *pātradhār*, as the former appears to hold the scheme of things in his hands and 'controls' the latter. Both these words are borrowed from Sanskrit and are widely used in the language written in Telugu newspapers, which indicates the Brahmanical influence on the field.

At the outset of the fieldwork, I realised the importance of the concept of 'journalistic capital' a stringer possessed and explained how it mattered for him to become *sūtradhār* from *pātradhār*. Considering various forms of capital agents possess or are in the process of accumulating, their dispositions and the relationships between agents occupying various positions and structures in operation within the field, it is possible to argue for a Brahmanical and Sat-shudra staffers and Dalit-Bahujan stringers pattern in Indian-language journalism.

By looking at the ownership patterns, which show that the majority of newspapers are concentrated in the hands of persons belonging to the dominant Sat-shudra category, and the journalistic practices that consistently reproduce graded inequality (Brahmanical version of social order), it is possible to frame an argument suggesting that there is a concurrence of *Sat-shudraisation of the media economy and Brahmanical media work culture* in the Telugu journalistic field, especially since the Green Revolution (Aloysius, 2010, p. 10; Washbrook, 1993, pp. 68–86; Bayly, 1999).[15]

The singular contribution of Sat-shudraisation appeared to be the breaking down of the previous rigid Brahmanical and Savarna order in the journalistic field, exemplified in some newspapers – *Andhra Patrika* and *Krishna Patrika* – in the form of an editor-publisher dual role, earlier held almost exclusively by the Telugu Brahmins. It democratised the entry into the field like never before, despite the discriminatory and casteist practices associated with it.

Even as the dichotomous proposition of Brahmanical and Sat-shudra staffers and Dalit-Bahujan stringers appears to be valid if one were to do a demographic survey of Telugu language journalists, stringers and editors across the Telugu-speaking states, it will not help in understanding *how* stringers continue to work in such highly exploitative, oppressive conditions in which they are subjected to symbolic and structural violence.

Some of the ways in which stringers from Dalit and OBC backgrounds take control of the situation were presented in the earliest description of the role played by YSS in the Gannavaram village assembly. Over a period of time, stringers develop a solid idea about 'editorial preferences' and push their stories in such a manner that they appeal to 'editorial sensibilities'.

Even stringers who remarked that they were mere role-players knew well how to position themselves in the field in such a manner that they became *sūtradhārs* instead of the desk person or rural in-charge. The crucial factor of experience in the field was realised to a great extent by senior stringers in Sangareddy and Gannavaram. Even as they work in small and medium-sized newspapers, they implant stories (for public good or personal gain or both) in big dailies by befriending stringers working in them.[16]

Even in the case of the editorial blunder made by their newspapers by omitting reports on the Ambedkar statue desecration incident, stringers with experience (MNR, KP and DD) 'successfully' managed to push their stories in different magazines and made their voices heard and even documented, a way of negotiating with issues related to social hierarchy and editorial staffers in the field. This tussle between being a *pātradhār* to becoming a *sūtradhār* could also be understood as a result of journalistic capital, a form of social capital, acquired by these stringers over a period of time.

Unlike the textual narratives woven by Savarna journalists in their own autobiographies or biographies of legendary editors about their 'uncompromising attitude' with the newspaper management, 'fearlessness in bringing truth to light' and 'adverse situations' they faced in the process, the reality appeared to be as journalist and editor Murthy (2003, p. 106) pointed out in his research work: 'Management or chairman of the board of directors are placed at the top of the organisational hierarchy'. This is an undeniable fact.

Just like a press card bestows social capital upon stringers in their *mandals* and small towns, running a media organisation helps in converting and consolidating (in some cases) economic capital into cultural and social capital for the owners. It gives them a passport to enter politics and helps push their economic interests, allowing them to accumulate more economic capital in order to gain social standing.

As much as the newspaper organisations set the agenda for news coverage (agenda-setting) keeping their own business interests and political affiliations, stringers too have their own ways of doing so at the level of local news production. If the journalistic field functions as a game with certain routines, rules and norms implicitly described but imposed by the management and editorial departments, then the logic of local journalistic practice suggests that playing the same game involves transforming, mending and manoeuvring those rules and norms. Stringers do that well, ensuring that they much more than merely survive at the bottom of the pyramid.

This intersection of caste with the economic and political fields helps in understanding the functioning of the journalistic field at the ground level along with the positions occupied in this hierarchy. In this chapter, I addressed the questions: how do they negotiate the obstacles of that position? What are the ways and means by which they develop a sense of agency and identity in a field occupied by powerful men who look down on them, despise them and have historically wielded violence over them?

Despite the prevalence of various forms of structural dominance, are the stringers merely passive victims? Does the journalistic field offer them a sense of agency and escape from the traditional strongholds of caste in the social, economic and political fields? How does the stringer manoeuvre his way in this minefield? These questions will be explored as I follow them further in the field.

Notes

1 The idea behind the rationalisation initiative was to maintain a healthy teacher–student ratio (one teacher for 30 students). In the process, schools (not per classroom or standard) running with fewer than 19 students were to be merged with nearby schools. Accordingly, teachers would be transferred and re-posted within the *mandal*/block.

2 *Eenadu*, *pakkagā hētubaddīkaraṇa vivarālu*: DEO (Data on rationalisation comprehensive, says DEO); Box item: *tandāllo pāṭhasālalanu nilapanḍi* (Safeguard schools in tribal hamlets), p. 11, Medak edition, 1 October 2014; *Namaste Telangana*, *pāṭhasālala hētubaddīkaraṇa vēgavantam* (Rationalisation of schools gains pace), p. 2, Medak edition, 1 October 2014.

3 *Andhra Bhoomi*, *pāṭhasālala hētubaddīkaraṇapai samīksha* [*sic*] (Review on rationalisation of schools), p. 7, Medak edition, 1 October 2014. The desk persons misspelt the Telugu word for school in the headline, a major blunder. Instead of *pāṭhasālala* (schools) they wrote *pākasālala* (kitchens or cooking places).

4 *Sakshi*, *prabhutva pāṭhasālala mūsivēta sarikādu* (Closing down schools incorrect) p. 11, Medak edition, 1 October 2014; *Andhra Jyothi*, *pāṭhasālala hētubaddīkaraṇapai punahsamīkshincāli* (Revaluate rationalisation policy), p. 12 Medak edition, 1 October 2014.

5 *Prajasakti*, *pāṭhasālala mūsivēta tagadu* (Closing down schools inappropriate), p. 8, Medak edition, 1 October 2014; *Visalaandhra*, *hētubaddīkaraṇa uttarvulu upasamharincāli* (Withdraw rationalisation orders: SFI), p. 7, Medak edition, 1 October 2014.

6 *Vaartha*, *Dalitulaku vidyanu dūram cēsēndukē pāṭhasālala mūsivēta* (Schools closed to deny education for Dalits), p. 7, Medak edition, 1 October 2014. *Surya*, *kramabaddīkaraṇa rājyāngaviruddam* (Regulation of schools unconstitutional), p. 3, Medak edition, 1 October 2014.

7 *Andhra Prabha*, *pāṭhasālala mūsivēta viramincukōvāli* (Closing down schools must be stalled), p. 5, Medak edition, 1 October 2014.

8 In the latter part of the interview, the editorial in-charge mentioned that there were a couple of instances in which he was instrumental in converting local reports filed by stringers into special stories in the Sunday magazine.

9 What the management person meant by *manci* story was to write a feel-good or feature article on how elderly persons from rich families are leading happy and peaceful retirement lives far from madding crowds and traffic jams in an old age home. This particular group of people belong to the 'farmer-capitalists' category Carol Upadhya (1988) writes about who remained in rural areas to safeguard their properties after the Green Revolution.

10 *Sakshi*, Krishna Rural, 10 May 2012, p. 5

11 *Prajasakti*, Vijayawada, 10 May 2012, p. 6. Pra. Vi. means *Prajasakti Vilekhari* (journalist).

12 *Dalita Poratam*, Vijayawada, RNI: APTEL/2010/32829 and *Dalitha Pragathi*, Guntur, APTEL/2012/59550. During my re-visit to Gannavaram, I learnt that KP shifted to Vijayawada as he was promoted as rural in-charge in *Sakshi* daily (9 September 2021). Callous

13 Thirumal and Tartakov (2011, pp. 20–39) rightly point out the need for digital equity but seem to disregard and overlook the laborious efforts of Dalit activists and organisations in archiving protests and information related to discriminatory events in the regional language print medium across the country. Often, these are the sources for material circulated on digital and even mobile networks.

14 Bodily hexis refers to the physical bodily attitudes and gestures that emerge as a result of the relationship between habitus of the agents and the particular field she or he belongs to (see Bourdieu, 2000, p. 141).

15 Dealing with land and labour issues in the eighteenth-century South India, Washbrook (1993) notes that the imperialistic drive to maximise revenue resulted in peasantisation of economy but retained and consolidated the Brahmanical notions of social hierarchy and culture. For Washbrook, this period in South

India, arguably, happens to be a 'golden age' for the pariah (the Dalit), at least in a relative way. This conception was furthered by Aloysius (2010) to delineate the endurance of Brahmanical power from historical times to the present.

16 Some rural in-charges of very large and large news dailies warn their stringers not to interact with them.

References

Aloysius, G. (2010). *The Brahminical inscribed in body-politic: A historico-sociological investigation of effective & enduring power in contemporary India*. New Delhi: Critical Quest.

Bayly, S. (1999). *Caste, society and politics in India from the eighteenth century to the modern age*. New York: Cambridge University Press.

Bourdieu, P. (1990). *The logic of practice*. Stanford: Stanford University Press.

Bourdieu, P. (1998). *Practical reason: On the theory of action*. Stanford, CA: Stanford University Press.

Bourdieu, P. (2000). *Pascalian meditations*. Stanford: Stanford University Press.

Bourdieu, P. (2018). *Classification struggles: Lectures at the Collège de France, 1981–1982, general sociology, vol I*. Cambridge: Polity Press.

Gerbner, G. (1972). Violence and television drama: Trends and symbolic functions. In Comstock, G. A. and Rubenstein, E. (Eds.), *Television and social behaviour, vol. 1: Content and control* (pp. 28–187). Retrieved from: https://web.asc.upenn.edu/gerbner/Asset.aspx?assetID=2584

Jeffrey, R. ([2000]2010). *India's newspaper revolution: Capitalism, politics, and the Indian-language press*. New Delhi: Oxford University Press.

Manor, J. (2000). Small-time political fixers in India's states: "Towel over armpit". *Asian Survey*, 40(5), pp. 816–835. DOI:10.2307/3021178.

Murthy, R. (2003). *Rural reporting in India*. Hyderabad: Prajasakti Book House.

Ninan, S. (2007). *Headlines from the heartland: Reinventing the Hindi public sphere*. New Delhi: Sage.

Reddy, G. R. and Haragopal, G. (1985). The pyraveekar: "The fixer" in rural India. *Asian Survey*, 25(11), pp. 1148–1162. DOI:10.2307/2644252.

Round Table India. (2012a). Desecration of Ambedkar statues: Truth is the first casualty. February 10. Retrieved from: https://www.roundtableindia.co.in/desecration-of-ambedkar-statues-truth-is-the-first-casualty/#:~:text=Truth%2C%20they%20say%2C%20is%20the,night%20of%2022nd%20January%3F.

Round Table India. (2012b). "We will do a Chunduru on you"! Desecration of Ambedkar statues: Truth is the first casualty (Part II). February 14. Retrieved from: https://www.roundtableindia.co.in/we-will-do-a-chunduru-on-you/.

Shaw, P. (2017). Who wants own Telugu news channels? *The Hoot*. Retrieved from: http://asu.thehoot.org/media-watch/media-business/who-wants-to-own-telugu-news-channels-10046.

Thirumal, P. and Tartakov, M. (2011). India's Dalits search for a democratic opening in the digital divide. In Leigh, P. R. (Ed.), *International exploration of technology equity and the digital divide: Critical, historical and social perspectives*. Hershey: Information Science Reference.

Upadhya, C. (1988). The farmer-capitalists of coastal Andhra Pradesh. *Economic and Political Weekly*, 23(27–28), pp. 1433–1442, pp. 1376–1382.

Wacquant, L. J. D. (2008). *Urban outcasts: A comparative sociology of advanced marginality*. Cambridge: Polity Press.

Washbrook, D. A. (1993). Land and labour in late eighteenth-Century South India: The golden age of pariah? In Robb, P. (Ed.), *Dalit movements and the meaning of labour in India*. New Delhi: Oxford University Press.

6

DAMAGED AND DAMAGING

The insecure masculinity of the small-town stringer

Udyōgam purusha lakshaṇam, adi pōtē avalakshaṇam (Employment is the definitive characteristic of a man; losing it is an inability/a character defect)

– A Telugu proverb

Introduction

I reached the venue at 8:40 A.M. where the annual meeting of the Andhra Pradesh Union of Working Journalists (APUWJ) was organised at Kanchikacharla *mandal* in Krishna district on 27 May 2012 (Sunday). A wedding hall in the open fields on the arterial Vijayawada-Hyderabad highway (NH-65) served as the venue. The meeting was attended by hundreds of working journalists from nearby districts along with journalists from Vijayawada/Krishna district. I identified myself to the organisers as I took their permission to audio-record the proceedings of the meeting, which started at 9:15 A.M. . . . As journalists in the audience were listening to the speakers driving home the point that they should stand united to fight for the rights of journalists . . . There was a tea break for half an hour at around 11 A.M. and everyone rushed to the washroom, which was full. I walked out of the hall and strolled towards the office room of the function hall to check if there were any other washrooms on the premises. The manager was watching *Satyamev Jayate*, a popular *TV* programme on a Telugu news channel and took a while to notice my presence. Without uttering a word, he raised his eyebrows enquiring what I wanted. I told him in Telugu that I was looking for a washroom as the one inside the function hall was full. He replied: 'Best thing . . . Go outside'.

I walked across the highway only to notice that scores of attendees at the meeting had dashed in different directions already to find a bush or a tree to relieve themselves in the

DOI: 10.4324/b23313-6

> open. The *en masse* urinating session blocked the traffic on the highway. An AP Road Transport Corporation bus stopped and male passengers got down to ease themselves, while their womenfolk stayed on board. It was only after looking at the stranded women passengers that I realised that *there were no women in the APUWJ meeting. They were not only absent on the dais but also in the audience section.* (Field notes, 27 May 2012, Kanchikacherla, Andhra Pradesh). Moreover, the women had to watch scores of men all around urinating in the open.

The act of 'urinating in the public' has social, cultural and economic significance laden with dense meaning outside of the 'Euro-American' contexts. The lack of social infrastructure in rural and small-town (even in urban) spaces points out the difficulties women have to face in their everyday life. The horrific nature of this scene of a bus with women in it, surrounded on all sides by urinating men is both a stark realisation and an evocative metaphor for the gendered field of Indian-language newspaper stringers. That it was utterly quotidian, a given, taken for granted, only underscores the embedded forms of patriarchy within and outside of the journalistic field the stringer inhabits which is exclusively male. There are no women stringers. Yet women haunt this space and shape the masculinity of the men in the public sphere in many ways, some of which I hope to show through ethnographic moments with stringers in the field. In this chapter, I examine how the emasculation and feminisation of the stringer by upper caste men and the demands of patriarchy that he faces on a daily basis on the one hand and the absence of women stringers in Telugu journalism on the other shapes the masculinity of the stringer that emerges in small-town spaces in AP and TS.

The working journalists' meetings in both the Telugu-speaking states helped me in familiarising myself with the journalistic field; building rapport with the who's who of the field; providing a platform to interview various agents in the field. A wide range of issues – political pressures, threats from the police, the precarious nature of jobs, welfare schemes for working journalists such as housing schemes and health insurance – were usually discussed in the meetings and workshops conducted by the journalists' unions.

However, issues related to gender equality and sensitivity, training and education to inculcate the idea were hardly discussed in the four journalists' meetings I attended or in the three workshops at various locations in AP and TS. The relative absence of women in Telugu journalism in general points to the particular nature of Telugu patriarchies that form both men and women but in the case of the stringers the stark absence of women stringers throws the masculinities of the stringers into sharp relief.

What I focus on is the dystopian women-missing-altogether space and the resultant gendered composition of the field of stringer journalism in small-town AP and TS. What are the anxieties, desires and embodiments of masculinity in the stringer and the field he inhabits? How do women feature in the imagination of the stringer? What are the languages of the precarious and slippery masculinities that the disenfranchised and economically deprived stringer speaks in relation to the upper-caste women they do encounter? These are some of the questions I explore by presenting ethnographic observations, documenting everyday utterances and practices in the life-world of small-town stringers in India.

Focusing on issues related to age, generation and sexism in Indian television newsrooms, Kanagasabai (2016, p. 676) rightly points out, 'While there is a significant amount of literature engaging with the representation of women in Indian media, there continues to be a lack of serious sociological scholarship on issues of gender and sexuality within the profession of journalism'. Even as the lack of sexual diversity in newsrooms and the profession is an important aspect while arguing for the need to achieve a critical mass of women's representation, an understanding of the social space and the caste and class dynamics in it are essential to further feminist scholarship on media studies in South Asia. Malik (2021) stresses on the same in her commentary on the state of affairs in Indian regional media.

Kumkum Sangari's (1995) formulation of multiple patriarchies yet overlapping in a different context is employed to understand how they 'function in three concurrent ways – systemic, shared, and differential'. Delving into the debate of the uniform civil code from a socio-legal perspective, Sangari (1995, p. 3384) pointed out that understanding the

> presence of multiple patriarchies involves an analysis of specific differences and similarities – their production, degree of structuration and content. The differences in types of oppression are not part of a realm of pure cultural diversity but differences between patriarchies, that may be more or less structured, and entangled with an even wider spectrum of social differences.

The peculiar nature of small-town journalistic field and practices of stringers allows us to address the 'dearth of ethnography specifically focusing on research sites where masculinities are performed by men marginalised or subordinated within the wider society' (Rogers, 2008, p. 80). Following Bourdieu praxeology (1989, 1990), I moved out of newsrooms and attempt to capture the ways in which women are intersected by class, caste and sexuality for the largely 'lower-class' and 'lower-caste' male stringers. To realise this, I engage Bourdieu's (2001) *Masculine Domination* to understand the givenness of masculine domination and the strategies of its reproduction in the field (legitimation), here, the journalistic field. This approach helped me understand that in the journalistic field, gender operates as a way of structuring social practice, inseparably intertwined with other social structures like caste, class and status.

A benefit of the field theory approach to understanding masculinities and multiple patriarchies in the field is its emphasis on the significance of everyday life practices in understanding how dominance and symbolic power operate in the most basic situations, contexts and behaviours in the social field (Thapan, 2009; Rogers, 2008). But it is equally important to understand complicity with and refusal to cleave from the symbolic or the non-material.

Anxious masculinity

> The exuberance among the journalists present at the first TUWJ meeting after achieving statehood was palpable at the venue. Giant posters and banners hailing the first Chief Minister of Telangana KCR and his party leaders were erected at the venue organised in a wedding hall. A Gajwel local DJ remix version of a popular song during the Telangana movement: *O gosh, these Andhra colonisers . . . looted wealth of our Telangana* was playing. I entered my name and the purpose of my visit and took permission from the organisers to record the proceedings. The meeting had a delayed start. There was one woman guest of honour on the dais along with TUWJ office bearers, ministers, and local political leaders. She was the first Deputy Speaker of Telangana Legislative Assembly M. Padma Devender Reddy. Speakers on the dais spoke at length about the issue of language, culture, Andhra domination . . . When her turn came to speak, the Deputy Speaker came straight to the point after extending greetings to one and all: '*Annalū, mirantā sakkaga Telangana bhasha gurinci maṭladirru. Kāni endanna okka āḍa biḍḍa ledu iḍa. Yiga mana Telangana vaccināka gūda aḍōḷḷa paristhiti gintēna?*' (Dear brothers, you spoke at length about Telangana language and culture. But there is not even a single woman in this meeting. Is this how the situation of women is going to be even after securing our own state?) As Reddy pointed out, she was the only woman present on the occasion as a dignitary. However, women sweepers were busy clearing the plastic cups and paper plates thrown on the ground near the snacks counter. *There were no women journalists at the meeting.* Women involved in menial labour were, as usual, invisibilised.
>
> (Field notes, 7 October 2014)

The enunciations made by the first Deputy Speaker immediately, in the logical sense, show the exclusive nature of the profession, lack of gender diversity and pernicious consequences of such an appalling male–female ratio in a democratic setup.[1] This dystopian picture at the meeting is a daily reality in the world of stringers on the ground. But it is not dystopian to the stringers at all but a taken-for-granted exclusivity.

This kind of exclusivity makes it challenging to understand the issue of masculinity in two overlapping ways: practical and methodological. The proposition made by Anandhi et al. (2002, p. 4397) that 'any study of masculinities needs to explore the complex interrelationship between competing notions of masculinities and femininities' appears practically unviable due to the near-total absence of women in the local journalistic field stringers inhabit. However, due to the heteronomous nature of the field, there were opportunities to witness instances when the masculine encountered the feminine, even though the latter did not have any direct stakes in the journalistic field. The methodological challenge then is to study masculinity in itself or by understanding the field's masculinism – 'the ideology that justifies and naturalises male domination' (Brittan, 1989, p. 5) but also to understand that the 'Exaltation of masculine values has its dark negative side in the fears and anxiety aroused by femininity' (Bourdieu, 2001, p. 51). This involves understanding the manner in which masculinities are produced and reproduced along with exposing the overt and covert masculinist operations implicated in everyday practices, visions and utterances in the field but also theorising the simultaneously disenfranchised and hegemonic masculinity of the stringers manifested in relations with women.

Understanding the entry of an agent into a particular field and allied barriers is an important component to be understood in the field theory approach. At the time of fieldwork, I gathered responses from the editorial and reporting heads of Telugu dailies about the absence of women at the local level, which ranged from 'sympathetic to sexist'. Some even sounded dismissive saying that 'there are more "serious" issues to study about journalists' or patronising, sermonising about ideal world situations. In fact, the language is such that reference to a stringer was always a default 'he' or 'him' in Telugu language. This was the case even while referring to an abstract situation involving a non-existent stringer.

The editorial in-charge of a leading Telugu newspaper based in Krishna district (AP) said that they tried 'experimenting' by recruiting a woman as a stringer and it 'failed', as she could not cope with the 'work pressure' and quit the profession in a very short time (GB, personal communication, 7 September 2012). The response of the editorial heads of other news dailies, including the progressive and left-leaning ones, to the same question was similar in both the Telugu-speaking states.

In a similar manner, a bureau in-charge of the Medak district edition at Sangareddy, VRK said that in his experience (of more than 24 years), he had not seen any woman from Sangareddy willing to work as a reporter or a stringer in the district *mandals*. 'Those who were educated and passionate about journalism look for opportunities in Hyderabad instead. Intelligent/sensible women (*telivaina āḍoḷḷu*) would not want to work as stringer', he said (VRK, Personal communication, 1 October 2014). Echoing the tone of a majority of salaried staffers, the rural in-charge of *Sakshi* daily in Krishna district, NS, said,

> We always recruit people on the basis of their abilities. If a woman was ready to work as a stringer, we never stopped her. But it would be very tough for women to travel alone or along with male stringers in villages to file stories or cover issues. This is the main reason for the absence [of women stringers and reporters].
>
> (Personal communication, 9 October 2012)

When asked why women were recruited more in desk jobs, a Telugu adage that was repeated by many stringers, staffers and editorial heads at multiple locations and instances was: *tirigi āḍadi tiragaka magādu cheḍatāru* (A woman loses her character by venturing out and a man by not doing so). More shockingly, a handbook for journalists (Reddy, 2016, p. 286) written in Telugu rephrased the above adage while describing the essential characteristics of reporter or stringer as: *journalisṭu tiragaka cheḍatāḍu* (A journalist turns useless by not venturing out). Notably, the gender of the journalist in the description was masculine. Bourdieu locates the principle of masculine domination in agencies such as 'the educational system or the state, and in their strictly political actions, whether overt or hidden, official or unofficial' (2001, p. 116).

A senior journalist explained that instead of heavy-duty reporting, many newspapers encouraged women to contribute or work in the family, women and the Sunday supplement sections of Telugu newspapers. Explaining the overtly masculine nature of the peer group and the field, a stringer with many years of experience in Sangareddy, PSR said, 'How can women maintain a working relationship with these *baṭṭebāzgāḷḷu* (shameless fellows)? Women's lives will be spoiled, as this is not an easy job to do'. The stringer implies that women may suffer material as well as symbolic losses when employed as local journalists. PSR also pointed out that sharing of information related to local news or dealings with government officials, businessmen and politicians was not possible with women in the journalism field at this level.

These responses about the recruitment of women entail a picture of dichotomy when juxtaposed with the earlier discussion on the eligibility criteria for recruiting stringers and journalists (Chapter 3). There appears to be a collectivist exclusionary tone while talking about women's recruitment, while it takes the form of an individualist inclusionary one when it comes to men. This dichotomy in strategies, under the mask of professional capabilities, seems to label women ineligible without considering their skills, credentials and allied competencies individually (or case by case) and thereby excluding them from entering the field.

In a way, the elite conduct themselves in a more 'acceptable' manner by slipping into patronising discourse when they discuss women and work or maybe sometimes as Tomar (2017, p. 258) noted, indulge in mansplaining.

While surveying biographies of veteran Telugu journalists for my doctoral research, only one senior editor Venkateswararao (2015) mentions recruiting women in a mainstream newspaper (*Eenadu*). He was one of the founding members of *Eenadu* editorial team, which was established in 1974. While recalling the recruitment and training process he oversaw in the newspaper, he (2015, p. 119) wrote:

> For the first time in the history of Telugu newspapers, we have recruited five women as sub-editors. I took great care regarding the safety of women journalists. I was almost like the head of the family. Even now when I see them (decades later), that feeling of being a proud father comes to the fore.
>
> (p. 119)

Even as this quote sounds patronising and invokes familial claustrophobia, this was the sentiment that most progressive men seemed to have held on to in newsrooms. Jeffrey (2010) noted a similar response about a woman journalist working in an Urdu daily based in Hyderabad, where she 'seemed to perform her tasks to the satisfaction of her editor and colleagues, who treated her presence as special – like having a daughter or sister working with them' p. 173).[2]

This invocation of familial notions while dealing with professional relations and practices is singular to the Hindu society which operates (depending on convenience) on the Laws of the Manu or centred on Brahmanical work culture. Moreover, the family is a 'realised category' (Bourdieu, 1996, p. 23) that tends to function as a field with its material as well as symbolic relations of domination and thereby becomes an important institution in reproducing masculine domination (2001, p. 85), which has been an important area of feminist research.

On the whole, there is a palpable indifference to employing women as reporters or stringers at the local level. The responses were either patronising or patriarchal and sometimes both, hinting at the presence of multiple patriarchies (Sangari, 1995) present in Indian society based on caste and division of labour.

Based on the ethnographic observations and the responses, it can be argued that the sexual division of labour in the journalistic field operates by (a) legitimising a dominant relationship based on crude physiological differences between female and male; (b) rationalising that the dominance is 'natural' and thereby justifying the absence of the women. This argument becomes clearer in the following two sections where I discuss the work culture of stringers and their views on women.

Misogyny, casteism and insecure masculinity

On many occasions, I accompanied stringers while they were interacting with women from different sections, officials, schoolteachers, nurses, wardens and local entrepreneurs among others. Passing an uncalled-for or lewd remark right after their work got done was witnessed, especially in case of relatively younger stringers. In one instance:

> I was with PR, a stringer in Sangareddy, who was in his early thirties, while he was at the animal husbandry wing of the district collectorate building on a Monday morning to collect data related to a story on new breed of disease-resistant chicken that the government was promoting for the benefit of poultry farmers in the district. The official concerned was a woman, who had been avoiding phone calls from PR and was not available to other stringers, as she was in the field inspecting various poultry farms in the district at that time. The discussion between them began with the official stating that she was busy the previous week and could not respond to any calls. PR conveyed to her that it was understandable in a deferential manner. The deference was visible not only in his speech and salutation but also in his body language. Before I could say anything, he introduced me to her as a reporter from Hyderabad on some work in the collectorate office. He gathered the required information from her about the poultry chicken story and thanked her. During the interaction, she was very considerate and even showed images of the farms on her mobile phone, which she took during inspection. We took leave of her and headed towards the media point in the same building. He informed the bureau in-charge of his newspaper that the story (centrespread) would be ready by evening. At the media point, we bumped into another stringer to whom PR narrated the entire episode and said: 'She's new to the place and doesn't know about me. She made me wait for more than a week to give this information. I know how to deal with her. Wait for some time. You will see how I retaliate for sure'.
>
> (Field notes, 7 October 2014, Sangareddy)

In this instance, PR, who was referring to the lady official as Madam, started body-shaming and slandering in her absence while talking to another stringer by using coarse Telugu expressions such as '*āmeku baa balisindi*' (temerity) and '*kotta kadā intē unṭundi*' (she resists because she's new). *Balisindi* literally translates as fattening of body parts (in this context).

While *kotta* neutrally translates as new or 'fresh', but the way it was intonated alludes to the virginity of a woman.

Such words were often referred to as 'double-meaning dialogues' in local parlance, which women very often face in both urban and rural areas. The manner of reference suddenly changed from the plural (formal/respectful) to the singular (casual/disrespectful). In Telugu, formal reference is in the plural form (*mīru*). This is the same stringer who was vociferous in his articulation against casteism in the field. This is not a one-off incident, rather a striking one to put across the case of relegated masculinity. I continue to use the concept of relegation to circumvent the rigid binary of hegemonic and subordinate (or subaltern), which may not be effective in understanding the layers of oppression (gender, caste and ability) relationally manifest in the journalistic field. The field and relationships between agents are so dynamic that what is considered as hegemonic masculinity in one moment slips into subordinate one and vice-versa.

In another instance at Gannavaram, I observed that a newly recruited woman horticulture officer was patronised by stringers while on her visit to assess crop damage caused by untimely rain in the summer season:

> The local landlord (*pedda raitu*) had organised a SUV for stringers to visit his mango orchard, where a horticulture officer along with her staff was on a visit to assess the damage in this part of district due to the rainfall. One of the stringers, DD, was informed about the officer's visit by the MRO staffer. He in turn alerted the landlord by 11 A.M. so that the landlord could make transport arrangements for them in the evening from Gannavaram centre to the farm, located at a distance of around 12 km. I travelled along with the stringers to the orchard in a car. DD mentioned that the officer was on her way from Agiripalle to Gannavaram and before that she was in Nuzvid (a *mandal* in Krishna district known for Banginapalli and Chinna Rasalu varieties of mango). Another stringer casually inquired DD, 'Anna, how do you know about all these details?' DD replied, 'The clerk told me that a new lady officer was appointed and I pulled some strings in the Vijayawada office to know her schedule'.
>
> From that moment, they started referring to her as *kotta piṭṭa* (new bird; colloquial usage for woman) in her absence. After reaching the spot, stringers took photographs of labourers picking up damaged fruits from the ground and the act of picking up fruits, as the not-so-well-dressed landlord was overseeing, was repeated till every stringer got a publishable image. The officer reached the farm in a jeep (horticulture department vehicle) and inspected the farm along with nearby ones. Stringers took photographs of the officers. When she was about to leave, stringers 'surrounded' her and were asking details about the official assessment of the damage incurred

to crops and compensation to farmers. The officer said that it was too early to talk about the compensation at that point; she would have to consult other officials after reaching Vijayawada.

At this point, one of the senior stringers in the lot and belonging to a Sat-shudra caste, ANR, intervened and said, 'Madam, you are new to this job. Reporters in Vijayawada don't care about agriculture issues. We cover these issues in detail and you might need our help too. Share some details with us'. The officer dispassionately shared the details and answered some of the queries and left saying that she needed to leave before it got dark. On the way back to Gannavaram centre, the stringers were all giggles when a stringer, pointing an imaginary remote towards ANR, remarked: '*Sār ki ladies button ekkaḍa nokkālō ekkaḍa vadalālō bāgā telusu*'. [Sir knows how to tame new officers, especially ladies. Literally, means where to press ladies' remote-control button].

(Field notes, 7 May 2012)

Here too the woman government official was new to the location or the job and some stringers sensed that it is their moment to play offense.[3] As much as they were focused on getting details about the crop loss from the official and writing a report favourable to the landlord (who not only arranged transport but also offered refreshments), indulging in misogynist banter against the woman official appeared to have occupied a place in the list of to-do things on the assignment. More than the nature of reporting, what was of concern here is the way some of these seniors set the example for relatively inexperienced who accompanied them or were acting as acolytes. The senior stringers had clearly left an impression on their juniors and set the precedence. Since most stringers do not have journalism education and 'learn' while on the job, incidents such as these could be seen as the ways in which masculinism gets produced and reproduced in the field. These, at the same time, also reflect the character of intragroup dynamics, which is vital in understanding relegated masculinities.

Often novice stringers show their write-ups to experienced stringers before sending the stories to the head office. In the event of any mistakes or blunders, the latter make fun of the former or 'chide' them by using expressions, which are ableist and sexist at the same time, such as 'Stop behaving like a woman', 'Speak up; is there "anything" stuck in your mouth', 'Don't make cry-face like a woman', 'retarded c@#t', to mention a few.

These are some ways in which the more experienced among them show that they are abler and superior, which often are loaded with symbolic violence. The inexperienced deal with the situation with a 'sheepish smile' or cut a sorry figure with their 'clumsiness' and 'inability' – the 'traits' which get classified as feminine in abusive utterances.

At both sites of research, there were instances in which senior stringers mildly hit juniors or acolytes on the tops of their heads or on their backs while supervising or overlooking their copy. If the hits and thuds suggest a physical, masculine assertion over the inexperienced who are feminised, slurs and sexist language mirror masculinity, which asserts itself only by degrading and projecting inability as feminine. Both the symbolic and physical gestures of violence seem to unmake 'lesser' men temporarily but tend them into the process of acquisition of habitus though practical mimesis or mimetic practices, which, in turn, result in the reproduction of masculine or sexual (di)vision (principles of vision and division).[4]

It is important to understand the symbolic effects of the humiliation suffered at the hands of more powerful men who control their words, livelihoods and lives and of not living up to the masculine ideals of their own societies, on the one hand, and their recourse to the language of patriarchal domination to assert some sense of self on the other for the largely 'lower-class' and 'lower caste' male stringers. Bourdieu's (2001) *Masculine Domination* is sensitive to this predicament. After showing how the dehistoricised and eternalised structure of sexual division produces the magnified image of man, Bourdieu points out that 'men are also prisoners, and insidiously victims, of the dominant representation' (p. 49) and that 'male privilege is also a trap' (p. 50).

What is noteworthy in the field observations is that the most visible displayers of masculinity on the ground are not always the most powerful social and economic elite. It was these relegated stringers, when located in the larger journalistic field, who give utmost respect to the staffers either in their presence or in their absence. They consciously or unconsciously relegate not only women in the social field but also their own peers to occupy a distinct social space and consolidate it in their own field.

Essentially, relegated masculinity can be located, captured and defined in relation to men, who are better placed in social and occupational hierarchies. Thus, masculinity coupled with caste becomes a channel through which discrimination streams and, to be more precise, the position of men as marginal depends on what is relationally considered dominant operating on the principle of graded inequality. It is possible to understand relegated masculinity only in relation to socially, professionally and economically more elevated (and thereby relegating) masculinity.

A dangerous zone

Whether it was in Sangareddy at the labour *aḍḍa* (pick-up point) on the highway centre or in the industrial estate (cottage industries) located near Surampalle village in Gannavaram and in the farmlands, women outnumbered men in heavy-duty work agricultural and construction-related works (Harriss-White, 2003, 2007). Also, women were seen carrying out 'soft works' such as running small shops, roadside eateries, *balwādi* (rural preschool setups) and *anganwādi* (rural childcare) centres.

However, the situation in journalism is different from other professions or jobs, as many stringers often expressed that journalistic work 'belonged to men' (*mogōḷḷadi*) and it was 'too hard for women to work in on a daily basis'.

Some of the responses in one of my earlier interviews during fieldwork in Gannavaram had a long-lasting impact and pushed me towards understanding the perceptions and imaginations of stringers, reporters and editorial staffers about women and their work. Their utterances and responses appeared like casteist and sexist riddles.

After sending reports to the district edition centre by 5 P.M., the then Gannavaram stringer for *Eenadu* daily ANR, agreed to give me an interview. Among many other things, he stressed that the reason why he entered this profession and continued was for *gouravam* and *maryāda* (respect and honour). What struck me was his 'statement' about the status of women in the profession, which he made while sucking on a peppermint candy: *Gurram chēsē pani gurram cēyāli, gāḍida cēsē pani gādida cēyāli* [A horse should do the job it was meant for and a donkey should do its job] (ANR, personal communication, 22 May 2012).

This particular utterance encodes a crude sexist and casteist idea of division of labour in Telugu society. It likens men to perform 'honourable' and 'competitive' functions in public (like horses), while women are reduced to perform menial and domestic jobs (like donkeys that assist local washermen [*cākalivāru* or *dhobis* belong to OBC community in AP and TS]).

In Sangareddy, on the eve of *Batukamma* – the major festival in the state – a stringer-cum-photographer PR was visibly overenthusiastic on getting 'colourful' photographs of women carrying *bonam* (offering). 'There should be some colour in our life too, which otherwise is filled with filing reports on financial frauds and farmers' suicides', PR said.[5] The front page of tabloid edition and the centrespread had women wearing gaudy and colourful sarees offering *bonam* to Goddess Durga. During the entire coverage of the festival, voices of women taking part in the festivities were absent but they were present only in images (Field notes, 1 and 2 October 2014).

Often, the imagination of women's ability for men working as stringers and reporters was almost a matter of ridicule or she was turned into an object of desire. When asked about how the situation would be if women were working as stringers, a stringer said, 'It will be nice, Sir. Women will bring a daily dose of entertainment in our everyday lives' (BMP, Field notes, 22 April 2012). This derisiveness, which comes in a very casual and natural manner, indicated the masculine domination coupled with misogyny in the journalistic field. Even the everyday language of various agents was sexist and would make women uncomfortable if they were to work in the field.

Also, it appeared as if men themselves feel uncomfortable in some situations with women working alongside them in this field. For instance, stringers as part of their everyday work while interacting with local politicians, businessmen, police and small-time bureaucrats indulge in gossiping about extra-marital affairs of locals, discussing strategies to outsmart their competitors/peers in government offices, nefarious businesses, and knowing both private and public information about persons in opposite political camps. These are conversations in which pertinent oppositions such as acceptable/unacceptable, pride/shame, public/private, legal/illegal, domestic/public, permissible/impermissible and inner/outer are temporarily suspended. This stems from deeper insecurities of men especially about their work and maintaining varying degrees of dominance over women in the social space.

The Goffmanesque (1956, pp. 72–74) frontstage and backstage behaviour of stringers in these situations can be better grasped in Bourdieu's *Masculine Domination* in which he (2001, p. 47) suggests:

> [T]he sexual division is inscribed, on the one hand, in the division of productive activities with which we associate the idea of work, and more generally in the division of the labour of maintaining social capital and symbolic capital which gives men the monopoly of all official, public activities, of representation, and in particular of all exchanges of honour – exchanges of words (in everyday encounters and above all in the assembly), exchanges of gifts, exchanges of women, exchanges of challenges and murders (of which the limiting case is war).

Along with these cultural and social aspects discussed so far to understand the absence or lesser presence of women in the journalistic field, the field revealed infrastructural absence and structural support to women. The non-applicability of the Sexual Harassment of Women at Workplace (Prevention, Prohibition and Redressal) Act, 2013, India too is a necessary corollary.[6] The primary reason for it was that stringers are not on the payrolls of the media organisation. Further, there is no workplace as such for stringers and sometimes even daily newspaper reporters since they are in the field most of the time, a condition which holds good for reporters based in urban areas, state capitals and the national capital too.

Addressing this aspect, Seshu (2011) observes:

> The sexual harassment women journalists face isn't just at the workplace, inside newsrooms, with colleagues or bosses. It happens even when journalists, especially reporters and correspondents, go out to work – in the field, during interviews or meetings with sources who hold out the promise of an exclusive tidbit. . . . Even as they report on sexual harassment elsewhere, they are as vulnerable to

> it at the workplace. They experience a low-level sexual abuse that they often ignore, not wishing to jeopardise a good assignment or be treated differently from their male colleagues.
>
> (Paras 1 & 2)

Most stringers were out at various locations in the *mandals* and villages during the day and filed their stories sitting under trees or in shutter shops at many makeshift media points. There were no facilities such as public toilets in small towns and villages at the time of fieldwork. Even in most government offices, schools and hospitals, the sanitary conditions were not congenial for women. Most stringers, all men, did not hesitate to attend to nature's call in the corners of streets or on farmlands.

With respect to the work culture, the everyday language used by locals, businessmen, clerks, constables, news sources and stringers themselves was abusive in nature at both the sites of research. This was not to suggest that women did not use abusive language in the sites of research.[7]

The tone of male stringers and reporters, while talking about women across sections, while on or off assignment, in the field was often derogatory and demeaning. At the same time, some stringers minded their own business or remained silent during the gossip sessions among stringers, while between assignments, over a cup of tea, smoke or lunch.

During fieldwork, I observed that stringers and sometimes even reporters would be courteous and cordial towards women if they happen to be a victim or in a helpless position to varying degrees, ranging from non-payment of monthly pension to untimely or accidental death of a husband. Girl student achievers or women folk playing during *Batukamma* (mostly upper-caste women) were others that commanded the respect of stringers. If the vulnerability of victims or helpless women makes a potential 'human interest' story for stringers, publicising women from influential or political families during festive occasions in villages helps in maintaining the caste hierarchy status quo.[8]

Misogyny in the field is not a result of the simple process of domino effect of power in the social and professional hierarchical chain from an upper-caste chief editor to a stringer with most disadvantaged disposition. Rather it appears to be an outcome of a more complex mechanism that emerges out of the Telugu journalistic field, which is marked by the concurrence of Sat-shudraisation of media economy and Brahmanical work culture.

There is evident masculine domination where the feminine was equated with inability and the underprivileged. While the editors and senior reporters felt that women might be recruited in 'soft' jobs on the desk or at best reporting in features, health and family section pages, stringers not only opined women are incapable but also viewed them as an object of ridicule. With varying degrees and tones of articulation, visions of most agents in field about labour were misogynist. When observed closely, the difference in tone appears primarily due to the positions agents occupied in social and professional spaces.

The sexist and masculinist utterances in isolation may appear illogical and inconsequential but contextually those are constructions of the social and the sexual and the ways in which masculinities and patriarchies are produced and reproduced in the field. These utterances are also the manifestations of positions occupied by agents and classification categories while constantly and relationally producing and reproducing the structures of oppression in the fields of power.

A vacillating masculinity

The culture and everyday language indicated that the local journalistic field in the Telugu-speaking states was wrapped up in casteist and classist misogyny. The informal and flexible nature of labour of a stringer and the material and symbolic insecurities emerging from the job results in the implicit and explicit symbolic violence in the form of a patronising misogyny and exertion of masculine domination over women within and outside the field.

The simultaneous operation of multiple patriarchies enmeshed in caste and class-based hierarchies within the field appears to be resulting in material and symbolic insecurities among stringers. It also appears in a way that the slippery masculinities that many of the agents in the field exhibit are not in fixed or absolute terms but in relational and comparative terms. The ethnographic observations and the documented utterances suggest that masculinity is displayed in front of fellow men as well as for men below themselves (either socially, i.e., caste-wise, or based on professional ranks). But in almost all the cases, this strategy is against women by projecting the field as a dangerous zone for the 'weak'. In addition, the misogynistic everyday language and compounded patriarchies might be seen as a response to the vulnerabilities and symbolic oppression men from marginal communities face from the so-called 'ritualistically' and professionally 'superior' upper-caste and Brahmanical men. Patriarchal masculinity becomes the bulwark that re-consolidates these men's senses of self.

This is not to excuse any of the behaviour and utterances of the stringers but to place it in context. Anandhi et al. (2002) and Rogers (2008) have examined this kind of sexism and misogyny from subaltern men in the context of rural Tamil Nadu and peri-urban Chennai, respectively. These scholars show a sensitivity to the context even as they do not excuse any of the sexist and misogynist behaviour. It is important to understand the stringer similarly as struggling to assert his identity which is disenfranchised and marginal in most ways, through the default male privilege patriarchy affords.

If the field is not fully open to able-bodied and influential caste women at the local level and even those holding positions in government offices face discrimination, one can imagine what the potential figure of a hijra stringer or persons belonging to sexual minorities would have to endure on a daily basis. But, more crucially for my purposes, it shows the damaged (and damaging) nature of patriarchal masculinities in general and of marginalised men in particular. There is very little work in sociology of journalism that seeks to understand and contextualise the violence – both on the self and on others, which patriarchy in both its disavowals and consolidations, inflicts on men and women. To understand the stringer, in a way, is also to understand the complexity of that violence.

Notes

1 By the early 1990s, this kind of argument about lack of sexual diversity gained prominence especially in the case of print journalism in India (Joseph and Sharma, 1991, 2006; Joseph, 2000; Sule, 2004; Murthy and Anita, 2010; Sharma, 2010; Jeffrey, 2010). Highlighting the point that the situation with respect to gender diversity has not improved even as we are well into the 2020s, I already presented secondary data collected from official sources to ascertain the female–male ratio in the Telugu-speaking states in Chapter 2 (see Table 2.11). A glance at Table 2.11 makes it obvious that women are under-represented in the profession in both English and Telugu language dailies in AP and TS. Even within the lesser percentages in both states, presence of women in the editorial (often referred to as desk) jobs is significantly higher than those working in the reporting vertical.

2 These accounts have a striking resemblance to Bourdieu's observations on masculinity masquerading as nobility when he points out that the 'world of work is full of little isolated occupational milieux functioning as quasi-families in which the staff manager, almost always a man, exercises a paternalistic authority' (2001, p. 58).

3 Stringers commanded a considerable amount of power at the *mandal* or village level and tended to bully new officials in general and new women officials in particular. Moreover, the women officials that I mentioned wielded modest power when compared to higher government officials like the district collector or district education officer. Such higher officials knew the means to tackle stringers by reporting their misbehaviour to editorial in-charges or bureau chiefs sitting in the district headquarters or head office. In one such instance, a woman circle inspector (CI) of police in adjacent Karimnagar district has put a stringer in his place for his 'misbehaviour'. This video went viral. See www.youtube.com/watch?v=QgJIp18742I

4 Bourdieu (2020, p. 164), while explaining the nature of symbolic power, elucidates, 'Acts of submission and obedience are cognitive acts, and as such they bring into play cognitive structures, categories of perception, patterns of perception, principles of vision and division'.

5 At the same time, this is also a strategy to gain confidence of the men from local upper-caste elite (mostly politicians) or gain favours (in cash or kind) from them that they gave sensual (*sakkamga*) coverage of their womenfolk.

6 A majority of media houses cutting across formats, languages and regions, in the first place, do not have any internal committees to deal with the issue. For an elaborate understanding about the seriousness of the issue, see NWMI (2020). The study found that more than one-third of all respondents experienced sexual harassment at their workplace, out of which 53 per cent of them did not report it anywhere.

7 Local women use abusive language in their day-to-day affairs too. At one instance, I was waiting for a stringer at Sangareddy Highway bus stop and a labour contractor was distributing daily wages among labourers. As he was distributing among male construction workers, a woman stepped in and yelled at him, '*nā baṭṭa*, these guys have ample time to drink and come back home. We have to go home and cook something for kids and these idiots'. The contractor sheepishly smiled and started giving wages to the women. [Field Notes, October, 2014]. *Baṭṭa* is a piece of cloth used by women from modest backgrounds during menstruation for the lack of sanitary pads. The word is derogatorily used by women against men and their work is often referred as *baṭṭebāz* (and thereby so shameless that they even do business with soiled pieces of cloth).

8 Bourdieu's field theory allows us to look at this patronising nature as 'Masculine domination, which constitutes women as symbolic objects whose being (*esse*) is a being-perceived (*percipi*), has the effect of keeping them in a permanent state of bodily insecurity, or more precisely of symbolic dependence' (2001, p. 66).

References

Anandhi, S., Jeyaranjan, J. and Krishnan, R. (2002). Work, caste and competing masculinities: Notes from a Tamil village. *Economic and Political Weekly*, 37(43). October 26, pp. 4397–4406.

Bourdieu, P. (1989). *Outline of a theory of practice* (Tr. by Richard Nice). Cambridge: Cambridge University Press.

Bourdieu, P. (1990). *The logic of practice* (Tr. by Richard Nice). Stanford: Stanford University Press.

Bourdieu, P. (1996). On the family as a realized category. *Theory, Culture & Society*, 13(3), pp. 19–26. DOI:10.1177/026327696013003002.

Bourdieu, P. (2001). *Masculine domination* (Tr. by Richard Nice). London: Polity Press.

Bourdieu, P. (2020). *On the state: Lectures at the Collège de France, 1989–1992* (Tr. by Peter Collier). Cambridge: Polity Press.

Brittan, A. (1989). *Masculinity and power*. Oxford: Basil Blackwell.

Goffman, E. (1956). *The presentation of self in everyday life*. Edinburgh: University of Edinburgh.

Harriss-White, B. (2003). *India working: Essays on society and economy*. New York: Cambridge University Press.

Harriss-White, B. (2007). *India's socially regulated economy*. New Delhi: Critical Quest.

Jeffrey, R. (2010). *India's newspaper revolution: Capitalism, politics, and the Indian-language press*. New Delhi: Oxford University Press.

Joseph, A. (2000). *Making news: Women in journalism*. New Delhi: Konark publishers.

Joseph, A. and Sharma, K. (1991). Between the lines: Women's issues in English language newspapers. *Economic and Political Weekly*, 26(43), pp. WS75–WS80.

Joseph, A. and Sharma, K. (2006). *Whose news? The media and women's issues*. New Delhi: Sage.

Kanagasabai, N. (2016). In the silences of a newsroom: Age, generation, and sexism in the Indian television newsroom. *Feminist Media Studies*, 16(4), pp. 663–677. DOI:10.1080/14680777.2016.1193296.

Malik, K. K. (2021). Media education and regional language journalism in India. *Media Asia* (Online). DOI:10.1080/01296612.2021.2009230.

Murthy, D. V. R. and Anita, G. (2010). Women in the media and their work environment. *Indian Journal of Gender Studies*, 17(1), pp. 73–103. DOI:10.1177/097152150901700104.

NWMI [Network of Women in Media, India]. (2020). *Creating safe workplaces: Prevention and redressal of sexual harassment in media houses in India*. Retrieved from: https://secureservercdn.net/198.71.233.33/13y.65a.myftpupload.com/wp-content/uploads/2019/02/CREATING-SAFE-WORKPLACES_compressed.pdf.

Reddy, K. S. (2016). *Jarnalisṭu karadīpika* (A handbook for journalists). Hyderabad: Vemana.

Rogers, M. (2008). Modernity, 'authenticity', and ambivalence: Subaltern masculinities on a South Indian college campus. *Journal of the Royal Anthropological Institute*, 14(1), pp. 79–95. DOI:10.1111/j.1467-9655.2007.00479.x.

Sangari, K. (1995). Politics of diversity: Religious communities and multiple patriarchies – I. *Economic and Political Weekly*, 30(51&52), pp. 3287–3310, pp. 3381–3389.

Seshu, G. (2011). *Harassed on assignment*. Retrieved from: http://asu.thehoot.org/media-watch/media-practice/harrassed-on-assignment-5393.

Sharma, K. (Ed.). (2010). *Missing: Half the story – As if gender matters in Journalism*. New Delhi: Zubaan.

Sule, S. (2004). Stepping in accessing jobs & appointments – Still a male bastion in language press & Work conditions as bad as for men. In Bhagat, P. (Ed.), *Status of women journalists in India*. New Delhi: Press Institute of India. Retrieved from: http://ncwapps.nic.in/pdfReports/Status%20of%20Women%20Journalists%20in%20India.pdf.

Thapan, M. (2009). *Living the body: Embodiment, womanhood and identity in contemporary India*. New Delhi: Sage.

Tomar, R. (2017). *Understanding women journalists: Experiences of working in Hindi print journalism in cities of Madhya Pradesh*. Unpublished Ph.D. Thesis. Mumbai: TISS. Retrieved from: http://hdl.handle.net/10603/174506.

Venkateswararao, P. (2015). *Vidhi nā sārathi* (Duty, my driving force). Hyderabad: Emesco.

7

INFORMAL LABOUR AND INVISIBILISED PRECARITY

Working lives of stringers before and after the global pandemic

Despite the challenging conditions in which they work, stringers retain a dry sense of humour. A sarcastic response capturing the ethos of a culture dominated by Telugu cinema from a Gannavaram stringer in Andhra Pradesh when asked about the wages and salary issues of stringers in newspapers was:

> Major Chandrakanth sinimālō NTR dialogue unṭundi telusā? Nīku dēśam ēmi cēsindi annadi kādu, dēśāniki nuvvu ēmi cēsavu anēdi mukhyam. Alānē mana patrikala vāḷḷu, mēmu nīku iccēdi ēntayya, nuvvu māku ēmi istunnāvu anēdi important. (Do you remember NTR's dialogue from the movie Major Chandrakanth? NTR says that what is important is your contribution to the country and not vice-versa. Even newspapers respond in the same fashion when stringers ask about salaries. They say, 'Don't ask what newspapers ought to give you, show what you can do/give to the newspaper'. That is important).
>
> [Personal communication, Gannavaram, 29 May 2012][1]

The monthly *gourava vētanam* (honorarium) most stringers receive from their news organisations in any part of the Telugu-speaking states is less than the monthly wages earned by a farm or construction labourer. Most stringers interviewed at the sites of research and those I interacted with during journalists' union meetings and training workshops complained about what they earned. Many pointed out that the advertisement revenue they generate is more than the wages and commissions they receive from the newspapers. Understanding issues concerning the *gourava vētanam* of stringers bring to the fore both the material and symbolic (non-material) conditions of news labour.

In his introductory textbook on Economics for Indian students, Omkarnath (2012, pp. 219–220) labels manual labourers, workers involved in illegal activities, orderlies in private and public establishments, casual labourers in medium and large industries and sex workers as informal workers in *petty production in the urban economy*. In effect, there are certain grounded ways to conceptualise and understand manual labour involved in

DOI: 10.4324/b23313-7

petty production in both rural and urban economies as part of 'employment accounting' in labour economics (Omkarnath, 2012, p. 233).

The majority of print journalism dailies and even media houses (television channels) function well within the formal sector of Indian economy. The very fact that the Goods and Services Tax (GST) applies to this sector proves this. Specifically, the newspaper as a 'good' invites no tax but as a service (sale of advertisement space) is taxed at 5 per cent (Government of India [GoI], 2017a, p. 11, 2017b, p. 22).[2]

How does one understand the 'informal' labour of stringers who actively take part in the news production process but are not present on the payroll of organisations which are part of 'formal' sector? What are the existing employment norms and pay scales or how to understand the lack thereof? How have recent developments in the form of the global pandemic and legislative Acts impacted the already precarious work of stringers?

Before delving into the aspects of informalisation and the resultant precarity of stringer's labour, I present some major events since my fieldwork began in 2012. They are (1) effective implementation of recommendations made by the Majithia Wage Board Committee for working journalists (wage fixation) in 2014 by a Supreme Court Order; (2) a global pandemic and the lockdowns in 2020 and 2021; and (3) revoking of the Wage Board Committee under the Working Journalists Act (1955) and the implementation of new Labour and Wage Codes, 2020 in 2021 (GoI, 2020a).

This chapter presents the aspect of informalisation of news labour in Telugu journalism, which has pioneered the 'localisation strategy' and led the way for media outlets in other Indian languages. It then discusses the different forms of precarity associated with the news labour of stringers, which was accentuated by the pandemic along with other related developments. The chapter discusses the role of journalists' unions and their collective action before pointing out the implications of the relationships between the state, media organisations and journalists' unions. Finally, it tracks the field during the pandemic and asks if the pandemic caused any special crisis for the stringer.

Informality and news labour: the dark side of localisation

The localisation strategy successfully administered by *Eenadu* in the 1980s and replicated by other newspapers within the Telugu-speaking regions and the country as a whole is the brightest possible version of the story. The strategy did result in the relative democratisation of news and broke barriers for many sections of society to enter the field, unlike in the Hindi heartland where journalism is still upper-caste bastion at all levels (Ninan, 2007, pp. 230–257; Neyazi, 2018, pp. 77–102). But it resulted in the violation of wage structures prescribed by various wage boards for working journalists, leading to precarious news labour in certain roles of news organisations. Professionalisation was compromised with some news establishments delegating non-journalistic work to journalists, violating journalistic standards.

Addressing the impact of localisation in the Hindi media in India, Neyazi (2018, p. 101) writes, 'the localisation of newspapers has mobilised local citizens, made them aware of their rights and allowed them to assert them when needed. It has also activated the administration to address local issues', while Ninan (2007, p. 29) says that it resulted in an 'evolving local public sphere' and helps 'local communities become more vocal and more conscious of their rights' (p. 111)

But both these book-length works do not shed light on the labour of stringers or local news gatherers who form the latent base on which the edifice of localisation rests and operates. In general, there is barely any literature that has attempted to address and present the working conditions of stringers in Indian-language print media.

Hanno Hardt's work brings the issues of labour and work relationships in the media and culture industry into focus. Hardt (1999, pp. 175–183) suggests that there is a need to reshape research agenda to the study of the intellectual labour of journalists, locating and identifying the boundaries and limits of journalism as a profession which is market-driven and whose autonomy is continuously challenged by political forces in society.[3]

Highlighting this issue in the Indian context, Remesh (2018, p. 134) notes the 'near absence of information or a conspicuous silence on the issues pertaining to work and working conditions of journalists themselves'. While dealing with the issue of unpaid and insecure work along with the paid news phenomenon, Remesh (2018, pp. 134–151) moved beyond the thesis of the 'Murdochisation of Indian media', pervasive in the academic understanding of the media industry.

It is possible to theorise the material conditions and informality of news labour from a field theory perspective, unravelling the connections between the economic, political and cultural fields and the journalistic field to offer a more dynamic account of the world of the stringer. The attempt is to show that the localisation strategy needs to be situated alongside issues of the informal nature of the media economy and casualisation of news labour by taking into account the material conditions of the journalistic labour of stringers, employment contract details, types of employment, professional differentiation within the field and the nature of news labour. These aspects are crucial to understanding the unorganised and informal nature of the media economy that fuels the field, even as it is erased from the final output of news production.

The first part of my fieldwork took place before the implementation of Majithia Wage Board recommendations for working journalists in India. During the second half, the Supreme Court gave directives to implement the Wage Board recommendations. I was presented the opportunity to understand and capture the changes and dynamics that took place before and after the judgement.

Even though the geographical areas of research were limited to Sangareddy and Gannavaram, journalists' union meetings and my interactions with union leaders and senior journalists across different regions and districts in both states helped in drawing a larger picture of the journalistic field. These interactions along with supporting archival work helped provide a better understanding, not just of the Telugu-speaking states but the pan-Indian context in general.

Normalising the informal: rise of news networks in language journalism

The localisation strategy was addressed in terms of local revenue generation and proliferation of newspapers and media, linking it with the increasing literacy rate in the country. Certainly, there is an emphasis on the content generated by stringers or local news gatherers in academic work (Ninan, 2007; Neyazi, 2018), but they do not highlight the policy changes and the need for changing the tone of state-led reports that concern the journalistic field.

Even as recruiting on a very large scale began in Andhra Pradesh in the early 1980s, this was quickly replicated in the Hindi heartland and even in other Indian-language newspapers such as *Sakal* (Marathi) by the early 1990s. Terming this notable development in news-gathering practices of Indian-language journalism as 'stringerisation' would risk limiting this phenomenon to the newspaper economy alone, whereas, in reality, it has strong linkages with the larger economy, society and polity as well.

Informal news networks of selected telugu dailies

Table 7.1 Telugu dailies

Sl. No.	*Newspaper*	*News Network*
1	*Eenadu*	*News Today*
2	*Sakshi*	*Newsline*
3	*Andhra Jyothi*	*Online*
4	*Andhra Prabha*	*KNN, Prabha News*
5	*Andhra Bhoomi*	*News Flash*
6	*Vaartha*	*Prabhata Vaartha*
7	*Namaste Telangana*	*T Media*
8	*Prajasakti*	*Not applicable*
9	*Visalaandhra*	*Not applicable*
10	*Surya*	*Major News*

Source: Fieldwork

What the report of the Kuldip Nayar Committee on News Agencies (GoI, 1977) envisioned in terms of news gathering from remote locations, villages and small towns, *Eenadu* with *News Today* (a proxy news agency) realised it on a grand scale with a profit motive by the end of 1980s with the launch of district tabloid editions across United Andhra Pradesh (EQC, 1999, p. 118). However, the guidelines suggested by the committee for the career growth of employees, democratic values and a non-partisan approach (independent) for correspondents and stringers were heavily compromised.[4]

The nomenclature (news network) was strategic enough to casualise the entire workforce. From the perspective of labour relations, this marked a watershed moment for journalists in the history of newspapers in this part of the globe. The stringer system of news gathering was consolidated and the newspapers which did not informalise the workforce lost the circulation race by the end of 1980s (for instance, *Andhra Patrika* and *Krishna Patrika*). Barring the left-leaning dailies (*Visalaandhra* and *Prajasakti*), almost every newspaper had established its own news network (see Table 7.1). In effect, the simultaneous establishment of a proxy news network, which was pioneered by Ramoji Rao, even by newly launched news dailies has become a 'norm'. One of the main reasons for the success of this kind of informalised recruitment in newspaper industry, popular as 'Ramoji model' among journalists' union leaders, is that the same workforce could be used for sister publications and allied businesses.

Effectively, Telugu news dailies were successful in circumventing successive Wage Board recommendations without engaging in any legal battles, unlike other news organisations in the country. This normalising of the informal newspaper economy or media economy was so smooth and effective that even English-language national dailies followed the pattern.

In their memorandum submitted to the Majithia wage board, news networks or services like Express News Service (affiliated to *The New Indian Express*) and Times News Network (*The Times of India*) figured in the list of in-house news networks (Annexure 16, APUWJ, 2009). Once the journalist unions sought legal means to prove that news networks should be considered agencies to ensure that prescribed pay scales are paid to working journalists and won the legal battle, the newspaper managements found a new way out. The modus operandi was to fudge the numbers or scale of gross revenue in their ledgers to ensure that the wage board recommendations were not applicable (APUWJ, 2009).

The 'normalising' of the informal economy in the newspaper industry resulted in the gross violation of the labour rights of journalists. Journalists (editorial and reporting) on the payroll of news networks as full-timers were denied salaries and benefits prescribed in the wage boards. For stringers, it was worse than full-timers, as they had as much work as full-timers but were not even on the payroll or written contracts of their employers. The magnitude of workload and the variety of work, both journalistic and non-journalistic, appeared to be much higher than that of full-timers (editorial and reporting staffers).

The terminology used in the state-nominated committees and wage boards and the language used by management personnel, along with a privileged core group of newspaper organisations, referred to stringers as part-time contributors, which did not do much justice to the full-time work they do on the ground. As a result, the duties mentioned in the part-time correspondent designation mentioned in the state documents had little relevance to the actual work of stringers in the field.

Despite having to undergo the process of recruitment, most stringers do not have any formal agreement regarding salary or any other specifications. Even in the case of some very large newspapers where there was an agreement between employer and stringer, it was clearly mentioned that the employees could be removed from the position without any prior notice. Regardless of the standing (*cinna* or *pedda*) of the newspapers, firing a stringer happened over a mobile phone call, which stringers termed as 'ousting orders over phone'. While informalisation resulted in the 'contractualisation' of staffers, it actually resulted in 'double informalisation' in the case of stringers (Harriss-White, 2020, p. 39).

As part of employment contracts, a majority of newspapers and periodicals insisted that employees would not form any union or federation to fight for their rights and would have to sign a declaration to that effect. Stringers had to deal with an informal job outside this purview even as they engaged in the work of newsgathering, unpaid and underpaid. They were forced to look for other sources of income also informal in nature.[5]

The concept of 'double informalisation' offers an explanation for stringers engaging in informal activities, including real estate, money-lending and self-employment activities, such as working as personal assistants to local politicians, labouring in rural employment guarantee schemes, running photocopy centres and selling subsidised newsprint in the black market after floating non-existing periodicals registered with the RNI (see Table 7.2).

A panoramic view presents a remarkable overlap of the timelines of informalisation becoming a norm, India embracing the neoliberal reforms and the Sat-shudraisation of the media economy and Brahmanisation of work culture in the Telugu journalistic field. More importantly, this overlapping took place in the Telugu-speaking regions (now states) in which the *masculine* political field was dominated by Sat-shudras.[6]

To understand the specific logic of practice in the journalistic field, the economic aspect of informality, habitus of agents, existing social and organisational hierarchies need to be laid out. It is only then that the issues of relegation and delegation along with the relation between the dispositions, habitus of agents and the positions they occupy in the journalistic field are revealed.[7] In effect, social reproduction takes place in the journalistic field with persons from modest backgrounds and marginal communities occupying lower

Table 7.2 Other sources of income for stringers

S. No	*Source*	*Count of stringers*
1	Private money lending/finance	2
2	Real estate agents	8
3	Small-time grocery store	2
4	Advertising and flex printing	3
5	Photo and Video studio	3
6	Ration (fair price) shop dealer	1
7	Electrician	2
8	Daily wage farm worker	1
9	Social work	1
10	Local cable operator	1
11	Temple priest and teacher	1
12	Photocopying centre	2
13	Total	27

Source: Fieldwork

positions or more precarious positions (stringers), while agents with considerably higher amount of social capital found themselves in relatively higher positions within the field, marked by informality and precarity.

Promise of wage boards: a view from the field

The localisation strategy employed by Telugu newspapers from the 1970s along with advances in communication technologies improved means of communication (transport), increasing competition in the industry and the growth of literacy appeared to have resulted in quantitative and qualitative changes in the effective news workforce. But there was little protection or security offered to stringers and part-time correspondents working in print journalism across the country by successive wage boards.

The six wage boards constituted following the Working Journalists Act (1955) are: (1) Divatia Wage Board Committee, 2 May 1956; (2) Shinde Wage Board Committee, 12 November 1963; (3) Palekar Wage Board Committee, 11 June 1975; (4) Bachawat Wage Board Committee, 17 July 1985; (5) Manisana Wage Board Committee, 2 September 1994; and (6) Majithia Wage Board Committee, 24 May 2007.

A reading of these reports reveals that the classification or grading of working journalists and non-journalistic newspaper employees along with the methodology to fix the wages was sophisticated, whereas, in practice, the implementation of the suggestions was diluted with each subsequent wage board. The reports, usually headed by retired Constitutional Court judges (the Supreme Court or High Courts), provide fine and detailed experiences of the work experiences of reporters and editors (desk), changes in the newspaper industry, along with technological advances, official categorisation of work location (that is, national/state capital, city or town or village) and, most importantly, the standing of the newspaper or periodical for pay scale grading purposes (Mishra, 2016, p. 127). However, I will limit the present discussion to the Majithia Wage Board recommendations, which (GoI, 2011, p. 71) suggests:

> Every part-time Correspondent and part-time Photographer shall be paid not less than 40 per cent, if he is posted at district headquarters and above and not less than 30 per cent, if he is posted at place below district headquarters, of the basic wage plus dearness allowance applicable to a full time Correspondent/Photographer at similar level, provided that no part-time Correspondent/Photographer will work for more than two newspaper establishments. In addition, payment shall be paid to him on column basis, the rate of which to be settled by mutual negotiations keeping in view the basic wages and dearness allowances drawn by a part-time Correspondent and part-time Photographer.
>
> (All upper/lowercases retained as in the original)

These recommendations were only on paper as managements did not wish to implement them for the benefit of working journalists. I measured the published news items and counted the published photographs of two stringers each in Sangareddy and Gannavaram to calculate the amount they ought to receive for their labour, as per the Wage Board recommendations. Given that Sangareddy happens to be the district headquarters, the stringer or part-time correspondent ought to have received 40 per cent of the salary a full-time reporter receives (basic pay INR 13,000). In the case of Gannavaram, the stringer ought to have received 30 per cent of the salary of the reporter, as it is placed below district headquarters.

In effect, Sangareddy stringers ought to have received INR 5,600 + lineage, whereas Gannavaram stringers ought to have received INR 3,900 + lineage. The tabulated lineage (Table 7.3) presented only 30 and 40 per cent of the basic pay and is not inclusive of the dearness allowance, to give a rough estimate. This is the payment or quantitative aspect. As mentioned in the Wage Board recommendations, the role of a stringer is not a part-timer 'journalist' as he is required to do non-journalistic work such as increasing the circulation numbers in the locality and procuring advertisements for the newspaper establishment in which he works.

In reality, no stringer receives even these meagre wages for his services to the newspaper establishments. In fact, many stringers did not receive the token of the lineage amount for months. At the time of fieldwork, many stringers did not bother to check their line account or enquire about the pending amount in the line account from managements. Instead, they focused on procuring local business and political advertisements. Most newspapers, instead of giving

Table 7.3 Lineage amount stringers ought to receive from newspaper establishments (Pre-pandemic)

S. No.	*Month*	*Date/credit line*	*Column-cm*	*No. of News articles*	*Lineage amount in INR*	*No. of published photos*	*Amount in INR*	*Min. pay*	*Total amount in INR*
GS-1	May 2012	Gannavaram	783	91	1,566	34	340	3,900	5,806
GS-2	May 2012	Gannavaram Urban	864	74	1,728	42	420	3,900	6,048
SS-1	Sept. 2014	Sangareddy	1,158	146	2,316	86	860	5,200	8,376
SS-2	Sept. 2014	Sangareddy	1,364	159	2,728	94	940	5,200	8,868

Source: Fieldwork

Notes: The number of photographs published in Sangareddy was relatively higher than Gannavaram due to the coverage of Bathukamma festival in the district tabloids. The number of articles published by the stringers was higher in Sangareddy because of its status as district headquarters. GS – Gannavaram stringer; SS – Sangareddy stringer. The column-centimetre lineage is measured physically using a ruler (scale) and while doing the same, headlines and blurbs were excluded, which is the existing practice.

salaries, offer a commission of 20–30 per cent of the advertisements. From time to time, stringers received reminders and alerts from managements setting 'target revenue' for upcoming events or festivals, which included May 1, International Labour Day. Their journalistic work was most often unpaid, while the non-journalistic work generates some income for stringers.

Payment of the commission amount to stringers is deferred in case of any mistakes in the content or placement of advertisements. In case of any blunders, stringers are fired without returning the caution deposit lying with managements and payable pending amounts from earlier advertisements. In Sangareddy, the stringer of a Telugu daily established in the 1930s misplaced a birthday wish advertisement of an ex-MLA. Instead of the ex-MLA's photograph, the stringer gave the name and photograph of an incumbent MLA. The desk persons, based in Hyderabad, carried it the following day (Field notes, 3 October 2014). The stringer was fired.

More importantly, Gannavaram stringers pointed out that if they fail to meet the target revenue twice or thrice consecutively, they are fired. In Sangareddy, in some newspapers, the pressure builds from the first failure itself, and for some stringers working in small or medium scale newspapers, it was based on an 'understanding' with managements. The view of management personnel on the non-implementation of wage board recommendations or flouting them, gathered from two lengthy interviews, might be summarised as: small-town journalists and especially stringers do not deserve the inflated salaries suggested from time to time by the boards (YKK & ChNR, personal communication, September 2014, Hyderabad).

The tone of these two interviewees working in the administration of two Telugu dailies was as harsh as the chairman and managing director of *The Indian Express*, Vivek Goenka, who said, 'I cannot think of anything more ridiculous', about the wage board recommendations (quoted by Jeffrey, 2010, p. 142). Commenting on the status and working conditions of journalists in Indian-language newspapers, Jeffrey (2010, p. 143) appropriately remarked, 'The life of many journalists was hectic, beholden and unsure'.

Making a generalised observation on the insecure working conditions prevalent across the world during an intervention – *Job insecurity everywhere now* – in Grenoble, France, Bourdieu (1998a, p. 86) points out:

> Casualisation of employment is part of a mode of domination of a new kind, based on the creation of a generalised and permanent state of insecurity aimed at forcing workers into submission, into the acceptance of exploitation. To characterise this mode of domination, which, although in its effects it closely resembles the wild capitalism of the early days, is entirely unprecedented, a speaker here proposed the very appropriate and expressive concept of *flexploitation*. . . . These submissive dispositions produced by insecurity are the prerequisite for an increasingly 'successful' exploitation.

Notably, Bourdieu stresses on the social, even as he was making an observation on the neoliberal market economy that continuously thrusts the workforce in a state of insecurity, which encapsulates the state of affairs of stringers. Yet in the Indian context, the news labour of stringers at the local level remains unacknowledged, not only by successive wage boards, which set their perspective aside while fixing the wages, but also in the larger journalistic field and in academia. My field observations at both locations revealed that the newswork performed by stringers is more or less quantitatively similar to that of full-time journalists.

Despite the fact that the wage boards allowed stringers or part-time correspondents to work for not more than two news dailies or publications, most of them 'officially' did not avail the recommendation. Instead, in the field, most newspapers had more than one stringer for the same location in Sangareddy and Gannavaram (urban and rural). This phenomenon was not restricted to Krishna and Medak districts; it has been prevalent in the Telugu-speaking states.

When a stringer gets fired from a newspaper, he approaches a fellow stringer asking if he might share a beat in the locality or goes to an old-timer in the profession asking him to recommend him to another newspaper.[8] On one occasion, Gannavaram stringer, ARP, who got fired from *Eenadu* without any prior notice, approached a senior stringer, DD, who in turn made a phone call and got the former appointed as a Gannavaram urban stringer, while the latter confined himself to the rural beat in the newspaper where he works. The entire hire-fire-and-hire episode highlights the informal nature of news labour within a formal sector and issues of casualisation and precarity in the field.

Stringers, politics of accreditation, journalists' unions

Based on an estimate by leaders of journalists' unions, there are around 20,000 stringers each in Andhra Pradesh and Telangana, with almost every Telugu news daily having at least one stringer in the tiny *mandals* of the districts (with and without accreditation). Most, like stringers in Gannavaram and Sangareddy, carry out their newswork along with other duties given to them by their managements without either written contracts or sometimes any stipulated wages or monthly salary.

What accounted for the burgeoning number of stringers in the Telugu journalistic field in particular, marked as it is by its informality and precarious working conditions? How were the journalists' unions and federations collectively addressing these issues to safeguard the basic rights of stringers in particular and journalists in general?

Riding around in the field with stringers and attending working journalists' meetings did not result in an extensive idea about the nature of the state (governing body). It was only while classifying the data that I realised that there were many faces of the state and how it operated in the journalistic field.

The workings of the state on the field were interesting and arbitrary as it was repressive and at the same time a welfare state. Apart from these two faces, it also had a third face, which allowed informality to thrive in the field – the neoliberal state. The responses to these different faces of the state from journalists' unions were: democratic protests against the repression, engaging with the welfare state, and monologue filled with parliamentary leftist rhetoric against the (neoliberal) state that sides with corporate media houses.

The APUWJ in united AP was one of the strongest unions in the country along with the Bombay Union of Journalists and Kerala Union of Journalists (Mazumdar, 2019, p. 38). While the state in its different forms (repressive, welfare and neo-liberal) continued to carry out peculiar jugglery, journalists' unions in Andhra Pradesh and Telangana engaged in making corresponding moves to push their 'demands', which could not be realised from the newspaper establishments in various ways with relative success. Some of them include: a) procuring accreditation cards for working journalists at various levels (*mandal*, district and state-level); b) housing schemes; c) medical insurance and allied facilities; and d) free transport facility for stringers and staffers in state-run road transport services.

A major factor for many stringers in Telangana to continue in the profession and get an accreditation card at any level is the electoral promise of double-bedroom *iḷḷu* (2bhk flats) for accredited journalists. Many journalists stay in the field only with the dream of securing a 2-bhk flat in the journalist quota.

Most schemes that applied to persons below poverty line (BPL) were being offered to stringers who were given accreditation cards at the *mandal* level (MRO) and some of them even provided with 1.5 to 3 cent area land (653–1306 sq. ft.) in the *mandal* they worked. While *mandal*-level stringers were given an AP or Telangana Road Transport Corporation bus pass to travel in the revenue division for free, district headquarter-level journalists avail free transport across the district, whereas, a state-level accreditation card would allow journalists to travel across the state at a very nominal tariff.

The collective bargaining of the members of journalists' unions with the governments enabled them to avail facilities such as *Aarogyasri* (a health scheme) or *Gruhakalpa* (housing scheme), otherwise allocated for persons from BPL in both Andhra Pradesh and Telangana. Some of these factors could be the possible reasons for the presence of a very large number of stringers in the Telugu-speaking states compared to other states (see Table 7.4).

This data was collected from the information and public relations website of every state and the number of publications of each state was procured from the RNI office. The accredited journalists' list of New Delhi was collected from the Press Information Bureau. One of the significant achievements of the working journalists' unions in AP (13,506) and TS (10,309) was making the accreditation rules as inclusive as possible.

Table 7.4 State-wise list of accredited journalists and registered publication in India

Sl. No.	*State*	*No. of accredited journalists*	*No. of registered publications*
1	Andhra Pradesh	13,506	3,319
2	Arunachal Pradesh	58	24
3	Assam	116	296
4	Bihar	690	489
5	Chhattisgarh	Not available	1,245
6	Goa	105	67
7	Gujarat	Not available	4,041
8	Haryana	1,197	864
9	Himachal Pradesh	396	169
10	Jharkhand	205	338
11	Karnataka	819	4,199
12	Kerala	905	1,639
13	Madhya Pradesh	3,998	8,314
14	Maharashtra	2,920	10,337
15	Manipur	42	39
16	Meghalaya	97	27
17	Mizoram	120	58
18	Nagaland	26	11
19	New Delhi*	2,441	5,566
20	Odisha	91	1,178
21	Punjab	228	721
22	Rajasthan	180	3,105
23	Tamil Nadu	Not available	3,465
24	Sikkim	Not available	83
25	Telangana	10,309	982
26	Tripura	111	62
27	Uttar Pradesh	137	9,425
28	Uttarakhand	Not available	2,554
29	West Bengal	Not available	1,547

Sources: www.arunachalpradesh.gov.in/press-media/ (Arunachal Pradesh); https://iprd.assam.gov.in/portlets/accredited-journalists (Assam); http://210.212.23.61/pdffiles/journalist.pdf (Bihar); https://dip.goa.gov.in/accreditation-of-journalists.php (Goa); https://prharyana.gov.in/sites/default/files/Media%20Corner/Accredited%20media%20persons%20of%20Haryana-website_sep%20 2018% 20(1).pdf (Haryana); http://himachalpr.gov.in/Default.aspx?Language=1 (Himachal Pradesh); http://prdjharkhand.in/iprd/apa/approved%20press%20accreditation1.pdf (Jharkhand); https://dipr.karnataka.gov.in/storage/pdf-files/Accounts/ANNUAL%20REPORT%202018-19(eng)%20.pdf (Karnataka); www.prd.kerala.gov.in/home-1 (Kerala); www.mpinfo.org/MPinfo Static/Hindi/Accreditation/Journalist-Card.asp (Madhya Pradesh); https://cmdashboard.maha rashtra.gov.in/scheme/facilities-registered-journalist (Maharashtra); http://diprmanipur.in/infoApp.aspx?par=Accredited%20Journalist (Manipur); https://megipr.gov.in/local_media.html (Meghalaya); www.pibaizawl.nic.in/pib/journalist.htm (Mizoram); https://pib.gov.in/newsite/AccMedia List/AccPressMediaNagaland.pdf (Nagaland); http://pibaccreditation.nic.in/acrindexall.aspx (New Delhi); https://enews.nic.in/pdf/STATE.pdf (Odisha); http://diprpunjab.gov.in/?q=content/media-list (Punjab); http://dipr.rajasthan.gov.in/content/dam/dipr/Accredited%20Journalist%20Informa tion/MediclaimCardList.pdf (Rajasthan); https://ica.tripura.gov.in/Accredited-Journalists (Tripura); http://information.up.nic.in/attachments/files/59f17ae5-b9d8-4ddc-abc4-402fc0b97065.pdf (Uttar Pradesh)

* Figures refer to the National Capital Territory of Delhi (NCT) and not National Capital Region (NCR).

These two states were followed by Madhya Pradesh (3,998) and Maharashtra (2,920), respectively. The next two states/UTs with the greatest number of accredited journalists were New Delhi (2,441) and Haryana (1,197), respectively. While AP and TS unions bargained for more democratic and inclusive accreditation rules, journalists' unions in Maharashtra pushed the government to come up with a legislative act that protects journalists from violence, which was accepted (GoM, 2019).

An important aspect which journalists' unions both AP and Telangana appeared to have conveniently ignored is the caste question. Very similar to the responses of the edition in-charges and management personnel, even the APUWJ or TUWJ (to an extent) did not wish to address discrimination faced by persons from marginal communities or any attempts to make the field more inclusive. Even leaders from AP Working Journalists' Federation (APWJF) and Telangana WJF, politically affiliated to the CPI (M) did not wish to engage with the question during my interactions with them.

Stringers from marginal communities in both Gannavaram and Sangareddy complained that even these facilities were given to persons from influential castes and backgrounds. 'I had to struggle for more than eight years to get a two-cent area plot under the BPL scheme, while a stringer from an influential caste got his third plot due to his position in the working journalists' union', Gannavaram stringer, SSS, informed me (Personal communication, Gannavaram, 18 May 2012).

A major criticism against the APUWJ and TUWJ leaders from stringers was that the unions were making the fourth estate dependent on the state in the collective bargaining process to secure basic entitlements and thereby compromising or losing their right to question it. A section of stringers at the APUWJ meeting held at Kanchikacharla in Krishna district raised slogans against the union before boycotting the elections for the local chapter of the union.

> No sooner the (then) APUWJ President D Somasundar proposed names of the candidates who wish to run for the office bearer positions for the district chapter than a section of stringers raised their voices against the union leaders demanding for a discussion on the issue of minimum wages for mofussil newsworkers. Despite repeated requests from the union leaders, agitating stringers gathered in front of the dais to stall the proceedings for elections. There was a pandemonium in the hall, when a union leader pointed his finger towards a stringer who was leading a group of protestors and warned him to behave properly (*mundu journalistula undatam telusuko*; learn how to behave like a journalist). Protestors, in turn, accused the union leaders of colluding with the YSR Congress Party and working only in the interest of *Sakshi* newspaper employees

with no concern towards the problems and everyday travails of stringers.

(Fieldnotes, 27 May 2012, Kanchikacharla, Krishna district)

When approached, the leader of the protestors, PDR fumed that the union leaders do not know the meaning of the fourth estate. He said:

> We are only asking the union to pressurise media organisations to pay minimum wages for stringers. Instead of doing that they (union leaders) were only interested in talking to successive governments for alms (*mushṭi*). We are not beggars to depend on government and urging that we collectively fight for what is rightfully ours from organisations. If we go on fighting for accreditation cards to avail government schemes, how can we report about corrupt activities and wrongdoings of local officials and politicians.

Another protestor told me that state-level union leaders were not aware of the clientelist activities of local (district-level) union leaders. Stringers at both sites often criticised the union leaders that they land from Hyderabad and preached about paid news or conduct of journalists without addressing the wage-related issues of stringers in remote and mofussil areas.[9] At the same time, many stringers on the sidelines of union meetings pointed out that the journalists' unions were successful only in proposing and securing bourgeois and superficial demands and failed to address the root cause of the problem – systemic failure (*patanam avutunna vyavastha*) and exploitation due to capitalist system (*pettubaḍidāri vyavastha*).

Forms of precarity in the journalistic field

> Journalism *mattu lekkanna. Okkasāri ekkināka e mattu vaduluḍu kashṭam* (Journalism is like a 'high'. Once it gets on, it is difficult to get rid of.)
>
> – Sangareddy stringer, NNK (Personal communication, 3 January 2022)

> *E vyasanāniki bānisalam ayipōyāmanḍi* (We became slaves to this addiction [journalism]).
>
> – Gannavaram stringer, DAR (Personal communication, 7 October 2012)

Economic aspects and material conditions of labour are privileged over non-material or symbolic ones when it comes to discussions of the precarity of a particular sector or any sphere of productive activity. Many studies address the issue of 'exploitation of labour' in factory settings, illegal markets, the unorganised sector, in general and even in the supposedly organised sector (see Routh, 2014; Mukhopadhyay, 2022). Little attention is paid to the non-material, cultural and legal aspects that aggravate precarity in the informal sector.

Śrama dōpiḍi is the Telugu expression to describe 'exploitation of labour'. Often, it was the initial response from stringers and reporters in the Telugu-speaking states during my fieldwork when asked about the issues, insecurities and problems stringers faced in their work life. Not even a single journalist union meeting concluded without at least one speaker uttering these two words. It was only after this initial response that stringers and journalists started talking about discrimination during formal interviews or informal interactions depending on their convenience. As discussed in the previous chapters, despite their marginalised status in the journalistic field, stringers commanded a considerable amount of capital in the limited area of their operation, however small compared to their counterparts in other media or staffers within their organisations.

At the time of fieldwork at both sites, the difficulty was more about how it was possible for vulnerable newsworkers to 'report' and 'bring to light' issues about even more vulnerable labourers, as I presumed that there was no solidaristic avenue or platform for them to express themselves. Partly, the difficulty was also about the fact that there was not much literature to understand the issue of exploitation in news or media labour, as pointed out by Hesmondhalgh (2017, p. 30).

A Sangareddy stringer, PSR during the period between the first phase of the lockdown (March 2020) in the country and January 2022, was either sacked or told to stop sending reports at three dailies. PSR said,

> I reported on illegal (prohibited) construction activities, negligence while carrying out duties by doctors at the local area hospital, and sale of illicit liquor during the lockdown. Either the ruling party leaders or Opposition party leaders were behind these activities.
>
> (Personal communication, 3 January 2022)

He said that the bureau in-charge had no option but to politely tell him to leave the organisation, as the daily may not get advertisement revenue if they continue publishing such reports. PSR continues to work in a small-time daily, precariously, only to ensure that his name is included in the district-level accreditation list.

How can we understand the issue of precarity in the relatively less autonomous journalistic field marked by informality along with existing social inequalities and political conditions? What is the impact of pandemic on the existing precarious nature of news labour?

The forms of precarity in the journalistic field that emerged from my research are: (1) symbolic precarity; (2) economic precarity; and (3) legal precarity. These forms as they appear are not mutually exclusive or watertight categories.

Symbolic precarity

This is a form of precarity that emerges from the insecurity faced by the agents within and outside the field based on non-material markers of discrimination such as caste, sex, gender, religion, region/space, ability/disability and many other factors. This study argues that this under-theorised form of precarity in the journalistic field has not been addressed adequately without which we cannot understand the lives of the stringers or the nature of news labour.

Initial responses from the stringers about the reasons why they have chosen this field include: 'Journalism is my passion', 'To raise public awareness (*prajā caitanyam*)', 'To contribute to a better society', 'To highlight social evils' and 'Opportunity to speak on behalf of the voiceless' and 'To bring about a change in the society' (Interviews, Stringers, Gannavaram and Sangareddy, 2012 & 2014). These were the responses from majority of aspiring journalists or students wishing to join a J-school. They have a rehearsed, artificial quality that sits uncomfortably with the actual lives of the stringers, how they and their reports are treated, and the extent to which they are devalued.

Stringers also mentioned that journalism is (a) 'a noble profession' (*udāttamaina vṛtti*); (b) 'a respectable job' (*gouravapradamaina pani*); (c) 'a way to get good recognition' (*manci gurtimpu*) in the society. These clichés were even starker in their contrast with the nobility, respectability and recognition not accorded to them. I was getting warmer but nowhere near the actual reasons. In their tone was some disillusionment, arising from the contradiction between their expectations before joining and the reality (social and professional pressures and economic constraints) the field offered or after realising the limited stakes they have in the field.

After developing a better rapport with stringers over a period of time, the reasons they revealed for 'continuing' in the field given the poor pay conditions and precarious nature of their jobs, changed a little; 'Journalism is my passion', 'There is no way out of this [profession]' and 'It has become an obsession/addiction (*vyasanam*)'.[10] Apart from the respondents in Sangareddy and Gannavaram, scores of stringers I met during the journalists' union meetings in both states used words such as *mattu* (high), *visha valayam* (vicious circle) and *bhramalalo batukutunnamu* (we live in illusions) in similar fashion in response to the question. How does one understand these clichés and their despite having a seeming disappointment or disillusionment?

A readymade rationale can be derived from the field theory concept of *illusio*, which is, 'the fact of being caught up in and by the game'. While addressing a sociological question about if a disinterested act is possible, Bourdieu (1998b) introduced the notion of *illusio* as,

> the fact of attributing importance to a social game, the fact that what happens matters to those who are engaged in it, who are in

> the game. *Interest* is to 'be there,' to participate, to admit that the game is worth playing and that the stakes created in and through the fact of playing are worth pursuing; it is to recognise the game and to recognise its stakes.
>
> (pp. 76–77) [Emphasis original]

The notion of *illusio* fell in line with the way stringers dealt with the disappointment regarding their news reports or articles being spiked by staffers at edition centres or being picked up by reporters working in the same organisation. Journalistic *illusio* was the manner in which the field tended to make the agent, here the stringer, believe that this was the only game available to them. Also, it was the feeling that they will succeed next time or the following day even in case they were to fail on a given day, which seemed to have kept them going.

Instead of the tennis match or gambling metaphors frequently used while discussing *illusio*, it appeared more appropriate to present an agrarian metaphor used by a Gannavaram stringer, who said:

> *Idi kūḍā vyavasāyam lāgānēnanḍi. Raitu koṭiswaruḍu ayipōdāmani sāguceyaḍu. Idi tappa vērēdi cēyaḍam teliyadu. Ante. Kākapotē ē sāri bāgā panḍutundi ani aśa. Tappuledugā?* . . . (Our job is akin to agriculture. A farmer does not till the land hoping to become a millionaire. The farmer continues to till the land because he does not know anything else. But he hopes that the produce/harvest will be better than the last time. There is nothing wrong with having hope, right?)
>
> (SSS, Gannavaram, 18 May 2012)

I discuss, briefly, two perceivable problems associated with the concept of *illusio*. First, it does not provide an explanation for the lack of paraphernalia for stringers to counter the forces emanating from the influential agents from other fields of power and their continuing in the journalistic field. Second, it does not fully answer the perennially subservient attitude of stringers in relation to socially, politically and economically influential persons present in the localities they operate in along with those whom they consider 'symbolically superior' within and outside of the journalistic field, even if the latter are physically absent in the immediate surroundings. In both cases, the stringer is perennially in a state of symbolic precarity, standing to attention as soon as a phone call arrives with a 'Sir, yes Sir?'

As much as the disparities in wage structure are based on social hierarchies (*peddā-cinnā* [big-small]), the issue of symbolic precarity was crucial in understanding insecurities faced by certain agents based on their social capital, the positions they occupy in the social space as well as the professional space ('mind your own business', 'know your limits'), as discussed earlier. This form of precarity, on occasion, could result from other fields of power as well.

The instance in which the ruling party TRS MLA, G. Mahipal Reddy threatened a Patancheru (Sangareddy district) local contributor, who belongs to the Dalit community, is a case in point. A case was booked under the SC and ST (Prevention of Atrocities) Act against the MLA for abusing and threatening the Dalit stringer for writing a story on a real-estate-related issue in which he was reportedly involved. This was carried by all major Telugu and English dailies and even journalists' unions demanded that the government take appropriate action against the MLA for abusing the stringer and his family members on the basis of his social and caste background.[11]

Symbolic precarity associated with the journalistic field also explained the absence of women as stringers and reporters in mofussil areas, persons from sexual minorities, and under-representation of persons from modest backgrounds in key roles along with the near-absence of persons from the Scheduled Tribe category. Hegde (2014, pp. 92–101) detailed how important the issue of 'gendered precarity' is in the complex intersection of media and power before suggesting that there was a greater need for transnational readings of the politics of gender and mediated environments. There was every possibility to deal with caste precarity, religious precarity and cultural precarity, among others, separately. But symbolic precarity encompasses such identity-based or non-material insecurities within and outside the field along with the overlapping of such categories.

Economic precarity

This form of precarity emerges from the exploitation of news labour in the informal media economy. The lack of job security and career growth coupled with the lack of protection of salary and allied economic problems faced by stringers and staffers comprised the sources of economic precarity in the field.

Even the mandatory benefits such as medical insurance and compensation in case of occupational accidents/deaths that many workers in other informal workspaces are entitled to are denied to stringers. As APUWJ leader, DS, pointed out that this issue of producing a backdated resignation letter or end of the contract was not limited to Sangareddy stringer SAK or the organisation in which he worked for and became prevalent since the 2000s in the Telugu print media. DS revealed that most of these employment contracts for staffers were written in English, which many aspirants fail to understand. He said:

> First of all, signing an employment contract with a monthly salary itself was a big thing for many [as stringers were not on the

> payroll]. In the same manner, we press the 'enter button' in the computer [accept software licence agreement] without any second thought, they sign contracts.

Even though the Supreme Court in February 2014 upheld the much-awaited Majithia wage board recommendations, which recommended that all full-time and part-time employees working in newspapers should be provided health insurance, it brought little cheer to the stringers. The Apex Court ordered:

> The wages as revised/determined shall be payable from 11.11.2011 when the government of India notified the recommendations of the Majithia wage boards. All the arrears up to March 2014 shall be paid to all eligible persons in four equal instalments within a period of one year from today and continue to pay the revised wages from April 2014 onwards.
>
> (GoI, 2014)

However, the Apex Court judgement resulted in two significant and unexpected changes in the Telugu print industry. They were (1) near-total 'contractualisation' of editorial and reporting workforce; (2) disappearance of news networks. This understanding emerged during interactions with agents of the journalistic field in Medak district, taking part in union meetings in various parts of AP and Telangana and informal interactions with scores of senior journalists and editors during literary and cultural events in Hyderabad.

The line accounts of stringers were maintained in separate books and at the time of fieldwork in Sangareddy, only three very large-scale newspapers, as per this study's classification, and one large daily, along with two left-leaning newspapers were giving compensation to stringers that ranged from INR 1,000 to 3,000. By the end of 2019, the situation of stringers in the Telugu-speaking states became even more precarious, as newspaper establishments started firing them if they did not meet the advertisement and other informal targets set every 3 months.

One of the reasons for the establishments being strict on revenue generation by any means from stringers was due to the over-availability of manpower willing to work at *mandal* and town levels by paying unaccounted-for and thereby non-refundable caution deposits. This situation was even more prevalent in television news channels. 'Depending on the location and establishment, an identification card from the news organisation could range anywhere from INR 10,000 to 50,000', an English-language newspaper reporter based in Sangareddy revealed (see Roy, 2011).

Box 1 The bane of contractualisation

Despite hailing from a 'police patel' family (an inherited police post during the Nizam rule; now defunct), SAK said that a love for literature and the arts ran in his blood. 'My grandfather worked in the Nizam's *Deccan Radio* and I shared the same fascination for radio programmes. Perhaps that was a major reason for my interest in the news and journalism field', he recalled and added that his father was an Urdu poetry aficionado and an admirer/follower of socialist and Urdu poet Makhdoom Mohiuddin.

He started his career in a local magazine as an intern for some months in 1996 and joined *Andhra Jyothi* as a stringer. Given his command over language and nose for news, he found himself working for *Eenadu* a couple of years later. In 1999, he was recruited as a reporter in *Vaartha*. 'It was a sensation in those days. Even my seniors in the profession were surprised to see me rise from the position of a stringer to a staffer in such a short time', he reminisced.

In January 2004, he was hit by a truck on the Mumbai highway while on the way from his village Gopalapuram to Patancheru to report an incident. He was rushed to the ESI Hospital at Ramachandrapuram. 'I saw the lorry at a distance and do not remember anything after being hit. I was in Ramachandrapuram hospital and by the time I gained consciousness, I could not feel my legs', SAK remembered.

It was only after shifting to Hyderabad for better medical treatment that he realised that his lower body was permanently paralysed due to his crushed spinal cord. The stringer-turned-reporter was always under the impression that monthly cuts from his salary were going to the employees' provident fund account, which was not the case, he said. SAK could not proceed legally as there were no salary slips or related proof of financial transactions with his employer.

Even the working journalists' union could not come to his rescue as the newspaper management produced a letter which stated that he resigned from the position 5 months before the date of the accident. With the help of union members and local politicians, he managed to receive an amount of INR 15,000 from the Chief Minister's Relief Fund. SAK continues to write for magazines and started working as a TV anchor in local channels. Apart from starting a disability rights organisation, he produces content for YouTube channels (personal communication, Sangareddy, 1 October 2014).

A vast majority of staffers had to sign a renewed written contract declaring that they were willing to work for the news organisation forgoing the wage board recommendations for a consolidated amount. Needless to add, newspaper establishments can terminate the contract with or without giving prior notice and did not provide medical insurance or provident fund, basic benefits and entitlements in the new situation.

Considering such 'prerequisites' for entering the journalistic field, it is possible to state that entering and sustaining in the profession had become more difficult for women and persons from marginal communities. This situation was similar to what Harriss-White hints at while talking about the relationship between social structure and labour in the informal economy in a different context. She says social identities 'affect the tasks most people do – the kinds, terms and conditions of contracts they are offered, and either settle for or refuse. They make for significant differences to the terms and conditions of work' (2003, p. 21). This observation is relevant not only for stringers in the Indian-language journalistic field but also for a vast majority of the workforce in the informal media economy in the country.

Legal precarity

The lack of legal protection for journalists from state oppression has resulted in the violation of human rights and killings, torture and illegal detention of journalists leading to violence, injury and death (see Seshu and Sarkar, 2019). Legislative Councils and Assemblies have passed press acts to regulate and control not only media organisations but also mediapersons, barring them from writing against the government.

There is a lack of any official grievance redressal mechanism or platform for journalists to present their case on a range of issues such as termination of services without prior notice, various kinds of discrimination within the field and from sources outside of it, and malfeasant media organisations that deny basic wages, which fell under the purview of state government were ignored conveniently.[12] Of these realities, the last affected stringers the most but all of these conditions constrict stringers in one form or the other.

The newly passed Labour and Wage Codes by the BJP-led NDA government are a cause of concern for journalists' union leaders, as they feel that the rights of journalists are at stake with the scrapping of a separate Wage Board for Working Journalists and including them along with other professions and sectors.[13] A member of the Veteran Journalists' Association, Hyderabad KLV with more than four and a half decades of experience in the profession said:

> It is unthinkable to witness that the Working Journalists Act, 1955 and Wage Board for working journalists are repealed through these

> Labour Codes. These are laws for which working journalists fought for to safeguard journalists and ensure they earn a decent livelihood by setting basic standards for the print journalism industry. Many founder members of APUWJ were instrumental in framing the earlier Acts and now they are placed under a Labour Code [on Occupational Health and Safety], which barely makes any sense.
> (Personal communication, 4 March 2022, Hyderabad)

In a way, for members of journalists' unions, these two repealed Acts are cornerstones for the industry and employees to maintain standards and sustain, respectively. TUWJ leader VAK pointed out, 'Without any legal protection the rights of journalists will be weakened. Hire and fire has already become a norm in the print and electronic media industries, as we have seen during the pandemic times'. He was hinting at the thousands of journalists in print media alone who were laid off by media organisations to 'minimise their losses'.

This is one part of the story. The global pandemic, which wrecked established systems and functions of legislature, judiciary, education, healthcare, law enforcing agencies and bureaucracy, had pushed even media organisations and journalists to unforeseen and dire situations. While the healthcare, electricity, sanitation, fire and other emergency service professionals were recognised as frontline workers, journalists were not given the recognition till May 2021. This effectively meant that journalists despite not getting vaccinated had to carry out daily reporting putting their own lives and those of their family members at risk throughout the first and second waves of COVID-19 in the country.

The state of affairs in the journalistic field concerning the insecure working conditions prompts one to ask two pertinent questions: (1) what is the reason behind the burgeoning number of stringers in AP and Telangana? (2) Are there any 'acts of resistance', collective or individual, on their part to deal with the precarious working conditions in their everyday lives?

Box 2 Tormented by police, hallucinating a better world

Bonala Ramesh was a stringer working with *Udayam* daily in the early 1990s. He was brought from Medak town to Gajwel to take part in the first TUWJ meeting ('Hello journalist, chalo Gajwel') organised in a function hall (Pragnya Gardens), attended by working journalists from different parts of the newly formed state.

Even before the audience (including myself) got to know about him, we could not miss his presence for his 'erratic' behaviour and for not maintaining decorum required at a union meeting. He went on sloganeering ('gibberish') at his will during a series of speeches, as two youngsters accompanying him were trying their best to pacify him. Before providing monetary assistance of INR 50,000, the then irrigation department minister T. Harish Rao (TRS) mentioned that Ramesh 'lost his sanity' due to police torture under Andhra leaders. The next speaker (union leader) after Rao revealed the details.

Ramesh joined the profession as a stringer in his early 20s in the newly launched *Udayam* in 1984. He travelled across the length and breadth of Medak district and reported on atrocities on weaker sections, state-sponsored violence and repression by the police. While some of his contemporaries either went missing or were booked under TADA, he was illegally detained several times and was tortured in the early 1990s. Even after several episodes of such violence, he continued in the profession with a progressive spirit. But he went missing for weeks in the first year of Chandrababu Naidu's (TDP, the year 1995–1996) rule.

Nobody knew what happened to him during that time but he was found picking up newspapers from streets and garbage dumping places to read. He lost his speech and regained it only after some years. With his sister's (a government employee) support, Ramesh was admitted into the Government Mental Health Centre, Erragadda in Hyderabad for treatment. His nephew told me that Ramesh keeps hallucinating that the people's party is in power (*prajā prabhutvam accindi*) or is under the illusion that he is still living in the 1980s or 1990s. The former scribe's age was around 50 but could easily pass off as a 65-year-old (Field notes, Gajwel, Medak [now Siddipet] district, 7 October 2014).[14]

We can't fall any further: the COVID-19 pandemic

During the series of lockdowns imposed due to the global pandemic, most Telugu newspapers stopped their operations for a week. Once resumed, almost all newspapers stopped publishing district tabloids or pull-outs, which used to have 8–12 A4 size pages, and started restricting news from mofussil areas to one side of a main page leaf.

This newly included page in the main edition of Telugu newspapers is made exclusive to each district in the Telugu-speaking states. On the whole, this meant a huge loss of publishing space for stringers. Table 7.5 presents the lineage amounts stringers in Gannavaram and Sangareddy ought to have received after the aforementioned changes that took place in the format of newspapers due to the pandemic.

Table 7.5 Lineage amount stringers ought to receive from newspaper establishments (pandemic)

S. No.	*Month*	*Date/credit line*	*Column-cm*	*No. of News articles*	*Lineage amount in INR*	*No. of published photos*	*Amount in INR*	*Min. pay in INR*	*Total amount in INR*
GS-1	August 2021	Gannavaram	548	70	1,096	24	240	3,900	5,236
GS-2	August 2021	Gannavaram	476	54	952	19	190	3,900	5,042
SS-1	Jan. 2022	Sangareddy	654	82	1,308	26	260	5,200	6,768
SS-2	Jan. 2022	Sangareddy	436	61	872	35	350	5,200	6,422

Source: Fieldwork

Interactions with stringers at both research sites during a re-visit in September 2021 and January 2022 revealed that initially they took time to get adjusted to the new layout of local pages and had difficulties convincing local businessmen and politicians for advertisements. More punishingly for stringers, their other sources of income took a hit during the lockdowns.

Some stringers had a tough time paying medical bills for family members affected by COVID-19. These conditions forced them to take *cēbadulu* (hand loans) from local politicians and contractors to keep their families afloat, which inadvertently may have had an impact on the reportage on the professional front.

Responding to my question about the impact of the pandemic, a Gannavaram stringer VSK said that there is no significant difference for us in the field during pandemic or before. In an unsentimental tone, he stated, 'Already *digajārina paristituḷḷonē unnāmu. Inka intakannā digajāraṭam kudaradu*' (We are at the rock-bottom level already. It is not possible to fall further down than this level).

This statement assumes significance when it is read in relation to the impact of the pandemic on journalists across the globe, who received pink slips, pay cuts and were sent on leave without compensation among other measures by media organisations to minimise losses. First, from the point of view of stringers, someone had to have a permanent job to be sacked and a regular salary to receive pay cuts, which they do not have. Second, stringers, unlike full-time employees, were perennially in a state of insecurity and the pandemic did not result in bringing about any earth-shattering changes for them.

Overall, the count of lives of journalists who died of COVID-19 in India stands at 625, as per the list compiled by various journalists and journalists' unions in association with NWMI (2022). Out of these, 146 journalists belonged to Andhra Pradesh, while 80 were from Telangana. Put together, these two states accounted to more than one-third of the deaths in the country.

This number in the Telugu-speaking states is higher than the rest because of the accreditation cards issued at *mandal*, district and state levels unlike in the rest of the country. But again, there are many stringers and journalists in both these states and country who were not accredited. This means that there will be no archive or data left about the faceless journalists and stringers who worked in media organisations, if in future one were to document the current history.

Another cruel aspect about the data regarding journalists who lost their lives is the fact that those belonging to urban centres, influential communities and castes (other than noted journalists) were documented in newspapers and on websites including photographs, while the 'lesser' journalists or mofussil stringers were given a bare mention due to lack of further details.

When viewed at a broader level, the working conditions and lack of basic entitlements in the contractual system in the informal media sector had become a part of what was considered as inherent and foundational principles of the field (doxa), as a whole. More importantly, there were no avenues or platforms to address issues concerning caste-based symbolic violence (ability/disability or sexual minority status).

Box 3 When a small-town stringer dies of COVID-19

The Novel Coronavirus during its second wave in India claimed the life of a Sangareddy stringer-cum-videojournalist Mirdoddi Rajendar (47). After complaining about chest pain and breathing difficulty, he was rushed to Hyderabad from Sangareddy and was admitted in a private hospital on 7 May 2021. For 24 days, Rajendar battled for life before succumbing to the virus on 31 May 2021. He is survived by his daughter and wife.

'We tried to admit him in government hospitals in Sangareddy and Hyderabad. But there were no beds and at that time there was severe shortage of oxygen (cylinders). Through known contacts, we managed to get him admitted into a private hospital at Bowenpally in Hyderabad. Let alone recovering from Corona, he could not get a minute of relief from pains and breathing difficulty', Rajendar's uncle, P. Chandrasekhar said during our interaction in Sangareddy. The hospital bill ran into lakhs of rupees and the family is now debt-ridden.

Discontinuing his undergraduate degree, Rajendar initially worked as videographer for a local studio to shoot marriages, family functions, and political meetings, where he developed an interest in news industry, in the town and nearby localities. He joined as a stringer in a small-sized Telugu daily in 2002 (*Andhra Bhoomi*), where he used to provide news and photographs to the newspaper from Sangareddy town. With the entry of 24×7 television news channels in (united) Andhra Pradesh in the 2000s, he shifted from print to join Gemini TV as videojournalist. He belonged to Gangaputra caste, which is categorised as OBC.

'He was very active in local journalists' union and even worked as an office-bearer in Manjeera Journalists' Union, (old) Medak district. Local politicians from across parties know him very well and he was popular among journalists in town. But when he was hospitalised, I did not receive any help from them', M. Anuradha, Rajendar's wife said. During my interview with her along with family members, she pointed out that there was no 'support system' for family members of local reporters to avail any help in case of emergencies.

After completing a dual Masters in English Literature and Education, Anuradha worked as a teacher in a private school in Sangareddy and continued her job even after marriage. She said that till Rajendar's peers visited him while he was in recovery, she had no idea about Telangana Working Journalists' Health Scheme. 'Rajendar was always busy either with journalistic work or union politics and was on duty during the lockdowns to cover news. He never informed me about the health scheme, which accredited journalists can avail. I ran from pillar to post to secure finances and approached the collector office (Sangareddy), while he was in the hospital. The collectorate personnel told me that they can offer help (medical insurance) as he is an accredited journalist', Anuradha said. But she said that the relief was short-lived as Rajendar died of Covid-19 leaving the family shattered and in a debt trap. Even at the time of the interview, she was clutching on to Rajendar's accreditation card in her right palm tightly and knew the card number (SRDD081) by heart and that it was valid till 30 September 2021.

After selling their home in Sangareddy, she along with her daughter moved to Hyderabad and currently stay in a small rented flat located on the outskirts of the city. 'I told him several times to find a better job and start a small business. But it is the double-bedroom (free 2bhk for accredited journalists, an electoral promise by the ruling TRS party) dream that made him stick to the profession. We are homeless now with zero savings,' Anuradha said and added that the only financial help they officially received was a sum of INR 50,000 through the Union government's *ex-gratia* policy for the families of people who died of Covid-19.

While she is hopeful of receiving help from the state government, Anuradha expressed that as much as the financial burden they face, it is the mental state of her daughter, who is an undergraduate student, that troubles her. 'She's not eating properly since her father's demise and wakes up in the middle of night weeping. I had to resign from my job to take care of her. I want her to complete her studies and lead an independent life', Anuradha said.

With help from her own friends in Sangareddy and relatives, Anuradha shuttles between Hyderabad and Sangareddy to produce proof and certificates to claim the financial compensation announced by the state government. Even though the Telangana government announced an *ex-gratia* of INR 2 lakh and a monthly pension of INR 3,000 for a period of five years, Anuradha expressed that it is proving to be a bureaucratic nightmare and said that she reached a point where she cannot even afford travel expenditure.

Ironically, it is stringers who usually help the needy to get pensions and *ex-gratia* amounts from local government offices. But their families have nowhere to look for help after their departure. Even more ironically, it is stringers who report about deaths in *mandals* and towns. But when they die, no newspaper or TV channel covers it (P. Chandrasekhar, personal communication, 22 March 2022, Sangareddy & M. Anuradha, Petbasheerbagh [Hyderabad], 3 April 2022).

Conclusion

The most glaring facet of the informalisation of workforce and the precarious nature of stringer's work in the journalistic field is the reluctance on part of the state to recognise and compensate the journalistic labour of stringers in particular and journalists in general. Even celebrated academic accounts of stringers and local news gatherers as torchbearers of expansion and localisation strategies on which the edifice of print Indian-language journalism rests do not account for the journalistic labour of stringers. They continue to carry out faceless labour, sometimes with neither *gouravam* (honour) nor *vetanam* (wage).

The tokenistic provisions bestowed onto stringers or part-time correspondents under wage boards evaporated with the new Labour and Wage Codes, leaving them with no security. This decade-long research on the wage issue of stringers has shown that the labour rights of not only stringers but journalists in general have been worsening, pushing them into a precarious zone.

While the informalisation of news labour jammed the stringer further into the ground, through all the previous chapters, I have shown how in the face of structural violence of different kinds, the stringer continues to be an indestructible figure in the journalistic landscape. The economic alone, while one of the most serious forms of violence cannot be seen in isolation from other forms of violence – caste, gender, status – or seen as determining the fate of the stringer. I have tried to argue that we need to engage with the ideas of symbolic as well as the legalistic aspects of precarity to holistically understand both the complexity of the webs that entangle the stringer and also his persistent struggles with them.

The global pandemic has accentuated the precarity associated with journalistic labour and hastened the implementation of new Labour and Wage Codes that have little regard for the welfare of working journalists, especially informal newsworkers like stringers. Due to the lack of such basic entitlements and amenities, stringers were forced to toe the line of those in power to secure accreditation, which is the only source of security to deal with medical emergencies under state-sponsored schemes. But the pandemic was not a particularly acute form of crisis for the stringer. It merely helped to highlight the permanent condition of precarity for the stringer.

Reliance on government schemes, acting as media managers for local politicians and contractors and carrying out other informal activities for sustenance indicate the loss of autonomy of the journalistic field at the grassroots but this situation is caused by the systemic and systematic marginalisation of grassroots journalists by the journalistic field. While the autonomy of this field has been compromised at all levels, the precarity of the stringer, which is endemic and only thrown into relief by the pandemic, remains invisible to all but the stringer himself.

Notes

1 Even though famous late Telugu matinee idol Nandamuri Taraka Rama Rao (NTR) does not utter this dialogue in the film, this quote by US President John F. Kennedy is popular in the Telugu speaking states and gets mentioned very often in the speeches on Independence Day or Republic Day in schools and educational institutions.

2 Also, services by way of transportation by rail or a vessel or a goods carriage from one place in India were not taxed (GoI, 2017b, p. 7); however, newspaper printing was taxed at 5 per cent (GoI, 2017b, p. 22).

3 While re-publishing a report of an international survey conducted by the International Labour Organisation (ILO) on the *Conditions of work and life of journalists (1925–26)*, Hardt (2005, p. 6) pointed out that the document was

> a reminder of the widespread plight of journalists as brain workers since the industrialisation of the press. As such the report is also a historical document that anticipates and reinforces the development of a professional model of journalism and offers insights into the social and economic determinants of a professional class as it is rising from its proletarian roots.

According to Hardt, some of the questions emerging from the ILO report, ranging from wages to work-culture, suggest the continuation of a struggle, in both developing and developed countries, for better working conditions, rights of journalists and recognition of journalists as an intellectual and creative labouring force (p. 7).

4 The Nayar Committee report, which in hindsight appeared to be acutely sensitive to caste/communal and linguistic issues, faced criticism from the industry as well as some of its members (GoI, 1977, p. 95) and was shelved (Shrivastava, 2007, p. 57).

5 These aspects of news labour in the journalistic field seemed to have a near-perfect adherence to the forms of informalisation encapsulated by Portes et al. (1989, p. 299), who suggest:

> First, economic activities may be informalised passively, through no fault of the participants, as it were. . . . Second, informality may come about through the efforts of firms and other private interests in a regulated

economy to gain market advantage by avoiding some state controls. . . . Finally, there is a process of informalisation which takes place precisely because formal rules and controls exist, through manipulation of their application for private gain.

6 It appeared as if the Second Press Commission report was resonating the inevitability of the changing trend in the press industry of those times, when it pointed out:

> Newspapers shall still be run by owners, whoever they may be . . . The production-relations of our society shall not leave them untouched. Even monastic Buddhism, let it be remembered, could not be delinked from the prosperity of trading Vaishya [Vysya] castes, whose emergence made it possible for this non-conformist religion to prosper. The concern of non-linked owners with profitability is likely to be more absolute and obsessive because being non-linked, they would have no other financial resources to cushion their losses, whether the non-linked owners would have any greater flair for or commitment to the profession of journalism is doubtful.
>
> (GoI, 1982, Para 36, p. 227)

7 Drawing on Bourdieu's field theory, Örnebring et al. (2018, pp. 1–21) propose a theoretical model or typology to understand the 'space of journalistic work'. They also attempt to address the issue of precarity in the journalistic field. But the social structure and historical conditions present in Indian or South Asian context make it difficult to 'measure' forms of capital or to come up with a typological model, which is based on the issue of economic class alone. See Harriss-White (2003, pp. 1–42, 2007) for the relationship between the social structure and the south Asian economy and Breman (1996, 2019) for an overview of the labour bondage, capital accumulation and issues of inequality in the Indian context, based on his extensive fieldwork in Gujarat, India for a little more than half a century.

8 This situation of asking a fellow stringer to spare a beat reminds one of Theda Skocpol's study on work, welfare and employment issues in the post-World War United States (1990, pp. 192–194).

9 APUWJ claimed credit for coining the word paid news in the country, which was asserted by former president of the union Devulapalli Amar on various platforms and occasions. Also, see Sharma (2013) and Mazumdar (2019).

10 Initially, I was baffled by this expression and the closest connection between journalism/newspapers and addiction was in an interview with Bourdieu, where he talks about alcoholism among journalists in France (Bourdieu, 2010, p. 327). Another link was by Adam Smith (2003, pp. 1091–1092), who suggests that taxation or stamp duties on newspapers should be on the lines of cards and dice (gambling) and consumption of liquor.

11 See www.deccanchronicle.com/nation/politics/101220/trs-mla-abuses-threatens-dalit-journalist.html; https://indianexpress.com/article/cities/hyderabad/trs-mla-booked-for-abusing-threatening-scribe-7098301/; www.newindianexpress.com/states/telangana/2020/dec/10/trs-mla-bookedfor-threatening-scribe-in-sangareddy-2234083.html. Even the recording phone call threatening the Dalit contributor went viral on YouTube: www.youtube.com/watch?v=MNX8uCmxGwY

12 An expert commentary on the first two kinds of insecurities emerging out of lack of legal provisions and related issues about journalism can be found in the writings of practising advocate and legal commentator Noorani (1982a, 1982b,

1984, 1987, 1992, 2000, 2006,2009). These select articles provided an excellent understanding of the concerns pertaining to the nature of work and the legality. The non-implementation of the Employees Provident Funds (EPF) and Miscellaneous Provisions Act, 1952 in newspaper establishments was a classic example even as it offered special provision for working journalists which was included in the Working Journalists Act, 1957 (see GoI, 1952, chapter X, Para 80, pp. 87–90).

13 The Occupational Safety, Health and Working Conditions Code (OSHWC), 2020 under the Labour Code, 2021, was diluted (GoI, 2020b). Without getting into details, I briefly discuss one single aspect of the OSHWC Code, 2020. Chapter X of this Code, applicable to all sectors, including the media industry, presents the 'Special provision relating to employment of women', which is all of two paragraphs. It (p. 39, Para 43) reads, 'Women shall be entitled to be employed in all establishments for all types of work under this Code and they may also be employed, with their consent, before 6 A.M. and beyond 7 P.M.'. Even during the times when the scrapped Working Journalists Act and Wage Board recommendations specifically mentioned the transport facility to be provided to women journalists working night shifts, it did not translate into practice on the ground. The OSHWC Code does not even mention a word on such a facility in their special provision for women's safety.

14 According to a report by human rights and civil liberties organisations, there was a bloodbath in north Telangana in the year 1996. The report stated that at least 161 extra-judicial killings took place in the then United Andhra Pradesh (PUDR, 1997, p. ii, p. 11).

References

APUWJ. (2009). *Memorandum submitted to Majithia wage board commission.* Hyderabad: APUWJ.

Bourdieu, P. (1998a). *Acts of resistance: Against the tyranny of the market.* New York: New Press.

Bourdieu, P. (1998b). *Practical Reason: On the theory of action.* Stanford, CA: Stanford University Press.

Bourdieu, P. (2010). *Political interventions: Social science and political action.* New Delhi: Navayana.

Breman, J. (1996). *Footloose labour: Working in India's informal economy.* Cambridge, UK: Cambridge University Press.

Breman, J. (2019). *Capitalism, inequality and labour in India.* New Delhi: Cambridge University Press.

ECQ [Eenadu Quality Cell]. (1999). *Eenadu: pātikeḷḷa akshara yātra.* Hyderabad: Eenadu Quality Cell.

GoI [Government of India]. (1952). *The employees provident funds and miscellaneous provisions Act.* Retrieved from: www.epfindia.gov.in/site_docs/PDFs/Downloads_PDFs/EPFScheme.pdf.

GoI. (1955). Working journalists and other newspaper employees (conditions of service) and miscellaneous provisions Act, 1955. In *The gazette of India.* New Delhi: Ministry of Labour.

GoI. (1957). *Report of the first wage board for working journalists* [Divatia Wage Board]. New Delhi: Ministry of Labour and Employment.

GoI. (1967). *Report of the second wage board for working journalists* [Shinde Wage Board]. New Delhi: Ministry of Labour, Employment, and Rehabilitation.

GoI. (1977). *Report of the committee on news agencies*. New Delhi: Ministry of Information and Broadcasting.

GoI. (1980). *Report of the third wage board for working journalists* [Palekar Wage Board]. New Delhi: Ministry of Labour.

GoI. (1982). *Report of the second press commission* (Vol. 1). New Delhi: Controller of Publications.

GoI. (1989). *Report of the fourth wage board for working journalists* [Bachawat Wage Board]. New Delhi: Ministry of Labour.

GoI. (2000). *Report of the fifth wage board for working journalists* [Manisana Wage Board]. New Delhi: Ministry of Labour.

GoI. (2011). *Report of the sixth wage board for working journalists* [Majithia Wage Board]. New Delhi: Ministry of Labour.

GoI. (2014). *Wage board for working journalists*. Retrieved from: https://labour.gov.in/sites/default/files/Wage%20Board%20for%20Working%20Journalists.pdf.

GoI. (2017a). *Rate of GST on goods*. Retrieved from: http://gstcouncil.gov.in/sites/default/files/NOTIFICATION%20PDF/goods-rates-booklet-03July2017.pdf [Last accessed on 15 December 2020].

GoI. (2017b). *Rate of GST on services*. Retrieved from: http://gstcouncil.gov.in/sites/default/files/NOTIFICATION%20PDF/services-booklet-03July2017.pdf [Last accessed on 15 December 2020].

GoI. (2020a). Code on wages, 2019. In *The Gazette of India*. New Delhi: Ministry of Labour and Employment.

GoI. (2020b). *The occupational safety, health and working conditions code, 2020*. New Delhi: Ministry of Law and Justice.

GoM [Government of Maharashtra]. (2019). *The Maharashtra media persons and media institutions (prevention of violence and damage or loss to property) Act, 2017*. Mumbai: Department of Law and Judiciary. Retrieved from: https://prsindia.org/files/bills_acts/acts_states/maharashtra/2019/2019MH29.pdf.

Hardt, H. (1999). Shifting paradigms: Decentering the discourse of mass communication research. *Mass Communication and Society*, 2(3–4), pp. 175–183. DOI:10.1080/15205436.1999.9677871.

Hardt, H. (2005). International labour office: Conditions of work and life of journalists. *Javnost – The Public*, 12(1), pp. 5–14. DOI:10.1080/13183222.2005.11008879.

Harriss-White, B. (2003). *India working: Essays on society and economy*. Cambridge, New York: Cambridge University Press.

Harriss-White, B. (2007). *India's socially regulated economy*. New Delhi: Critical Quest.

Harriss-White, B. (2020). India's informal economy: Past, present and future. In Chen, M. A. and Carré, F. J. (Eds.), *The informal economy revisited: Examining the past, envisioning the future* (pp. 38–44). Abingdon, Oxon: Routledge.

Hegde, R. S. (2014). Gender, media, and trans/national spaces. In Carter, C., Steiner, L. and McLaughlin, L. (Eds.), *The Routledge companion to media and gender*. London: Routledge.

Hesmondhalgh, D. (2017). Exploitation and media labor. In Maxwell, R. (Ed.), *The Routledge companion to labour and media* (pp. 30–39). New York: Routledge.

Jeffrey, R. ([2000] 2010). *India's newspaper revolution: Capitalism, politics, and the Indian-language press*. New Delhi: Oxford University Press.

Mazumdar, S. (2019). Journalists and trade unions in Kolkata's newspapers: Whither collective action? *International Journal of Media Studies*, 1(1), pp. 22–45. Retrieved from: www.efluniversity.ac.in/Journals-Communication/IJMS1_Mazumdar.pdf.

Mishra, A. (2016). Protection of the interests of the employees of media industry and freedom of speech and expression. *Indian Law Institute Review*. New Delhi: Indian Law Institute. Retrieved from: http://ili.ac.in/pdf/paper7.pdf [Last accessed on 15 December 2020].

Mukhopadhyay, I. (2022). *Employment in the informal sector in India*. Singapore: Springer.

Neyazi, T. A. (2018). *Political communication and mobilisation: The Hindi media in India*. New Delhi: Cambridge University Press.

Ninan, S. (2007). *Headlines from the heartland: Reinventing the Hindi public sphere*. New Delhi: Sage.

Noorani, A. G. (1982a). A journalist and his sources. *Economic and Political Weekly*, 17(22), pp. 898–899.

Noorani, A. G. (1982b). Bihar press act. *Economic and Political Weekly*, 17(33), pp. 1306–1307.

Noorani, A. G. (1984). Policemen and journalists. *Economic and Political Weekly*, 19(9), p. 372.

Noorani, A. G. (1987). Interrogation of journalists. *Economic and Political Weekly*, 22(16), p. 685.

Noorani, A. G. (1992). Can a source sue a journalist? *Economic and Political Weekly*, 27(8), p. 386.

Noorani, A. G. (2000). The press and the police. *Economic and Political Weekly*, 35(17), pp. 1420–1421.

Noorani, A. G. (2006). The constitution and journalists' sources. *Economic and Political Weekly*, 41(27/28), pp. 2964–2965.

Noorani, A. G. (2009). The press council: An expensive irrelevance. *Economic and Political Weekly*, 44(1), pp. 13–15.

NWMI. (2022). *In memoriam: Journalists and media workers lost to Covid-19 in India*. Retrieved from: https://docs.google.com/document/d/e/2PACX-1vTkXC1UzWBeXiz39WHroeqleYml9WJui-SbQIu7nANl0zjC-c0jp_maF0XeTNAqOg/pub.

Omkarnath, G. (2012). *Economics: A primer for India*. New Delhi: Orient Blackswan.

Örnebring, H., Karlsson, M., Fast, K. and Lindell, J. (2018). The space of journalistic work: A theoretical model. *Communication Theory*, 28(4), pp. 403–423. Retrieved from: https://doi.org/10.1093/ct/qty006 [Last accessed on 15 December 2020].

Portes, A., Castells, M. and Benton, L. A. (Eds.). (1989). *The informal economy: Studies in advanced and less developed countries*. Baltimore: Johns Hopkins University Press.

PUDR. (1997). *Murders most foul: A report on the extra-judicial killings by the police in north Telangana*. November 11. Retrieved from: www.unipune.ac.in/snc/cssh/HumanRights/02%20STATE%20AND%20ARMY%20-%20POLICE%20REPRESSION/A-%20Andhra%20pradesh/24.pdf.

Remesh, B. P. (2018). Unpaid workers and paid news: Working conditions of journalists in India. In Athique, A., Parthasarathi, V. and Srinivas, S. V. (Eds.), *The Indian media economy, Vol. II: Market dynamics and social transactions* (pp. 134–151). New Delhi: Oxford University Press.

Remesh, B. P. (2021). News hunters or ad gatherers? Precarious work of rural stringers in print media. *Economic and Political Weekly*, 56(15), pp. 36–41.

Routh, S. (2014). *Enhancing capabilities through labour law: Informal workers in India*. Oxon: Routledge.

Roy, S. (2011). Television news and democratic change in India. *Media, Culture & Society*, 33(5), pp. 761–777. DOI:10.1177/0163443711404467.

Seshu, G. and Sarkar, U. (2019). *Getting away with murder: A study on the killings and attacks on journalists in India, 2014–2019, and justice delivery in these cases.* Retrieved from: www.thakur-foundation.org/report-on-attacks-on-journalists-in-india-2014-2019.pdf.

Sharma, A. (2013). *In need of a Leveson? Journalism in India in times of paid news and 'private treaties'*. Oxford: Reuters Institute for Study of Journalism.

Shrivastava, K. M. (2007). *News agencies: From pigeon to internet*. New Delhi: New Dawn Press.

Skocpol, T. (1990). 'Brother can you spare a job?' Work and welfare in the United States. In Erikson, K. and Vallas, S. (Eds.), *The nature of work: Sociological perspectives* (pp. 192–213). New Haven, CT: Yale University Press.

Smith, A. (1776/2003). *The wealth of nations*. New York: Bantam Classics.

8

CONCLUSION

By way of conclusion: small-town stringer and the journalistic field

The aim of this decade-long research that culminated in this book is to offer a dynamic and complex account of mofussil stringers working in Indian-language newspapers. What began as a conjecture that there was not much research concerning small-town spaces in India and the journalistic figures in it, especially in Communication(s) and Journalism Studies with not much literature in the discipline and sub-disciplines, turned into a study that required sustained engagement with a deeply structured and yet equally volatile field.

The overriding concern for me as I delved further into the field was not to reproduce an economistic and linear view of the field. I saw the importance of culture and the social as being as important as the economic. Without an engagement with the cultural, the social and the symbolic, the figure of the stringer would not be understood in his fullness at all.

I began this book by introducing the stringer in mofussil areas as an important figure and tracked how 'he' deals with publics and influential people such as bureaucrats, politicians and businessmen. Raymond Williams' insight into the importance of the study of culture and Bourdieu's field theory for media studies offered valid methodologies to operationalise this ethnographic research and delineate the figure of the stringer in the local journalistic field, which is influenced by and influences other fields of power. An implicit but consistent engagement with Bourdieu's field theory forms a running thread that holds the arguments and formulations I generate based on the primary data.

Not ignoring the structuring hierarchies that operate in the journalistic field such as caste, class, space and gender, I presented them in great detail but also attempted to show how they are not determining, asphyxiating the stringer in a static hierarchy or fixed position. Chapter 2 offered a description of these structuring structures by presenting a cross-section view, to use

DOI: 10.4324/b23313-8

an anatomical metaphor, of the journalistic field in relation to the social, political and economic fields.

While the arduous task that I undertook in the field was to capture the simultaneity of the 'workings' of the fields of power on the news labour of the stringer and vice-versa, it was the cautious dissection of each of the forces (with their varying degrees of emphasis at any given point) in the field that I realised in writing to present an understanding of the journalistic field. In other words, this chapter took up the challenge of conveying and translating the 'feel for the game' of the agents into a wider academic understanding.

A meticulous mapping of the 'principles of vision and division' (*nomos*) inherent in the field(s) demonstrates the pertinent relationship between the forces of domination present in the field and struggles not just to survive but to achieve distinction or difference by stringers (agents) through a variety of practices. This helped in breaking away from the crude structural dyad of the dominant and dominated and to further explore how stringers actively forge relationships with other agents within the journalistic field and with agents from other fields. This sometimes leads to relative transformation and at other times the perpetuation of unwritten norms.

This mapping is further explored in Chapters 3 and 4, in which I showed how the journalistic field refracts the social (caste), economic (class) and political hierarchies outlined in Chapter 2. I presented the ethnographic experience of the recruitment process of stringers to explain the possibilities and impossibilities of their 'professional growth'. By offering an analysis of the relationship between the forms of capital that shape them, the social space of stringers and their position in the journalistic field, I engaged with the concept of relegation. In the first instance, a look at the dispositions of stringers and their positions in the field may immediately lead to the conclusion that it is overtly a case of social reproduction in the journalistic field (or social structures determining the journalistic field). I specifically deployed the concepts of relegation and delegation to delineate the homologous nature of the field as perceived by stringers and how they mediate it in practice.

I captured the relations of news production enmeshed within hierarchies and roles in the journalistic field visible in the form of utterances and perceptions ('lift irrigation', torture and kismet) to offer an account of asymmetrical power relations (especially caste) that stringers have to deal with on a daily basis to show how these are negotiated, navigated and mediated by the stringer. The attempt was to show that this is by no means a wholly pessimistic account of the journalistic field in which the stringer is a down-and-out figure. It is a picture of a challenging minefield comprising unwritten 'rules of the game' and latent 'norms of the field' that the stringer treads, circumvents and sometimes subverts while carrying out everyday newswork.

As much as the stringer internalises the externalities, he externalises his internalities, while transforming one form of capital into the other in the journalistic field. This dynamic relationship between dispositions of stringers (internalities) and the rules of the journalistic game (externalities or the field) is constitutive of journalistic practices. I presented the interplay of these aspects in the form of ethnographic vignettes, events and utterances in Chapter 5. In this chapter, I argued that stringers mediate a difficult field, where there is visible oppression based on caste, class, gender and status but at the same time, I put forth the logical proposition that it is by no means a complete unfreedom that stringers endure in the field.

While the proposition Sat-shudraisation of media economy and Brahmanical media work culture mirrors the state of the journalistic field, the dramaturgical formulation of stringers contriving to become *sūtradhārs* from being mere *pātradhārs* in the field encapsulates the logic of local journalistic practice. This chapter also documented the ways in which stringers bend the very rules, norms and routines that are thrusted upon them to their advantage on occasion, rather than merely surviving in the margins of the field, in which the distinction between journalistic and non-journalistic work often gets blurred. While it is not possible to become a *sūtradhār* on a daily basis or even every instance, what keeps stringers continuing in the field is the hope and possibility of becoming one (journalistic *illusio*) by constantly trying rather than being inert 'cog in the wheel'.

Flaunting an overtly dominating masculinity appears to be one of the ways in which stringers exhibit some power and to build an image (perception of self) in their immediate localities and the world of work where they are emasculated and feminised. While Brahmanical ideology in the form of oppression and inequality constantly damages the stringer, his escape from it, in turn, takes the form of misogyny and the other discontents of hegemonic masculinity, evident in utterances and interactions with women and men. Moving away from the obvious argument that representation of women in the journalistic field is appallingly meagre, in Chapter 6, I present the slippery and vacillating masculinities of the stringer in the journalistic field.

The informality and 'flexploitation' associated with the journalistic field, instrumental in creating both material and symbolic insecurities among stringers, indirectly lead to masculine domination and preservation. I point out, in this chapter, that along with women even 'lesser' men are at the receiving end of this symbolic violence. The contradictory dialectic of being damaged by Brahmanical and masculinist ideologies and damaging 'others' through an internalisation of them as the symbolic marks the slippery masculinities of the stringers and the patriarchal nature of the field.

Chapter 7 outlined the informal news labour of stringers in the journalistic field, which is marked by informality from the inception. Despite the recommendations of successive wage boards in independent India, the part-time contributor or mofussil stringer struggles to make his ends meet. Yet the resilience of stringer is evident despite several forms of precarity piled against him. Either by individual efforts or by collective action, the stringer is not averse to pleading with the state, navigating the underbelly of the state and doing whatever he can to survive in the field. What accentuates the enigmatic character of mofussil stringer is the way he continues to struggle against the odds, so much so that the global pandemic that impacted every sphere of life was not a great rupture to him as his existence is a kind of permanent pandemic.

The forms of precarity he deals with on a daily basis – social, political, economic and symbolic – make clear that there is no radical sense of freedom either or a portrayal of stringer agency that circumvents all power. By dynamic I mean that the stringer is not determined or fixed in structures of power. This means that there is a possibility of negotiating and engaging with those established and sedimented historical forms of power. This change may well be slow and incremental but it offers hope to both the stringer and the journalistic field.

Implications for future research

Some of the observations and formulations I made in this book will be useful to understand the working lives of journalists and newsworkers in a rapidly converging media environment, especially the ones that focus on the logic of journalistic practices, relations of news production, relationship between journalistic field and other fields of power. Before discussing some research possibilities that could emerge from this book, I would like to present some methodological concerns.

By presenting narratives from the two small-town formations in AP and TS, this research points out that Journalism Studies, in the Indian context, need to engage at mezzo-level as opposed to macro (nation, global) or micro-level (individual) formulations. Journalism cultures and economies in India are closely linked to caste, matriarchy/patriarchy and communal groupings, which are highly regional in character. Thereby, carrying out mezzo-level journalism research could be one of the ways to avoid misleading and sweeping generalisations.

One of the possibilities of this research is to extend it by studying stringers, freelancers and reporters working for online platforms, as informalisation is increasingly becoming a trend in the journalistic field. Despite the increasing digitalisation of news, catalysed during the global pandemic, news organisations and agencies need persons to do 'leg-work'.

Another related prospect is to carry out an intense engagement with the idea of precarity and journalistic labour, which appears to be the need of the hour in the years to come. Given the challenges of learning from past experiences, due to lack of a proper prosopography (collective biography) of journalists, this is an opportune moment to carry out documentary work on the tendencies and counter-tendencies in the journalistic field. Especially in these times when religious and cultural nationalism is on the rise and even the rank and file of media organisations also are being replaced, bringing the ideological motives to the fore, such work will have significance and prove to be resourceful in the near future. Managing or muzzling the media is taking new forms in the current economic and political scenario, which the orthodox political economy approach may not address adequately.

This book explicitly suggests the need for a comprehensive survey of journalists by documenting the constitution of journalists' union office bearers and press clubs to assess the diversity issues such as gender, caste, ability and region/space factors in the journalistic field. It reiterates that such a research, which considers the whole social and political orders, would contribute to the progressive withering away of domination.

A field-based/ethnographic approach to understanding ethical and moral issues in journalistic practices appears to be an untapped area of research in this part of the globe. This helps in bridging the gap between theorisations and observations on 'principled ethics' and 'functional or operational ethics' along with the issues related to the autonomous and heteronomous nature of the journalistic field.

Appendix

PROFILES OF RESEARCH SITES AND KEY ASPECTS OF TELUGU NEWS DAILIES

Some important elements and key aspects of Telugu dailies

Telugu is a prominent Dravidian language, widely spoken in two states in India – Telangana and Andhra Pradesh – by about a population of over 81 million (8.1 crores), as per the Census of India report (2011). It is rated as the fastest-growing language in the United States and ranked as the 15th widely spoken language in the world.

I tabulated circulation figures of the top 20 dailies in Indian languages as well as English in India to present the standing of Telugu newspapers in the country sourced from the Audit Bureau of Circulation (Table A.1). Similarly, Tables A.2 and A.3 present the circulation figures of the top three Telugu dailies and readership bases in Andhra Pradesh and Telangana.

Since the focus of the study is on stringers working in daily newspapers, this section presents some of its key components and elements. Almost all Telugu dailies have two parts: (a) broadsheet, often called as 'main paper'; (b) a tabloid, known as *zilla* or district edition or mini. The *zilla* edition (tabloid size) is a 6–12-page pull-out tucked in the folded broadsheet, which in turn comprises 8–14 pages depending on the circulation and readership of the newspaper (and thereby advertisement revenue).

Apart from the regular state, nation/world, edit, business and sports pages, there is a page dedicated to 'women readers' (commonly referred to as 'family page') and a cinema page. Dailies with fewer pages compromise on nation, world and sports pages, but not on family/cinema and business pages. Some newspapers have family/cinema and business pages in one standalone centre page (a single two-paged leaf and not a centrespread). The logic of advertisement positioning is the same as any language newspaper in the world, that is, a preference for odd-numbered pages (*recto* or right-handed) for visibility purposes and the edit page is usually positioned on an even-numbered page (*verso* or left-handed), which does not have advertisements.

Table A.1 Highest circulated newspapers across languages

Sl. No.	*Publication*	*Language*	*Circulation in 000s*
1	*Dainik Bhaskar*	Hindi	4,579
2	*Dainik Jagran*	Hindi	3,614
3	*The Times of India*	English	2,880
4	*Malayala Manorama*	Malayalam	2,308
5	*Amar Ujala*	Hindi	2,262
6	*Hindustan*	Hindi	2,221
7	*Rajastan Patrika*	Hindi	1,788
8	*Eenadu*	Telugu	1,614
9	*Daily Thanthi*	Tamil	1,473
10	*The Hindu*	English	1,416
11	*Daily Sakal*	Marathi	1,264
12	*Mathrubhumi*	Malayalam	1,231
13	*Punjab Kesari*	Hindi	1,106
14	*Patrika*	Hindi	1,095
15	*Hindustan Times*	English	1,073
16	*Sakshi*	Telugu	1,065
17	*Anand Bazar Patrika*	Bengali	1,047
18	*Divya Bhaskar*	Gujarati	792
19	*Dinamalar*	Tamil	768
20	*Vijayavani*	Kannada	757

Source: Audit Bureau of Circulations (2019a)

Table A.2 Top-3 highest circulated Telugu dailies

Sl. No	Publication	Circulation in 000s
1	*Eenadu*	1,614
2	*Sakshi*	1,065
3	*Andhra Jyothi*	664

Source: Audit Bureau of Circulations (2019b)

Table A.3 Readership figures of top-3 Telugu dailies in both states

Sl. No.	*Publication*	*State*	*Readership in 000s*
1	*Eenadu*	AP	6,391
2	*Eenadu*	Telangana	5,149
3	*Sakshi*	AP	5,756
4	*Sakshi*	Telangana	2,593
5	*Andhra Jyothi*	AP	3,056
6	*Andhra Jyothi*	Telangana	1,565
7	*Namaste Telangana*	Telangana	1,616

Source: Media Research Users Council, India. (2020, p. 41)

The organisation and structure of *zilla* editions is more complicated than the main page. Like the main page, even the *zilla* edition has a front page, specifying the location, where every stringer of that particular district wants 'his' story or news item to get published. This front page in mofussil areas is of two types: city edition and rural edition. The second page is usually filled with crime news from all parts of the district. The centrespread of the tabloids is designed at the newspaper headquarters and is common for all districts, again on an average and normal day. Every newspaper has a special booklet on Sundays.

Every district page has a sheet, which covers the overall Legislative Assembly constituency news on one side and news from the constituent *mandals* on the other. This effectively means that some parts of the district edition are hyper-local, published exclusively for that particular Assembly segment. Readers outside of that segment would read different pages (their own locality news). The only way to access the pages from other Assembly segments was through the free e-paper on the newspaper website.[1] At the time of fieldwork, there were 10 districts in Telangana and 13 districts in AP, and the numbers have swelled to 33 and 26, respectively, by 2022. Apart from the edition centres located within the two Telugu-speaking states, some newspapers have metro editions in New Delhi, Mumbai, Chennai and Bangalore, catering to the Telugu readership in those cities.

Demographic and socioeconomic profile of Gannavaram, AP

Gannavaram – a *mandal* which falls under the Nuzivid administrative division in Krishna District, Andhra Pradesh – is located on the arterial National Highway-5 (Chennai-Kolkata). Roughly 16 km away from Vijayawada city, it is one of the fastest developing assembly constituencies in the district. There are 23 villages and one hamlet (Savarigudem) in this *mandal* with an estimated population of 87,027 (DCO, 2011a, p. 460). Gannavaram is surrounded by Agiripalle *mandal* on the North and Vijayawada Rural on the West. Bapulapadu and Kankipadu *mandals* surround Gannavaram on the East and South, respectively.

The NH-5 divides the *mandal* with upland (*meṭṭa*) area on one side and delta area on the other. The Gannavaram Airport, built during World War II, is located on the upland side in Kesarapalli village. However, Gannavaram never witnessed industrialisation, except for one small-scale industrial estate at Surampalle, due to the strong presence of Left parties and labour unionism. Other major commercial activities apart from irrigation and quarrying are aquaculture, sericulture and hatcheries.

Residents of the upland (*māgāṇi*) area are completely dependent on the Brahmayya Lingam *cheruvu* (lake) that has a storage capacity of two thousand million cubic feet (TMC) nestled in the middle of the mountains.

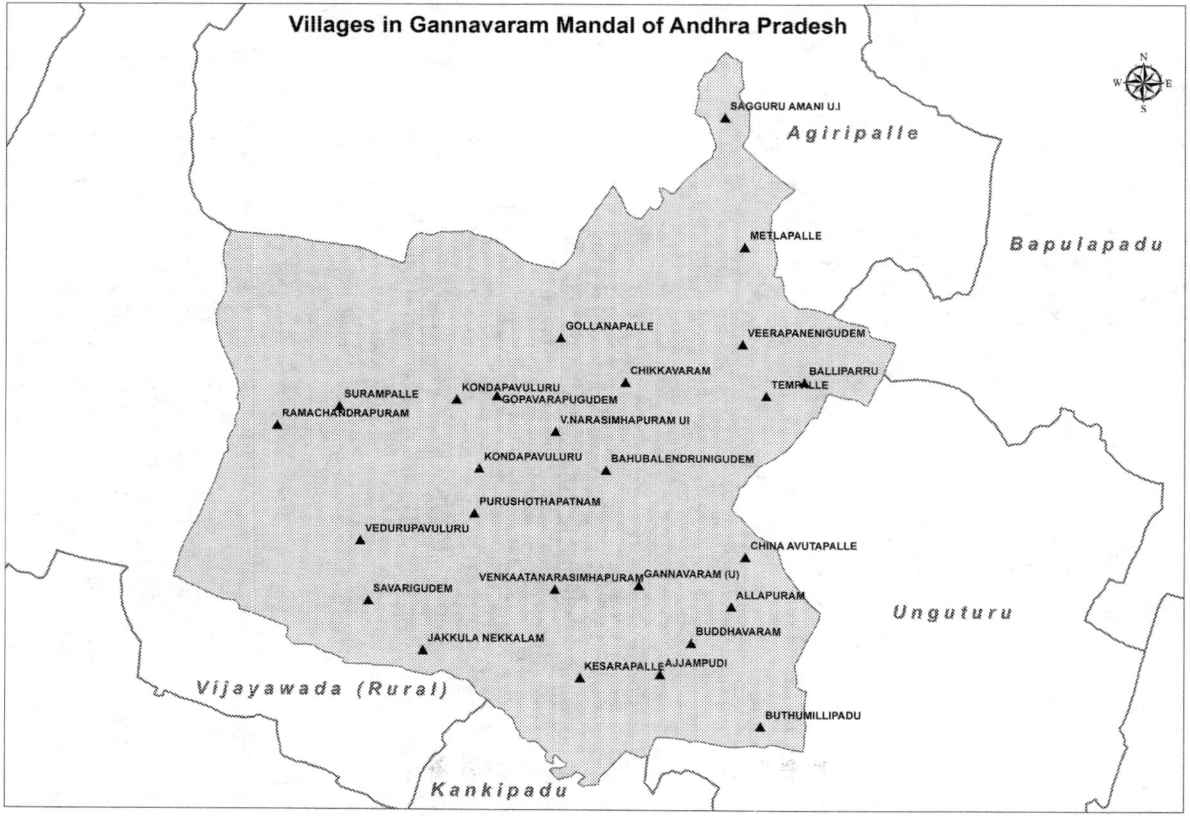

Map A1 Villages in Gannavaram *Mandal* of Andhra Pradesh.

Source: Author.

This massive natural water tank with an area of more than one thousand acres has an ayacut of nearly 10–12 thousand acres. Located by the side of Brahmayya Lingam cheruvu, was another naturally formed tank by name Sagguru amani, with a water spread area of 200 acres. As there was no presence of any settlements or hamlets near the lake, the lake is pristine. Around 30 towns rely upon this lake water for their development, including for agriculture.

Cotton, groundnut, vegetables and mango orchards are the major crops in this part of the *mandal*. This part of the *mandal* is one of the most sought-after real estate areas in the district, as an IT park on the lines of Hitec city (Hyderabad Information Technology and Engineering Consultancy City) of Hyderabad is established. Stone quarrying is also one of the important commercial activities. Across the highway, the delta part of the *mandal*, which gets water from Eluru canal on a regular basis, is a paddy-rich area. Farmers have a minimum of two crops of paddy in *rabi* (winter crop) and *kharif* (monsoon crop) seasons of the year.

K. Balagopal (1984, p. 1901) describes the towns on the NH-5 in the coastal Andhra region, which captures the essence of the political economy of the region:

> On either side of the route are villages laid end upon end, many of them really small towns; with neatly thatched and tiled houses, and quite a few good buildings, they do not seem to be part of this land of the wretched; but the pride of place is taken by the twin symbols of coastal Andhra: cinema halls that look like rice-mills and rice-mills that look like cinema halls, give or take a chimney stack. The resemblance will no doubt offend any decent architect, but it is true to its salt, for all the surplus that is generated by the delta agriculture goes in exactly two directions: agro-based industry and trade, and film production, distribution and exhibition.

On the political front, Gannavaram was a bastion of the Communist Party of India (Marxist) till the advent of the Telugu Desam Party (TDP) in 1983. From then the political contest has been between Congress (I) and TDP with CPI (M) playing a crucial role in forging alliances. However, left parties are fast losing their hold in this area.[2]

It was obvious that a lion's share of wealth was generated from agriculture and allied businesses in this part of Andhra Pradesh. Explaining the accumulation of wealth by a particular dominant caste, which he labelled as the 'propertied class', Balagopal (1984, p. 1901) noted:

> This wealth resides in a class, a class that is predominantly (but by no means exclusively) Kamma by caste and agrarian in its origins, which came of age in the period of the nationalist movement and

> the agrarian struggles against the Zamindars and the British Raj. These struggles that attended its birth have also given it the largest share of participation in radical movements; socialism, rationalism, atheism, communism, and Radical Humanism – you name the heterodoxy and they have seen it. Over the period, they have also grown substantially rich, and have multiplied their riches since the Green Revolution. But while wealth has come their way, they have been systematically kept out of the prime seats of power at Hyderabad. They lost it symbolically when they had to concede the name Visalandhra (in favour of the Hindi-ised Andhra Pradesh) for the state for which they fought the hardest, and had to simultaneously concede their demand for making Vijayawada the capital city: and they lost it substantially as part of the general 'Congress culture' of keeping the economically dominant classes and communities in the states away from the seats of political power.

Even though both Gannavaram *mandal* and constituency are traditionally dominated by Kamma community leaders, there was a strong numerical presence of Yadava, Muslim, Christian, Mala and Madiga communities. Major religious centres in this *mandal* were Mustabada Mosque, Joseph Thambi Church at Peda Avutapalli village and Brahmayya Lingam Temple at Chikkavaram village. The NTR College of Veterinary Sciences is located in Gannavaram.

Local issues that frequently made their way into the newspaper were: political, irrigation and agriculture, real estate ventures, dignitaries at the airport, the airport, highway accidents, crimes, protests, *rasta roko* (block the road) and Brahmayya Lingam cheruvu.

Demographic and socioeconomic profile of Sangareddy, TS

Sangareddy district has an inter-state border with Karnataka on the west. The neighbouring districts of Sangareddy are Kamareddy, Medak, Medchal, Rangareddy and Vikarabad in Telangana. Sangareddy *mandal* shares a boundary with Pulkal and Hathnoora *mandals* on the north, Jinnaram and Patancheru on the east. Sadashivpet and Kondapur *mandals* share boundary with Sangareddy on the west, while Shankarpalle *mandal* is on the south of Sangareddy *mandal*.

Manjeera, a tributary of the River Godavari, is an important drainage flowing in the district on which the Nizam Sagar dam was constructed. The other important streams are Haldi and Kudalair which flow in the eastern half of the district (DCO, 2011b, p. 16). While on a drive on the National Highway-65 or Hyderabad-Sholapur Highway that connects Hyderabad to Sangareddy, the moment one crosses Bharat Heavy Electricals Limited at Ramachandrapuram, s/he enters one of Asia's largest Special Economic Zone (SEZ): Industrial Development Area (IDA), Patancheru.

One cannot miss the ubiquitous presence of pharmaceutical, industrial chemicals, forest produce, ceramic, polymer, pipes and tubes, wires and cables and alloy industries among others on either side of the highway. The 'other side of industrialisation' in the IDA, Patancheru or Patancheru SEZ, is quite depressing, to say the least (Vijay, 2003, pp. 5026–5030).

Talking about the perils of development that resulted in Patancheru after giving permissions to establish a Special Economic Zone (SEZ) that flout environmental guidelines in this part of Sangareddy district, a former civil servant, Sarma (2007, p. 1901) lamented:

> The industrial units in an SEZ would not only drain surface and groundwater resources at the expense of the local communities, but also their effluents (sic) could pollute the local water bodies. The industrial estate at Patancheru (sic) is a standing example of what could happen, if stringent environmental norms are not enforced.

The civil servant went on to say that this was a clear attitude of 'Help the Rich, Hurt the Poor' on the part of successive governments that made Patancheru one of the most dubious cases of perils of 'development'. He (2007, p. 1901) opined that SEZs are imposed on the local people without any prior consultation.

Talking about the environmental pollution that pharmaceutical companies have created in this part of the world, Stan Cox in *Sick Planet: Corporate Food and Medicine* observed:

> Clearly, the drug companies have no intention of calling off their quest to accelerate the growth of pill-popping. That means more trouble ahead, and not just for the patient. In recent years, the pharmaceutical industry has become so tightly integrated across the planet that a patient in Madison, Wisconsin is connected directly through doctors, pharmacists, and sales reps from companies based in New Jersey or North Carolina or Switzerland to ingredient suppliers in India and China, and through them, to workers and farmers in some of the world's most impoverished and polluted places. One such place is Patancheru, India.
>
> (2008, p. 33)

Perhaps the best possible way to describe the sorry state of affairs about the IDA in Patancheru, which is just 23 kilometres away from Sangareddy zero milestone, in Cox's (2008, p. 37) own words: 'The word "Patancheru" has acquired multiple meanings: a lake, a town, a region, and, in more recent years, an ecological catastrophe'.

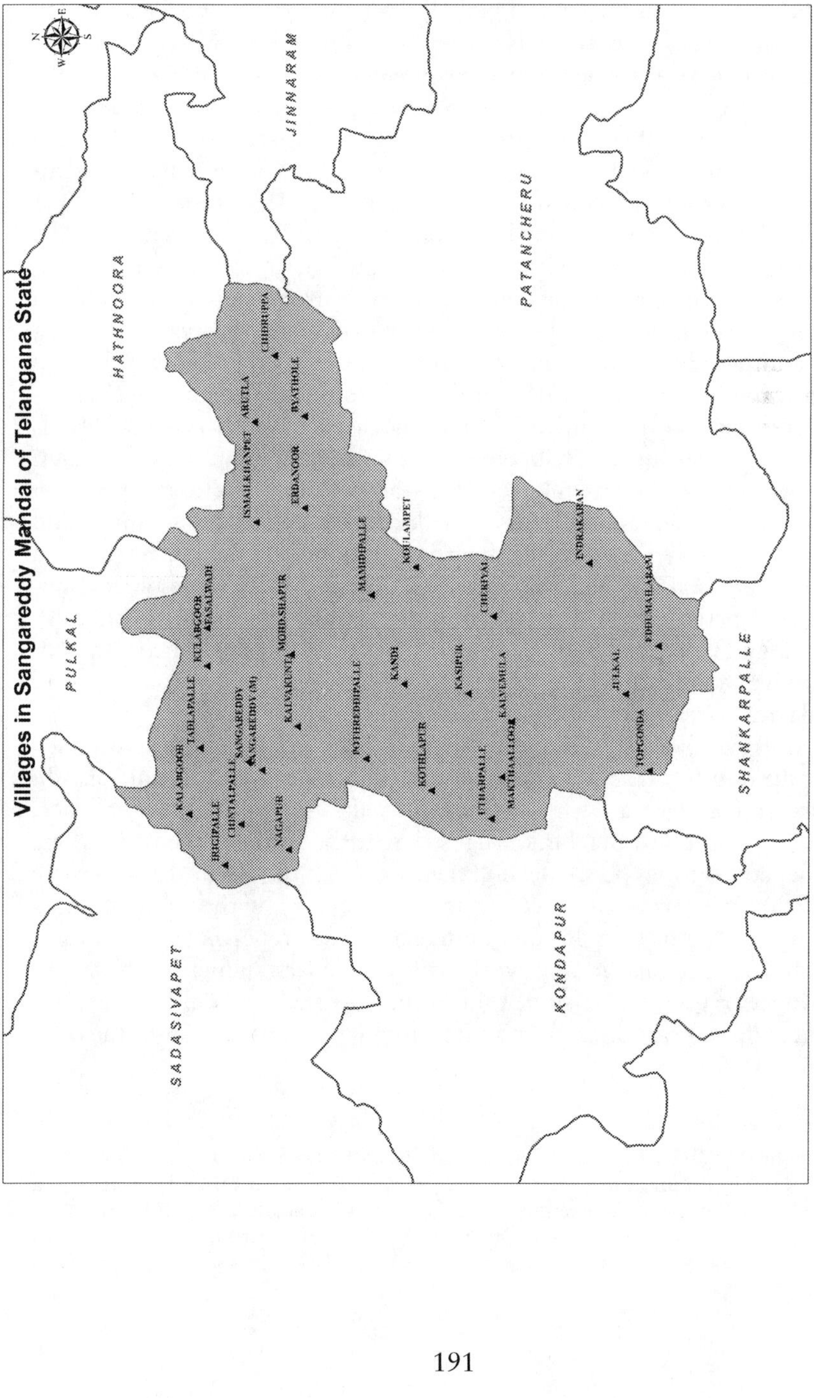

Map A2 Villages in Sangareddy *Mandal* of Telangana State.

Source: Author.

While the situation on the eastern side of Sangareddy district is described in Kafkaesque prose, around 62 kilometres on the NH-65, Pastapur village in Zahirabad *mandal*, which is on the western side of Sangareddy, presents a poetic voice of struggle against globalisation and for autonomy over food production, seeds, natural resources, market, and, more importantly, community media by a women's collective (*Sangham*), under the aegis of the Deccan Development Society (DDS) for more than three and a half decades.

Established in 2008, the Sangham Radio at Pastapur is India's first community-owned and community-operated radio station managed, principally, by a group of Dalit women.[3] The Pastapur Declaration in 2000, a watershed initiative in the annals of community radio movement in India, took shape in the Medak district. The declaration urged the Government of India 'to take the current government policy of freeing broadcasting from state monopoly to its logical conclusion by expanding the available media space and permitting communities and organisations representing them to run their own radio stations' (Pavarala and Malik, 2007, pp. 281–282).

Local issues that frequently make it to the district as well as main editions of newspapers include: development and workers' union issues surrounding IDA, news and press releases from the district collectorate including government initiatives, accidents and deaths on NH-65, agriculture and irrigation, school education, health and sanitation and fauna in and around the Manjeera Wildlife Sanctuary, among others. Most events or developing news emerging from prestigious institutes like the Indian Institute of Technology-Hyderabad and ICRISAT were covered by special correspondents from Hyderabad, while stringers from Sangareddy either follow up the next day or cover 'sidelights' of such news stories.

As already noted, stringers came from modest backgrounds and joined the profession to make a living. The profession serves as a means of subsistence rather than a leisure activity to make the world a better place. However, the notion of 'the journalist has to be in the thick of it' along with fidgety editorial personnel and their interventions deemed appropriate meant that newswork involved stringers negotiating with different agents in the society (immediate locality), interacting with reporting staffers/heads and editorial persons on any work day. An understanding of newswork by stringers requires an assimilation of the knowledge of cultural settings, social contexts, practices and structures from within and outside of the field.

Notes

1 After the COVID-19 lockdown in the last week of March 2020, except for *Sakshi* (a daily), almost all newspapers stopped printing the district tabloids. Instead of a separate pull-out, they started including one extra broadsheet page for local news of that particular area. Some newspapers shut down operations altogether. This, however, was for a brief period and Telugu news dailies in some districts, based

on revenue potential, were back to 'normal' business by the end of first quarter of 2021.

2 Puchalapalli Sundarayya, the chief architect of the contestable political geography *Viśālāndhra* (not to be confused with the newspaper *Visalaandhra*) was elected thrice (1955, 1962 and 1978) for the AP Legislative Assembly from Gannavaram. This is birthplace of former People's War Group leader and revolutionary poet K.G. Satyamurthy or Satyam. Popularly referred to as *udyama nelabāluḍu* and Sivasagar, he has inspired a generation of activists and poets in Telugu literary field after he parted ways with the Naxalite armed-struggle (see Bag and Watkins, 2021, pp. 61–63; Gidla, 2017)

3 See www.ddsindia.com/www/default.asp

References

ABC [Audit Bureau of Circulations]. (2019a). *Highest circulated dailies amongst member publications (across languages)*. Retrieved from: www.auditbureau.org/files/JD%202019%20Highest%20Circulated%20(across%20languages).pdf.

ABC. (2019b). *Highest circulated daily newspapers (languages wise)*. Retrieved from: www.auditbureau.org/files/JD%202019%20Highest%20Circulated%20(language%20wise).pdf.

Bag, K. and Watkins, S. (2021). Structures of oppression: Querying analogies of race and caste. *New Left Review*, 132. November–December, pp. 55–82.

Balagopal, K. (1984). A false resurrection: Rise and fall of Rama Rao. *Economic and Political Weekly*, 19(45), pp. 1901–1904.

Census of India. (2011). *Language: India, states and union territories*. New Delhi: Office of Registrar General, India. Retrieved from: http://censusindia.gov.in/2011Census/C-16_25062018_NEW.pdf.

Cox, S. (2008). *Sick planet: Corporate food and medicine*. London: Pluto Press.

DCO [Directorate Census Operations]. (2011a). *Krishna District census handbook*. Andhra Pradesh: Census of India.

DCO. (2011b). *Medak district census handbook*. Andhra Pradesh: Census of India.

Gidla, S. (2017). *Ants among elephants: An untouchable family and the making of modern India*. New York: Farrar, Straus and Giroux.

Media Research Users Council, India. (2020). *Indian readership survey, Q4 2019*. Retrieved from: https://mruc.net/uploads/posts/cd072cdc13d2fe48ac660374d0c22a5d.pdf.

Pavarala, V. and Malik, K. (2007). *Other voices: The struggle for community radio in India*. New Delhi: Sage.

Sarma, E. A. S. (2007). Help the rich, hurt the poor: Case of special economic zones. *Economic and Political Weekly*, 42(21), pp. 1900–1902.

Vijay, G. (2003). 'Other side' of new industrialisation. *Economic and Political Weekly*, 38(48), pp. 5026–5030.

INDEX

Aloysius, G 121, 124n
Ambedkar, B.R. 18, 20, 28–29, 46, 96
Ambedkar's statues 22, 106–108, 121
Andhra Bhoomi (newspaper) 94, 147
Andhra Jyothi (newspaper) 41n, 63, 94, 147
Andhra Patrika (newspaper) 57, 69n, 121, 148
Andhra Prabha (newspaper) 94, 147
AP Working Journalists' Union (APUWJ) 30, 61, 148, 155, 157, 166, 174

Balagopal, K. 38, 68n, 188–189
Bayly, Christopher 5
Bayly, Susan 20, 29, 121
Benson, Rodney 11
bodily hexis 118–119, 123n
Bourdieu, Pierre 10–12, 65–66, 69, 88, 98n, 109, 114–115, 128, 130, 142, 153, 174; *bodily-hexis* 14n; capital 26–27, 69n; caste 15n; field 76; interviewing 15n; journalism 96; masculine domination 138, 141n
brahmanical 41n, 98, 120–121; ideology 140, 181; view 63, 93, 123–124n; work culture 120–121, 132, 139, 181
Breman, Jan 174n

capital: forms of 11, 27, 35, 96, 109, 115, 120, 174n, 180; *see also* cultural capital, social capital, economic capital, journalistic capital
Carey, James 4, 8, 68n
caste 20, 39–42n, 99n, 136, 157, 188–189; based identity 48–49, 53, 106, 162; as capital 25–28; discrimination 104–106; in everyday life 22–25; feeling 89, 91; as hierarchy 93–95, 117, 139; and news production 80–81, 108; in politics 30–39 (*see also kulamu*); and recruitment 62–65
casualisation 146, 153–154; *see also* contractualisation
Census of India 7, 20, 22, 184
census town 7, 14–15n
contractualisation 3, 6, 149, 163–164; *see also* flexploitation
Cox, Stan 190
cultural capital 27, 30, 49, 95, 114–115

Dalit 20–21, 23–24, 39, 39–40n, 64, 81, 94, 124n; magazines and periodicals 108, 123n; organisations 106–107; women 192; *see also* Scheduled Castes (SC)
Dalit-Bahujan 39, 103, 108, 121
delegation 13, 104–105, 109, 146, 149, 180; *see also* flexploitation
Dirks, Nicholas 20
dispositions 11, 20, 65, 69n, 75, 96–97, 109, 114–115, 121, 139, 149, 153, 180–181
doxa 11, 64–65, 76, 88, 96, 118, 170
Dube, SC 24
Dumont, Louis 20

economic capital 27, 95, 109, 113, 122
Eenadu (newspaper) 48, 57–58, 61–63, 67–68n, 94, 132, 145, 147–148, 185
ethics 51, 118–119, 183
ethnography 1, 6, 8, 10, 12–14, 128

fields of power 11, 13, 34, 85, 90, 115, 120, 140, 161–162, 179–182
field theory 11, 142n, 174n, 179
fixers 3
flexploitation 153, 181; *see also* informality
freelancer 3, 64, 182

Gandhi, MK 6–8, 21, 29, 40n
Gannavaram, profile of186–189
gift 115, 120, 138
Goffman, Erving 138
Gundimeda, Sambaiah 21, 26, 40–41n

habitus 11, 27, 34, 39, 65, 81, 88, 95–96, 106, 114, 123n, 136, 149; *see also* capital
Hardt, Hanno 146, 173n
Harrison, Selig 22
Harriss-White, Barbara 136, 149, 165, 174n
Harvey, David 8
Hegde, Radha 162
hierarchies 13, 39n, 41n, 48, 75, 85–86, 102, 114, 136, 140, 149, 161; internalisation of 20; newspaper 93–96; professional 89–90, 98n; social 22, 89–90

Ilaiah, Kancha 19, 22, 39n, 41n
illusio 114–115, 120, 160–161; *see also* journalistic *illusio*
inequality: principle of graded 96, 102, 121, 136; *see also* Ambedkar
informalisation 13, 145, 149, 172, 173n, 182; *see also* casualisation
informality 145–146, 149–150, 154–155, 159, 173n, 181; *see also* precarity
Innis, Harold 4–5

Jeffrey, Craig 42n
Jeffrey, Robin 2, 68n, 77, 90, 132, 141n, 153
Joseph, Ammu 141n
journalistic capital 10, 95, 109, 113, 118–121
journalistic *illusio* 114–115, 161, 181
Journalistic practices 27, 51, 75–76, 81, 86, 90, 93, 102, 115, 120, 122–124

Krishna Patrika (newspaper) 121, 148
kulamu 53; *see also vargamu*

lift irrigation 73, 75, 180; *see also* news labour, stringers' perception
line account 2, 78, 151, 163
lineage 2, 104, 151–152, 167–168
localisation strategy 2, 13, 67n, 145–146, 150, 170; *see also* informalisation

Madiga (caste) 19–21, 23–24, 39n, 48, 106, 189
Mala (caste) 21, 23–24, 35, 39n, 94, 189
Malik, Kanchan 90, 128
Mana Telangana (newspaper) 94
mandal (administrative unit) 2
Manor, James 110; *see also pyraveekar*
masculinity 13, 27, 31, 35, 126–140, 141n, 149, 181
Massey, Doreen 8
McLuhan, Marshall 5, 8
mofussil 2, 6–8, 12–13, 14n, 77, 97n, 104, 179, 182

Namaste Telangana (newspaper) 94, 147
Nava Telangana (newspaper) 94
Nehru 6–8, 49
news labour 4, 63, 159–160, 162, 180; conditions of 144–146, 154; informalisation of 172, 173n; stringers' perceptions of 63, 66
Newswork 4, 6, 10, 13, 72, 77, 79–80, 95, 109, 114, 154, 182, 192
Neyazi, Taberez 145–147
Ninan, Sevanti 2, 7, 67n, 95, 99n, 145–146; *see also* localisation strategy

OBC (Other Backward Classes) 10, 22–24, 40n, 53, 64, 92, 121

pandemic 6, 144–145, 152, 159, 166–169, 172, 182
pātradhār 102, 120–121, 181
patriarchy 127–129, 132, 136, 140–141, 181; *see also* masculinity
Pavarala, Vinod 192
Prabhata Velugu (newspaper) 94
Prajasakti (newspaper) 94
Prasad, Madhav 42

precarity 6, 64, 144–145, 154, 159; economic 162–165; forms of 13, 158–159; legal 165–167; symbolic 160–162
pyraveekar 110–111

Rajagopal, Arvind 3
Rao, Ramoji 48, 62, 68n, 94, 148
Rau, MC 6, 8, 99
recruitment 13, 27, 49, 148; and caste 63, 68; of stringers 55–62, 149, 180; of women 131–132
region 1, 3, 14, 21, 49, 77, 90, 91, 108, 160, 183; and caste 30, 32, 36–38, 41, 89, 93–94; delta region 27, 29–30, 89; and media 91, 93–94, 99, 123, 128, 145, 147; Telugu-speaking 22, 24, 30, 31, 42, 89, 107, 149, 188, 190
regional 23, 27, 28, 30, 48, 93, 117, 182
regionalism 27
relations of production 5, 80, 180, 182
relegation 13, 64, 69n, 76, 91–92, 96, 108–109, 134, 149, 180; *see also* delegation
Relli (caste) 39–40n
Remesh, Babu 3, 146
reproduction 13, 42n, 85, 93, 128, 135, 149, 180; *see also* inequality
rituals, journalistic 27, 115, 117, 120
roles 10, 13, 20, 75–78, 80, 83, 90, 96, 102, 110, 145, 180
Round Table India (website) 106–107
Roy, Srirupa 2, 163

Sakshi (newspaper) 30, 53, 58, 61, 68n, 94, 147, 157, 185
sāmājika vargamu 53; *see also* caste
Sangareddy profile 189–192
Sangari, Kumkum 128, 132
Sat-shudraisation 121, 139, 149, 181
Sat-shudras 22, 27, 121; in journalistic field 81, 92, 94, 96, 104, 135; and media economy 121, 139, 149, 181; in political field 29–32, 34–35, 38, 149
Satyamurthy, KG 193n
Scheduled Castes (SC) 20–21, 39–40n 48, 54; colonies 22; in/of journalism 6, 8, 92; *see also* Dalit
secularism 28, 42n
Shudra 20–22, 40n
Skocpol, Theda 174n
small town 7–9; *see also* mofussil
Smith, Adam 174n
social capital 26–27, 34, 38, 76, 93, 109, 113, 121–122, 150, 161
Soja, Edward 8
Srinivas, MN 20
Srinivas, SV 26, 42n
Statutory town 7, 14–15n; *see also* census town
stringers: definition 2; education of 48–50; payment 2; social background of 49–55; work experience of 51–52
Sundarayya, Puchalapalli 33, 193n
Surya (newspaper) 94, 147
sūtradhār 102, 120–121, 181; *see also* *pātradhār*
symbolic annihilation 91, 106, 108
symbolic capital 34, 138
symbolic insecurities 140, 181
symbolic power 129, 132, 141n
symbolic violence 39n, 90, 96, 106, 121, 135–136, 140, 170, 181

Telangana Union of Working Journalists (TUWJ) 31, 129, 157, 166
Telugu language 184
Thapan, M 129
Thirumal, P 123n
Tuchman, Gaye 99n

Upadhya, Carol 69, 123

Vaartha (newspaper) 94
Vaishnav, Milan 38
vargamu 53; *see also sāmājika vargamu*
varnashrama dharma 20
velivada (Dalit ghetto) 108
Visaalaandhra (newspaper) 94

Wacquant, Loïc 69, 76, 108
wage board 145–146, 148–151, 153–154, 163, 165, 173, 175
wages 60, 114, 142, 144, 150–151, 154, 157–158, 163, 165, 173n
Washbrook, David 121, 123n
Watkins, Susan 193n
Williams, R 4–5

Printed in the United States
by Baker & Taylor Publisher Services